JESUS—HEALER & TEACHER

JESUS—HEALER & TEACHER

A discursive study of the Ministry of our
Lord based on the Synoptic Gospels

W. F. BARLING

THE CHRISTADELPHIAN
404 SHAFTMOOR LANE
BIRMINGHAM, B28 8SZ

2005

First published 2005

ISBN 0 85189 148 9

Printed by
Cromwell Press Limited
Trowbridge
England

PREFACE

TO some readers the contents of this book will be familiar, being a reprint of previously duplicated notes, but for the benefit of new readers a few words of introduction are not out of place. The notes recorded the substance of twelve lectures given by the author in the autumn of 1952, to a Bible Study Class in Central London, numbering just over a hundred regular members. With the invaluable help of a small band of stalwart fellow-workers they were first made available in weekly instalments to the members of this Class, being designed as memory-aids to those who heard the lectures, and as a guide to those who could not be present on all occasions.

The writer is painfully aware of their shortcomings. An adequate treatment of the Ministry of Jesus is clearly impossible in only twelve lectures, and much has inevitably had to be omitted or left only cursorily examined. On grounds of style and arrangement, too, they have in places little to commend them, for they were written at a pace which ill becomes any subject, let alone one so exalted as "Jesus Christ and him crucified". Yet, because the views expressed have had to be set down hurriedly, it must not be thought that they were either hastily or rashly adopted. They are, in fact, the fruit of prolonged study and reflection. Naturally, the writer is not so bold as to assume that they will all meet with unqualified assent or approval, but he hopes that wherever they prove to any of his readers to be disconcertingly novel they will at least command respect for what they are—honest attempts to resolve problems which are more often avoided than resolutely faced. Where he is found to be in error he has no excuse to plead except the fallibility of his own memory

and judgement, and he leaves his readers to sift the wheat
from the chaff with which they may find it to be encum-
bered. For him and for all who have helped him, if the
notes inspire in the heart of anyone a greater love for
Jesus, the labour of making them available in their present form will have been amply recompensed.

W. F. BARLING
December, 1952

FOREWORD

THIS study of the Lord's ministry is described in the sub-title as *'discursive'*. This can mean *'rambling'*, indicating a random wandering from one topic to another. However, a cursory glance at the Contents, will assure the reader that the adjective in question is used here in the philosophical sense—that is, going from premise to conclusion in a series of logical steps. The progression from the first apparently audacious claims to be the Messiah, to the dying breath upon the cross, is faithfully followed. Jesus is shown to be at the centre of all things from the first to the last—the Alpha and the Omega. The journey is suspended at the crucifixion—the fact of the resurrection, although not directly studied, is implied throughout as the driving force behind the gospel records.

Events are pieced together from the Synoptic gospels in order to maximise the lessons to be drawn from them—a synthesis rather than an analysis. This is necessary because the extraordinary selection of material by the Gospel writers precludes them from being independent biographies of the Lord. Indeed they have no conventional literary category, *'being in their own way as exceptional as the One of whom they testify ...'*. Inexplicable differences of emphasis in the records are brought before us, not in any critical or analytical sense, but in awesome recognition that these unique records are each capturing a facet of the Lord's work. As records, they are wonderfully subservient to the One whom they portray, and the author ensures that our minds are focussed on the revealed Christ, rather than on the means of revelation.

While passing through the phases of Christ's ministry, the author concentrates with considerable insight on the reactions of those who came into contact with Jesus; indeed this is a fascinating and most rewarding feature of the study. In the process, Jesus is shown elevated as supreme Lord and Master over his disciples, and the one with ultimate power over his enemies. We are caused to think searchingly of our own relationship with the Master, and an Epilogue details the practical outworking of Christ's teaching in the lives of his followers.

The premise is that Jesus, the carpenter's son is the Christ. The conclusion to which we are led by this examination of the miracles and teaching of the Master, is that truly this is the Son of God. *'It is of such an one'* (declares the author) *'that we have come to enquire and learn more in this study. Only with awe and utter humility ought we to approach so exalted a task. Let us then, as it were, put off our shoes from off our feet, for the place whereon we stand is holy ground, sanctified by the revealed Presence of God Himself.'*

Birmingham   COLIN WALTON
                                                    2005

CONTENTS

1
LISTEN, O ISLES, UNTO ME

The Lord's assumption of ultimate authority

NO authentic historical information is available to us regarding Jesus other than what is to be found in the New Testament, and there, except for one or two details, it is concentrated into the four gospel records of Matthew, Mark, Luke and John. Each of these accounts has its own peculiar features which distinguish it sharply from the rest. Particularly is this true of John's Gospel whose idiosyncrasies—apart from the fact that it clearly presupposes a thorough acquaintance with the other three—are so pronounced that there are decided advantages in studying it on its own. The rest, on the other hand, despite their divergences, are best examined in conjunction with, rather than independently of, one another. By arranging them in parallel columns it is possible to survey at a glance the large amount of material common to them all—a fact which has led to their being given the apt designation "the Synoptic Gospels"—and to abstract from them a composite portrait of Jesus which gives a fuller meaning to John's Gospel.

To fill in as many details as possible of that portrait is the prime object of this study, and our researches will accordingly be confined to these first three gospels. Yet it is not the gospels, as gospels, that we shall study. It will be upon Jesus himself, upon his sayings and doings rather than upon any particular presentation of them, that our attention will throughout be concentrated.

This is as it should be, and moreover as the gospel writers themselves meant it to be, for not one of them even included his own name, as author, in the text of his gospel, so at pains was he to avoid diverting the attention of his readers to himself from the majestic figure to whom he wished to bear testimony. Even where Luke (1:1-4) and John (21:24) did in fact make direct allusion to themselves it was with a transparently honest intent which excused them completely from the charge of vanity. They did so purely from a desire to stress their credentials as witnesses, and thereby bring more solemnly home to their readers the truth of the marvellous story which they had to tell. Thus, interesting and profitable though it would be for us to make a special point of isolating the characteristic features which distinguish one gospel from another, or to trace evidences of a special editorial purpose determining each author's choice of subject and phraseology, we shall be able to spare these important matters no more than an occasional passing reference. Our study will in fact entail a synthesis rather than an analysis, of the three gospels which form its basis, for what we need to bear uppermost in mind is that all four accounts—John's Gospel as well as the Synoptics—were written about one single and outstanding person who is clearly recognisable in each as one and the same individual. He alone is the unifying factor in them all, and the compelling need to tell men of him serves as the sole and all-sufficient justification for their existence.

It was precisely the Evangelists' sense of that need that made them so often indifferent to details of time and place; what Jesus said and did, not when and where he said and did it (except where these factors conditioned his words and actions) was what most urgently concerned them, and they, in pursuit of their chosen purpose, deny us much circumstantial detail which we would gladly know of, though generally for no better reason than simple curiosity. Thus both Matthew (23:37) and Luke (13:34) recorded a lament uttered by Jesus over Jerusalem for so often rejecting his overtures of mercy, yet neither felt the need to mention any of the many visits to Jerusalem which that lament implied, far less give details of them. Or again, the same writers, in recounting Christ's denunciation of Chorazin as one of the unrepentant cities where he had performed most of his mighty works, saw no necessity to specify what those works were, or whether among them were some that they actually mention in their records (Matthew 11:20,21; Luke 10:13).

That is, the gospels are fragmentary records, and avowedly so. They are not complete chronicles, as the many attempts made to write biographies of Jesus (each with its own peculiar chronological scheme), or to devise satisfactory harmonies of the gospels, go to show only too convincingly. Where they are silent it is therefore pointless for us to resort to conjecture. As literary productions they in fact defy classification. They are in a category of their own, being in their way as exceptional as the One of whom they testify—and inevitably so, precisely because it is of him, and of no other, that they testify.

Alpha and Omega

Who, then, was this Jesus? To those who first heard him and saw what he did, merely a carpenter turned preacher and healer—a local artisan who had with mysterious suddenness forsaken workshop and home to enter on a new career as a religious teacher and reformer. For this task he was, in their estimation, singularly ill-qualified. He had received no schooling in any of the great rabbinical colleges of Jerusalem, nor had he in its place any influential family connections to commend him to his contemporaries. Yet, despite these disadvantages, he performed his work with a brilliance and power which excited the envy of the ablest leaders of his nation, and made him an enigma to all his erstwhile acquaintances. "Many hearing him were astonished, saying, From whence hath this man these things? and what wisdom is this which is given unto him, that even such mighty works are wrought by his hands? Is not this the carpenter, the son of Mary?" (Mark 6:2,3). Thus did he, who had once seemed so normal, and who had lived unobtrusively among them right through childhood and early manhood, become by his unwonted abnormality a challenge to all with whom he came into contact. They knew not what to make of him, but ignore him they could not. Many he repelled, but all were fascinated by him, and a faithful few actually relinquished everything they possessed to become his constant companions. In stark contrast to their fidelity, however, stood the implacable hostility of the Jewish hierarchy. Only for three odd years did those envious men allow his activities to continue, and then they brought his career to an abrupt end by engineering his judicial murder at the hands of Roman soldiers.

As he hung upon the Cross, and they gloated at their cunningly won victory, it seemed that his brief labours had come utterly to nought. So they gleefully thought, and so his disillusioned followers despairingly concluded. But appearances belied the facts and both groups, the hostile and the devoted, were alike mistaken. Little did either of them then realize that the revolution which he had set in motion in so short a while was soon to rock the mighty Roman Empire—whose soldiery had done him to death—to its very foundations, and in every subsequent generation would continue to reverberate throughout the world, conditioning fundamentally the development of human society and thought even in the remotest corners of the earth. He whose career had been so brief, and whose end so untimely and ignominious, was to prove the greatest force with which mankind had ever had to reckon. Myriads, throughout the ages, would come to think of him less as a historical figure than as Lord of their lives and Saviour of their souls—one to whom they owned a personal loyalty and with whom it would be their constant delight to enter into the closest fellowship.

For such an effect—an effect which was then only a future prospect, but is now indelibly written on the pages of history—there must have been an adequate cause, and, for all that the modernist may choose to say, one alone suffices to explain it—the Resurrection. He who thus died a martyr's death rose again to life unending; and it was the realization of this staggering fact which so transformed the situation for his dispirited disciples, rousing them from the torpor into which his death had plunged them, and quickening their memory of what he had repeatedly told them of the course which events were to follow (see John 14:26). Before, all had been mystery and frustration; but afterwards it was as though scales had fallen from their eyes. They now once more saw sense in what the Cross had seemed to reduce to nonsense, and at once it became their urgent pursuit to recover the facts about his Ministry from the oblivion into which they had been wistfully prepared to let them slip. As a result many in fact took in hand "to set forth in order a declaration of those things" of which the Cross had apparently made a hideous mockery, but which had now, in the light of the Resurrection, come to be "most surely believed" among them (Luke 1:1). Nothing that they had heard Jesus saying, or which had been reported to them as a genuine utterance of his, now seemed too far-fetched to warrant recording for the information both of their contemporaries and of posterity.

Among "the many" in question were our four Evangelists. Like all the others, therefore, they wrote under the overwhelming influence of the Resurrection. They could not do otherwise, and if we read their records sympathetically we can sense their almost inexpressible relief and wonder that the Crucifixion had not after all belied the truth of what Christ had said, nor denied the significance which it had seemed logical to attach to his mighty works at the time that he performed them. The gospels in fact pulsate with joy and awe: a note of triumph and of serene confidence sounds through them all from end to end. Through long familiarity we have come to read them with a phlegm and impassivity which are in sharp contrast to the amazement felt both by those who came into actual contact with Jesus, and by those who first read those gospel accounts of him. The result for us is grievous loss, so to repair this loss must be our conscious endeavour from the outset. Let us then begin by allowing Jesus to strike us now as he struck men then, by submitting ourselves to the full impact of his personality as it is presented to us by those who tell us of him. This we shall best be able to do if first we listen to him talk, and then briefly observe him at work. We shall as a result anticipate summarily much that we shall have to examine again in a fresh context as our study proceeds, but the disadvantages of repetition must be accepted if we are to appreciate properly the vivid, photographic qualities of our records. And if we succeed in doing this we shall realize, as never before, how much in character are the words of Jesus as recorded in the Book of Revelation, "I am Alpha and Omega, the first and the last", and how appropriate is his designation of himself there as "the Amen, the faithful and true witness, the beginning of the creation of God" (Revelation 1:11; 3:14).

Hearken!

Wherever Jesus went crowds flocked to see and hear him. "Come ye yourselves apart into a desert place, and rest a while", he said once to his Apostles, Mark adding by way of explanation, "for there were many coming and going, and they had no leisure so much as to eat" (Mark 6:31). Proceeding once as far afield from his usual sphere of activity as the borders of Tyre and Sidon, "he entered into an house, and would have no man know it". "But", says Mark, "he could not be hid. For a certain woman, whose daughter had an unclean spirit, heard of him, and came and fell at his feet" (Mark 7:24,25). On his return journey many (mostly Gentiles, too, on this occasion, it would seem) followed him from those distant parts even as far as Decapolis (Matthew 15:21, 29-31; Mark 7:31). This stir which he everywhere caused was no doubt due to the remarkable cures which he performed. It was not only because "Jesus went about all Galilee, teaching in their synagogues, and preaching the gospel of the kingdom", that "his fame went throughout all Syria", but because he also went "healing all manner of sickness and all manner of disease among the people" (Matthew 4:23-24). But that fact does not minimise the power of his preaching, for time and again "the people were gathered thick together" to hear him (Luke 11:29). He had a strange personal magnetism which riveted men's attention on him (Luke 4:20), and in the end he was obliged to adopt the novel expedient of preaching from a boat moored offshore (Mark 4:1), when "the people pressed upon him to hear the word of God" (Luke 5:1). On at least one occasion "there were gathered together an innumerable multitude of people, insomuch that they trode one upon another" (Luke 12:1), and another famous occasion was that on which the woman with an

issue of blood sought to take advantage of the fact that the
multitude "thronged him and pressed him" to obtain healing unobserved (Luke 8:43-48). We can be sure, too, that
not once only, but many a time, did men wonder at "the
gracious words which proceeded out of his mouth" (Luke
4:22), as they listened to him discoursing.

Such in fact was his fame as a preacher that it won for
him the unsolicited title, Rabbi. It was a custom of the
times for Jewish children to be brought to a Rabbi for his
blessing upon them on their first birthday. It was therefore
in spontaneous recognition of his right to the title that
enthusiastic mothers once brought their infants to him
that he might lay his hands upon them (Matthew 19:13;
Luke 18:15). But what is more, he encouraged the ascrip-
tion of the title to himself. "Be not *ye* called Rabbi", said he
to his disciples, "for one is your Master", the emphasis
alone making it clear who that Master was (Matthew
23:8); and to the astonishment of the scribes and
Pharisees—they who were so habituated to treating others
as pupils—he not only adopted the rabbinical formula, "Go
ye and learn what that meaneth", as though his right to do
so was beyond question, but he even turned it against
themselves, bidding them, as pupils not as teachers, seek
out afresh the true meaning of the prophet Hosea's words!
(Matthew 9:13). We can scarcely appreciate how those
words must have stung, nor how unwarrantably overbearing the use of them must have seemed in their eyes. His
calm assumption of the right to teach people, when in their
eyes he had none, drove them to madness, and when he
resorted even to teaching in the sacred Temple porticoes
they would forthwith have done him to death had they
dared, but fear of the people stayed their hands. They
"could not find what they might do: for all the people were
very attentive to hear him" (Luke 19:48). The common
people knew greatness when they met it even if their
better qualified rulers did not, and they gave proof of their
appreciation by coming "early in the morning to him in the
temple, for to hear him" (Luke 21:38). It seemed natural,
in view of the powerful impression which he made upon
men, for them to liken him to Elijah, or Jeremiah, or one of

7

the prophets, or even John the Baptist come to life again, and the very fact that they thought him to be so many different persons serves to show how his versatility had made its mark. Here, for them, was the teacher of teachers.

The Evangelists, by their careful preservation of his sayings, show us why they took him to be so, for almost every saying they record is couched in the first person singular. Right from the outset of his Ministry Jesus spoke with an imperiousness, a self-assurance, a certitude, which filled men with amazement. An unforgettable memory for many in Capernaum was the Sabbath day when he first taught in their synagogue. "They were astonished at his doctrine: for he taught them as one that had authority, and not as the scribes" (Mark 1:21,22). He invoked his own authority in a fashion which implied that it needed neither assertion nor demonstration: it was something which they, like himself, were to take for granted. In the most startling fashion he defined what was the true meaning of the Law (Matthew 5:21-28), and even revoked the rights which it conceded to men (Matthew 5:31,32,38-42), as though none could gainsay his authority to do so and all he used in self-justification was the simple formula, "But I say unto you"! He even went to the utmost limit of asserting that life lived in disregard of the counsel which he had to give was bound to end in eternal ruin: only by heeding his prescription of righteousness could men attain to ultimate salvation. Small wonder, on this account alone, that "the people were astonished at his doctrine" (Matthew 7:24-28).

But the most astounding thing of all was the calm way in which he asserted, not only that men's response to his teaching would decide their eternal destiny, but also that the very one who would pronounce the final verdict upon them would be none other than himself. Having said, in order to bring home to men the grim consequences of spiritual barrenness, that "Every tree that bringeth not forth good fruit is hewn down, and cast into the fire" (Matthew 7:19), he proceeded forthwith, in what was clearly for him a natural and altogether right and proper way, to intimate that it would be himself who would visit final judgement upon such barrenness. "Not every one that saith *unto me,*

Lord, Lord, shall enter into the kingdom of heaven; but he that doeth the will of my Father which is in heaven". He, the very one who sat there addressing them, was to be their Final Judge, and he would have them know it, not for his own glorification however, but solely because it was of such vital importance to them all to realize the fact. "Many will say to me in that day, Lord, Lord, have we not prophesied in thy name? and in thy name have cast out devils: and in thy name done many wonderful works? And then will I profess unto them, I never knew you: depart from me, ye that work iniquity" (Matthew 7:21-23). "To me ..." — the gasp of the crowd at his audacity can almost be heard as the words are read; if they are read sympathetically.

Or was it audacity? The very form of his teaching — implying as it did such profound claims for himself — presented his listeners with a stupendous challenge. Was he an impostor, or true — a vainglorious charlatan or indeed the ultimate arbiter? He left men to decide for themselves, but he warned them — as indeed one who was destined to be the Final Judge had perforce to do — of the consequences of a wrong decision reached at for mere regard for present worldly advantage. "Whosoever therefore shall confess me before men, him will I confess also before my Father which is in heaven. But whosoever shall deny me before men, him will I also deny before my Father which is in heaven" (Matthew 10:32,33). As for himself, he constantly implied that there was no penal Judgement for him to fear. He was not as other men: "ye being evil", was an expression which aptly summarised the common servitude to sin of even his dearest friends, but it spoke volumes as to his own exemption from that servitude. He could teach them to pray, "forgive us our debts", but in a context which rendered incongruous any request by them that he should make the same petition. Vexed by the faithlessness of his disciples and the perversity of his enemies, he poignantly asked, "O faithless generation, how long shall I be with you? How long shall I suffer you?" (Mark 9:19). Even in such words as these, greatness was issuing a challenge to men, for who could speak with such detachment but one who in a genuine sense stood apart from that generation? And once men admitted the propriety of this distinction which he drew between others and himself, nothing sounded more natural upon his lips than the imperious summons (hinting at a unique profundity attaching to what he had to say) with which he called upon men to ponder his words, "He that hath ears to hear, let him hear" (Matthew 11:15; 13:9,43). "Hearken!" was his terse, arresting, almost peremptory, introduction to the parable of the Sower (Mark 4:3), suggesting that something was to follow that was of momentous significance to every member of his audience. It was always like that with him—not for some vague general reason, but because he himself was the speaker. His words were instinct with the most staggering claim—both implicit and explicit—to uniqueness.

You, my friends

The very way in which Jesus spoke to, and of, his disciples in particular was characteristic of one who was sublimely conscious of his own greatness. "Blessed are they which are persecuted for righteousness' sake: for theirs is the kingdom of heaven", said he, propounding first a general law governing God's dealings with men. Then came the added comment, with its significant change of pronoun, "Blessed are *ye,* when men shall revile you, and persecute you, and shall say all manner of evil against you falsely, for my sake" (Matthew 5:10,11). Here was a new factor: they were not as other men; but for one cause only were they different because they were related to him, and loyal to that relationship. "Rejoice, and be exceeding glad", he added, "for great is your reward *in heaven*"—an explanation that took for granted the supreme privilege of attachment to himself as did his further comment, "for so persecuted they the prophets which were before you". "The prophets", we note: how audacious, yet how natural and in character it was for him to liken his followers to the illustrious figures of Israel's past—audacious because it seemed so pretentious (for if they were as great as the prophets, what was he who sent them forth?); yet natural because it seemed so proper for him to do so.

Here, as always, it was he who made the difference, for to exult in being reviled, persecuted, and falsely accused has no intrinsic blessing attached to it, and comes naturally to no one. "For my sake"—that was the operative factor that so radically altered the situation. "For whosoever will save his life", said Jesus, "shall lose it: and whosoever shall lose his life for my sake shall find it" (Matthew 16:25). Here is a rule to which no man readily subscribes, for it runs counter to our human experience. Instinct tells us with compelling urgency that to lose one's life is to lose all, and that to preserve it is man's first and most sensible duty. But Jesus inverted this standard of values—not, however, for the mere sake of doing so, or even to propound a general moral maxim. It is indeed common sense, in a time of mortal crisis, to preserve life itself even at the cost of losing everything that makes life (life in the purely animal sense) worthwhile, for otherwise in seeking to save the accessories of life, life itself can be lost, as was the case with Lot's wife. So Jesus, recognising this fact, laid it down as a general rule that "Whosoever shall seek to save his life shall lose it; and whosoever shall lose his life shall preserve it" (Luke 17:31-33).

But what he wished his followers to realize (as a greater law which comprehended this lesser truth) was the worthwhileness of suffering—even where suffering entailed death itself—*for his sake*. God is mindful of every sparrow that dies, said he. "But of your head," he added, with significant emphasis, "the very hairs are all numbered. Fear ye not therefore, ye are of more value than many sparrows" (Matthew 10:30-31). Their preciousness in God's sight depended solely on the fact that they were followers of him, we note. As such, he forewarned them, "Ye shall be betrayed both by parents, and brethren, and kinsfolks, and friends; and some of you shall they cause to be put to death". There was a starkness about the warning "to death". "But", he added paradoxically, "there shall not an hair of your head perish". So it was not immunity from martyrdom that he was promising them, but the privilege of triumph over it even when it had been undergone! "In your patience possess ye your souls" (Luke 21:16-19), was

11

his cheering reassurance, so pregnant with meaning for being so calmly offered.

Then, again, there was his special promise to the Apostles, "Verily I say unto you, That ye which have followed me, in the regeneration when the Son of man shall sit in the throne of his glory, ye also shall sit upon twelve thrones, judging the twelve tribes of Israel". Here, once more, Jesus was not propounding a general, but a special, rule. Some only would be so blessed—those whom he addressed as "Ye"; and what bestowed those exceptional privileges on them was the fact that they were "Ye which have followed me" (Matthew 19:28).

Such language was bound to make men ask, Who is this that he should so speak? He was clearly no normal person if he spoke true; yet how criminally he misled men if he spoke falsely! They, with understandable hesitancy, at first shrank from automatically accepting his opinion as law. He, however, boldly predicted that events would prove him true. He himself would suffer death before his followers (Luke 17:25); but death would be powerless to undo his work or destroy his living influence. It would in actual fact further that work and enhance that influence, for they would be brought even before kings and rulers "for my sake" so important a person was he (Luke 21:12). And when this befell them they would find themselves speaking with preternatural eloquence. Not in their own strength, however. In whose, then? In his, of course. "*I* will give you a mouth and wisdom, which all your adversaries shall not be able to gainsay nor resist", said he (Luke 21:15). Such a reassurance was either monstrous impudence or unchallengeable fact. Experience not long afterwards convinced them which it was, but we must appreciate how at this stage the element of uncertainty must have haunted their minds. He, however, with commanding self-assurance, brushed their misgivings on one side, and boldly foretold how his personal influence would in due course sanctify their corporate life as his Church: "for where two or three are gathered together in my name", said he, "there am I in the midst of them" (Matthew 18:20). This, which for all succeeding generations of believers has been a gracious

promise and a cheering reassurance, must have struck his
first hearers as an astonishing declaration, laying the sorest test upon their faith. Yet the very tone in which he
uttered it must have made any uneasiness they felt seem a
shameful thing in their sight, so overpowering was his personality.

The King

Jesus could not bring home too often to his disciples the
tremendous privilege of their relationship to him. "Unto
you", he said, "is given to know the mystery of the kingdom
of God" (Mark 4:11), and, "Whosoever shall give you a cup
of water to drink, because ye belong to Christ, verily I say
unto you, he shall not lose his reward" (Mark 9:41). The
special and exclusive sense in which he used that pronoun,
"you", served to emphasize his own greatness even more
than theirs. Who but the King himself would congratulate
them on having learned from him the mystery of the
Kingdom, or who but the Anointed could guarantee their
benefactors an automatic reward? His royal status in fact
betrayed itself to a greater or lesser degree in his every
pronouncement on the Kingdom. When he said, "Blessed
are the poor in spirit: for theirs is the kingdom of heaven",
he spoke as one who had exclusive knowledge of a secret;
and he did so again, when he added, "Blessed are they
which are persecuted for righteousness' sake: for theirs is
the kingdom of heaven" (Matthew 5:3,10). But he took
more upon himself still than that, for in stating who was
least, and who was great in the Kingdom, he spoke as only
the King in person could (Matthew 5:19). It was therefore
natural for him to let men into the secret of what the King
would actually say to men on Judgement Day (Matthew
25:34), and to approve of a scribe's spiritual perception by
declaring, "Thou art not far from the kingdom of God"
(Mark 12:34); natural for him also, when sending forth his
Apostles and his disciples to preach, to address them as
personal messengers of the King. In every city they were to
heal the sick and say unto them, "The kingdom of God is
come nigh unto you" (Luke 10:9). Even if their message
was rejected they were to stress their commission as the

envoys of the King, saying, "Even the very dust of your city, which cleaveth on us, we do wipe off against you: notwithstanding, be ye sure of this, that the Kingdom of God is come nigh unto you" (verse 10-11). And in further declaration of his own majesty he added the sombre comment, "But I say unto you, that it shall be more tolerable in that day for Sodom, than for that city" (verse 12). The reason for this lay in the fact that any who heard them heard him, so that any who despised them also despised him; and since "he that despiseth me despiseth him that sent me", his denunciation of a city for its rejection either of him, or his envoys, was not a vindictive outburst but a solemn pronouncement of certain judgement from heaven upon that city for its wickedness. When the King spoke, none could hinder the fulfilment of his word: that was the implication on every occasion.

This was as true of his public utterances, made oftentimes to his enemies, as of his confidences to his disciples. He would have them realize that rejection of him was rejection of God Himself, and he did so by speaking as though God spoke to them directly through him. "Behold, I send unto you prophets, and wise men, and scribes" (Matthew 23:34), he said. The language was simple but its implications were staggering, for all that men saw standing before them was a young man, barely thirty years of age and of humble origin. They did not know then what we know now, or what the Evangelists knew by the time they came to record the words. If we are to appreciate the drama of the situation we need therefore to bear that fact consciously in mind, for even as Jesus spoke he knew that the enmity with which his stinging rebukes were filling his foes would soon cut short his life and that the stillness of death would shortly make his words sound the hollowest of mockeries. But say it he had to, none the less, because it was unalterably true and the Gospel writers recorded it for that very reason. In doing so they were able in retrospect to appreciate the irony of the situation to the full—an irony which had escaped all but Jesus himself at the time, since only he knew that the very death which his enemies were plotting would spell utter ruin not to him, but to them. He being what he was, his death would be the consummation of the nation's long record of wickedness and therefore bring down upon them the direst of judgements (verse 35).

Even their revered Temple would be brought to ruin, as he intimated enigmatically, saying "Behold, your house is left unto you desolate". With these words he took his leave of them, but, as Matthew indicates for us by his simple comment, "And Jesus went out, and departed from the temple" (Matthew 24:1), there was once again an irony in the situation which escaped them. Matthew saw that the physical departure of Jesus for the last time was an immediate desolation of that House, though none but Jesus himself was aware of it, and that the circumstances which led to that departure would lead to its eventual desolation by the Romans, amid fire and blood. Already the glory had departed and unbeknown to them the Temple had become no more than a garish hulk which had outlived its purpose. All the more pathetic therefore, as Matthew saw, was the enthusiasm which led his disciples to draw his attention to its grandeur and beauty. How chilling must have been his response, "Verily I say unto you, there shall not be left here one stone upon another, that shall not be thrown down" (verse 2). Furthermore, in a way which they did not then appreciate, but which later they would come to realize, those sombre words threw his own greatness into relief as much as it did the uselessness from then onwards of the Temple.

Even in this very method of confessing his own limitations Jesus calmly and carefully emphasized that greatness. Moving on in his discourse to the time of his coming in glory, he declared, "But of that day and hour knoweth no man, no, not the angels of heaven, but my Father only" (verse 36). Mark reports the words more fully, "Of that day and that hour knoweth no man, no, not the angels which are in heaven, neither the Son, but the Father" (Mark 13:32). The Angels, the Son, the Father—such was the order of ascent, signifying that Jesus claimed to be superior in status to the angels, not in some flamboyant way, however, but as though it was the most natural thing for him to do so. The Kingdom was his, not the Angels'; there was therefore no real immodesty in his assuming their inferiority to himself, but a definite fitness that needed no laboured demonstration.

I came

This constant self-assertion of Jesus was not something which men could react to as whim dictated, but something which demanded a decision. For Jesus himself it was all of a piece with the reason for his existence and to be accepted by men as an essential declaration of his mission, for he could not tell men too emphatically that his advent was no accident, but that he was for everyone of them the Man of Destiny. Yet he could not declare himself to be this without appearing to some to be the most gigantic fraud of all time. What cool effrontery it must have seemed to many when they heard that he had said, "Think not that I am come to send peace on earth: I came not to send peace, but a sword" (Matthew 10:34). Within hearing of great multitudes he had likewise said, "Think not that I am come to destroy the law and the prophets: I am not come to destroy, but to fulfil" (Matthew 5:17). On each occasion the caution given was doubly significant. "Think not" implied both that he assumed that men held decided views about him and thus conceded that he possessed a greatness which they felt they could not ignore; and also that his mission was of such transcendent importance that it was essential for men to understand it aright in their own eternal interest.

If men did not write him off at once as a deluded egotist, intoxicated by his own vanity, they were bound to wonder who could speak with such confidence other than one who was unique among men. And if he was this, they would accept as both essential and inevitable the fact that he should constantly be talking in such terms of himself and making such uncompromising demands upon men. It would not be unreasonable that, with threefold emphasis, he should lay down as law that men's attitude to him was the only valid criterion of their personal worth, "He that loveth father or mother more than me is not worthy of me: and he that loveth son or daughter more than me is not worthy of me. And he that taketh not his cross, and followeth after me, is not worthy of me", adding, once again, these words that spoke such volumes; "He that findeth his life shall lose it: and he that loseth his life *for my sake* shall find it" (Matthew 10:37-39). On the other hand how vain these words must have sounded in the ears of those who, having heard them spoken so confidently, later saw him impaled upon the Cross. Yet, in contrast, how precious they became when he demonstrated their truth by showing himself alive after his passion by many infallible proofs (Acts 1:3). And for that reason, also, with how bold a challenge they confronted men. All this Jesus anticipated. Though persecution, contumely, and even death itself, were all that he declared that he could then offer men as the consequence of attachment to him, yet his appeal was that they should submit cheerfully to any or all of these experiences, because over and above and beyond them he could also offer what no other was capable of giving— peace, final and absolute. "Come unto me, all ye that labour and are heavy laden, and I will give you rest" (Matthew 11:28).

The paradox must have startled men—turmoil, yet rest! But those who acted upon it found his promise of rest to be immediately true: attachment to him at once brought an exhilarating experience of peace and assurance which was a foretaste of the greater experience of the life to come. He, as it were, brought forward the future into the present, transcending the barriers of time. In that confidence he could say, as he entered the home of penitent Zacchaeus, *"This day* is salvation come to this house". Salvation had come because *he* had come—"come" not only in person, but come in a greater sense still, to save the world at large. "For the Son of man is come to seek and to save that which was lost" (Luke 19:9-10). So important did he know himself to be on that account, that when the Pharisees, vexed by his enthusiastic disciples' acclamation of him as Messiah, requested him to silence them, he retorted, "I tell you that, if these should hold their peace, the stones would immediately cry out" (Luke 19:40). He had no hesitation in claiming to be greater than the Temple (Matthew 12:6), greater than Jonah, greater than Solomon (verses 41,42). "Heaven and earth", said he, "shall pass away, but my words shall not pass away" (Matthew 24:35). And all this, so far as his listeners were concerned, came from an obscure Galilean, a mere carpenter, and a young one at that, with no dignity of years to add weight to his words. Yet that he was infinitely more than appearances suggested, his personal powers proved beyond all doubt. He could overawe the largest and most enthusiastic crowd and persuade it to do his bidding (Matthew 14:22). He could read men's inmost thoughts with disconcerting effect (e.g. Matthew 9:3,4), and perhaps there is no example of dramatic irony more exquisite that his exercise of this power in the house of Simon the Pharisee. Simon was aghast that Jesus should permit a prostitute to lavish attention and affection on him. To Simon she was a familiar figure, but to Jesus a stranger. In Simon's sight however, this fact, far from excusing Jesus' action, invalidated his claims. "When the Pharisee which had bidden him saw it, he spake within himself, saying, This man, if he were a prophet, would have known who and what manner of woman this is that toucheth him: for she is a sinner". Poor man! In the swiftest and most decisive manner the falsity of his logic was exposed to his utter confusion. Without stating the fact in so many words Jesus made it abundantly clear that he did in fact know what kind of woman she was for he knew what a false conclusion Simon had secretly based on his knowledge of her (Luke 7:36-47). The awe which men felt in the presence of Jesus on such occasions must have been overwhelming. Yes, truly, this was no ordinary man, as the sequel quickly proved to all but the obdurate.

Who is this?

The altercation with Simon ended no less interestingly and challengingly than it had begun. Sinner though the woman had been, she was such no longer, and that was what was of paramount importance to Jesus: her penitence had cancelled her debt before God. So turning from Simon to the woman, Jesus, like a sovereign declaring an amnesty, said, "Thy sins are forgiven" (Luke 7:48).

The reaction of the other guests was automatic, but so much did they by now stand in awe of him that they carefully concealed their feelings from him. They "began to say within themselves, Who is this that forgiveth sins also?" The unspoken answer to their question only served to expose their folly in asking that question silently and not aloud, for Jesus was as aware of what they were thinking as he had been in Simon's case. So, pointedly answering their question for them, he said further to the woman, "Thy faith hath saved thee; go in peace." His confidence and boldness were bred of knowledge of his absolute right to say this to her and wise men would appreciate the fact (verses 49,50).

With the same finality and with perhaps even starker dramatic irony, if that is possible, the same question was provoked and answered on yet another occasion. The friends of a paralytic had stopped at nothing to lay him at the feet of Jesus and invoke his healing power; and when Jesus had seen their faith he had "said unto the sick of the palsy; Son, thy sins be forgiven thee" (Mark 2:2-5). To many this calm fiat seemed altogether natural and proper —coming from him. "But there were certain of the scribes sitting there, and reasoning in their hearts, Why doth this man thus speak blasphemies? who can forgive sins but God only?" (verses 6,7). How right they were to think that none can forgive sins but God only—for is not all sin ultimately rebellion against His will; so that forgiveness of it must of necessity be His prerogative alone? Yet—and herein lay the intensity of the dramatic irony—how wrong, how pathetically wrong, they were to accuse *Jesus* of blasphemy, as his next action so signally demonstrated. "Immediately when Jesus perceived in his spirit that they so reasoned within themselves, he said unto them, Why reason ye these things in your hearts? Whether is it easier to say to the sick of the palsy, Thy sins be forgiven thee; or to say, Arise, and take up thy bed and walk? But that ye may know that the Son of man hath power on earth to forgive sins, (he saith to the sick of the palsy), I say unto thee, Arise, and take up thy bed, and go thy way into thine house". We can imagine all sections of the crowd, the

19

sympathetic and the hostile alike, waiting open-eyed to see what would happen. "And immediately he arose, took up the bed, and went forth before them all; insomuch that they were all amazed, and glorified God, saying, We never saw it on this fashion" (verses 8-12). Matthew's summary comment is, "But when the multitudes saw it, they marvelled, and glorified God, which had given such power (i.e. authority) unto men" (Matthew 9:8). Luke goes further, and draws attention to the element of fear in their amazement; "And they were all amazed, and they glorified God, and were filled with fear, saying, We have seen strange things today" (Luke 5:26).

The reason for their fear is obvious. "This man blasphemeth", said the scribes, meaning that he was usurping the prerogatives of God. 'I am certainly *exercising* prerogatives which are properly God's alone, but as for *usurping* them, no!', was in effect the answer of Jesus, as expressed enigmatically in the act of freeing the man from his infirmity. The miracle established his claim that he could do on earth what God did in heaven, and what He had hitherto done in heaven alone. That is, implicit in the performance of the miracle was a characteristic claim to uniqueness, a uniqueness predicated on a special and unprecedented relation to God and it was precisely this that struck fear into men. It brought them face to face with God.

God hath visited His people

In the incident of the impotent man we find word and action mingled, the one vindicating the other. The same was equally true of every other miracle, for each was charged with the same significance in attestation of Christ's claims. This will be established in detail later. Here it suffices to state the fact summarily and to appreciate that in the case of the miracles also, dramatic irony was rarely absent. There is, for example, the raising of the widow's son at Nain. When Jesus saw the pathetic spectacle of this woman bereaved of her only child, "he had compassion on her, and said unto her, Weep not. And he came and touched the bier: and they that bare him stood still. And he said, Young man, I say unto thee, Arise". The effect was instantaneous. "He that was dead sat up, and began to speak. And he delivered him to his mother". Luke adds, "And there came a fear on all: and they glorified God, saying, That a great prophet is risen up among us; and, That God hath visited his people" (Luke 7:11-16).

God had indeed visited His people, not only in the sense which they gave to their own words, but in another which as yet escaped them. Not only had a great prophet risen among them, one who could associate his name with that of Elijah and Elisha as a mere matter of course (Luke 4:23-27), but someone who was much more than a prophet. This fuller and unintentional meaning attaching to their words had become plain by the time the gospel writers wrote. It was, in fact, precisely on that account that they wrote their records, and we who read them miss much of their meaning, and fail properly to understand either the gospels or Jesus himself, unless we appreciate this fact, for the dogmatic significance with which the records are charged was not of the Evangelists' own devising; it lay in the facts themselves as they occurred. The purpose of the writers was simply, by careful selection and presentation, to make that significance all the more obvious and arresting. They did not set down the ethical teaching of Jesus only out of respect for his qualities as the greatest moral teacher of all time. He was that for them, certainly, but only as a matter of course, because he was so much more besides. They considered it so essential to preserve with scrupulous fidelity what he had said, because they had come to see that he never made sententious pronouncements or expressed general moral maxims after the fashion of moral philosophers, but that all his utterances derived their relevance—an *eternal* relevance—from the fact that it was he, and no one else, who had made them. They treasured his sayings not so much for their intrinsic wisdom and greatness as because they were no one's but his; he it was that gave them their distinctiveness and their absoluteness, by virtue of what he was. Thus the Golden Rule—"as ye would that men should do to you, do ye also to them likewise" (Luke 6:31)—was treasured by the early Christians, not only as a neat and pithy definition of the wisest and

21

noblest way of living, but also as a solemn declaration of every man's positive duty, since, originating with Jesus, it had the force of divine law, binding upon all. For them it was nothing less than a revelation direct from God, because they had come to realize that his advent was not just the rise of another prophet in Israel, but a unique visitation of His people by God—a divine epiphany. It was this which enabled them to catch the dramatic irony of those situations in which men had groped after the proper explanation of what Jesus said and did, without espousing it, either through spiritual blindness or through fear. Mark, for example, is obviously impressed by the fact that a demented man intuitively recognized Jesus for what he was—the Holy One of God— before Jesus had even cured him, whereas the sane, after actually witnessing his cure, could only question among themselves, "What thing is this? what new doctrine is this? for with authority commandeth he even the unclean spirits, and they do obey him" (Mark 1:23-27), and shrank from giving the only satisfying answer to their own enquiry. Or, again, that a blind man, without being able to see Jesus, had recognised him for the Messiah (Mark 10:46-52), whereas those who prided themselves on their spiritual perception disowned him and slew him as an impostor. And nowhere do the Synoptists (and the same is true of John) demonstrate their truthfulness to better effect than in their frank exposure of the Apostles' dimness of spiritual sight. They above all should have appreciated in whose company they were (cf. Luke 18:34 & 35-38).

On one unforgettable occasion Jesus and they were crossing the Lake of Galilee in a boat. "And there arose a great storm of wind, and the waves beat into the ship, so that it was now full. And he was in the hinder part of the ship, asleep on a pillow: and they awake him, and say unto him, Master, carest thou not that we perish? And he arose, and rebuked the wind, and said unto the sea, Peace, be still. And the wind ceased, and there was a great calm. And he said unto them, Why are ye so fearful? how is it that ye have no faith? And they feared exceedingly, and said one to another, What manner of man is this, that even the wind and the sea obey him?" (Mark 4:37-41).

The wonder of this incident can so easily escape us. But not those who witnessed it. They, from their long familiarity with the Lake, knew that there had been no coincidence here. There was something uncanny in the event which they had witnessed. Many a time before had a violent squall suddenly swept the Lake, lashing its surface into surging foam, and as quickly subsiding, but only to leave its waters disturbed by a heavy swell for a long period afterwards, heaving like the sides of some exhausted monster panting for breath. But on this occasion not only had the wind ceased when bidden, but the sea also had become still and unruffled. And what was more, on the other side of the Lake Jesus was soon to demonstrate that he could exercise the same absolute control over brainstorms as over the fury of the elements. When he spoke it was done, and in circumstances where no mere man could do the same, because such a thing lay utterly beyond a normal person's power.

The conclusion was inescapable—this was no mere man. But what was he then? For in the Scriptures it was written of God, not man, "Thou rulest the raging of the sea: when the waves thereof arise, thou stillest them" (Psalm 89:9), yet before their very eyes these words had suddenly become as true of this man, as of God Himself! God alone, according to Scripture, "stilleth the noise of the seas, the noise of their waves, and the tumult of the people" (Psalm 65:7), but in rapid succession they saw the words take on fresh meaning with the stilling of the storm and the healing of the Gadarene demoniac. Storm-tossed, they had turned to him in terror to save them, but of other sailors it was written, "They mount up to the heaven, they go down to the depths: their soul is melted because of trouble. They reel to and fro, and stagger like a drunken man, and are at their wit's end. Then they cry unto the LORD in their trouble, and he bringeth them out of their distresses. He maketh the storm a calm, so that the waves thereof are still" (Psalm 107:26-29). The novel, awe-inspiring fulfilment which these words had all at once received in their presence would strike them with something akin to terror. In whose company exactly did they find themselves at that moment? Or, again, when they saw him, during another storm, walk serenely over the raging billows? For Job had said of God that He "alone ... treadeth upon the waves of the sea" (Job 9:8), yet here was a man, seemingly no different from themselves, who showed himself capable of the very same thing. Who, or what, then was he? In the wilderness the wandering Israelites would have perished had not God satisfied the multitude with the bread of heaven (Psalm 105:40), but they saw a multitude twice satisfied in desert places by one who was in all essentials a normal man? But how could he be just a normal man in face of what he did? We can imagine, then, how they wondered and mused, wanting to believe yet fearing to believe, that God was with them there and then on earth, for everything this man said and did seemed to make that impossible conclusion possible. He spoke as one who was familiar with happenings in heaven, divulging God's purposes and motives with the greatest assurance (Luke 11:48-50), and revealing that the conversion of every sinner gave personal joy to every angel in God's presence (Luke 15:3-9) with a simple, "I say unto you" as an all-sufficient guarantee of the truth of what he said (verse 10). It was axiomatic for the disciples, as for their fellow Jews, that "the Kingdom is the LORD's; and He is the governor among the nations" (Psalm 22:28), but here was a man who could speak of the Kingdom both as the Kingdom of God (Mark 9:1) and as that of the Son of man, i.e. his own (Matthew 16:28), leaving men to draw the obvious doctrinal inference deeming no word of explanation necessary. Even in giving to men his promise of rest for their souls he was appropriating to himself powers which, very properly, men considered to belong to God exclusively, for He had shown Israel the way to it (Jeremiah 6:16). Whereas Isaiah had said, "Hear the word *of the LORD*, ye that tremble at His word; Your brethren that hated you, that cast you out for my name's sake said, Let the LORD be glorified: but he shall appear to your joy, and they shall be ashamed" (Isaiah 66:5), Jesus had seen fit to use almost identical language *in his own right.* "Blessed are ye, when men shall hate you, and when they shall separate you from their company, and shall reproach you, and cast out your name as evil, *for the Son of man's sake.* Rejoice ye in that day, and leap for joy: for, behold, your reward is great in heaven ... But woe unto you that are rich! For ye have received your consolation" (Luke 6:22-24).

Was all this sheer brazen blasphemy, the outcome of a disordered brain, or unchallengeable truth? Such were the questions that were inevitably prompted by that air of finality with which Jesus always spoke: everything he said and did constituted a challenge to men to reach a decisive conclusion. But to help them reach the right conclusion, convincing substantiation of his claims was always present in some form or other. The cursing of the barren fig tree was a symbolic repudiation of Israel as the chosen nation—outwardly an undoing of God's own work. Yet its immediate withering confirmed the authority with which he thus intimated the eclipse of Israel's privileges before God (Matthew 21:17-20). Even where less palpable proof was not in evidence, there remained the permanent witness of his works to add weight and finality to what he said. There was no gainsaying his right to speak with an imperiousness that none could flout. He merely assumed that absolute authority of which Isaiah had testified in advance, when witnessing that One would come who could —and would—proclaim, "Listen, O isles, unto me; and hearken ye people, from far", and who would be able so to do because he could in truth declare, "The LORD hath called me from the womb; from the bowels of my mother hath he made mention of my name" (Isaiah 49:1).

The gospels are at pains to show how slowly that great truth broke in upon men, but we who today acknowledge this authority of Jesus as unquestionable can so easily fail to appreciate what a staggering enigma this man proved to be at the time to disciples, enemies and the merely inquisitive alike, in all that he said and did. The shock of each encounter left them stunned and bewildered, so radical a transformation in their thinking did the task of coming to understand him and trust in him demand of them. Then, at last, the degradation of the Cross, seemed to deepen the enigma beyond all hope of resolution.

Thank God, all in due course, became plain. Those who had committed themselves to him in faith learnt that an angel's words had in advance confirmed his right to speak and act as he did, and had in the process even necessitated the suffering of the Cross. The Psalms had testified, "Let Israel hope in the LORD; for with the LORD there is mercy, and with him is plenteous redemption. And *he* shall redeem Israel from all his iniquities" (Psalm 130:7,8); but no less an authority than a divine messenger from heaven had pronounced to Joseph, "Joseph, thou son of David, fear not to take unto thee Mary thy wife, for that which is conceived in her is of the Holy Spirit. And she shall bring forth a son, and thou shalt call his name JESUS: for *he* ("he", is emphatic here) shall save his people from their sins" (Matthew 1:20,21). Two vital factors here served to explain everything about this remarkable man—the manner of his birth, and the secret of his death. His death, far from invalidating his claims (as men thought), confirmed them to the uttermost, as the Resurrection so soon afterwards proved (Acts 2:23,24), and brought out the full significance of his name. And not of his name only, but equally of his unique birth, for it was this which explained—and warranted—his assumption of divine prerogatives. As Matthew put it, "Now all this" (i.e. the visit of the angel to Joseph and the fulfilment of his words in the birth of Jesus) "was done, that it might be fulfilled which was spoken of the Lord by the prophet, saying, Behold a virgin shall be with child, and shall bring forth a son, and they shall call his name Emmanuel, which being interpreted is, God with us" (Matthew 1:22,23).

In this statement, made before ever Jesus had been born, let alone his Ministry begun, all the tension in men's minds which the Ministry created was resolved in advance. He was not God Himself, but God *manifest*; nor was he merely a man, though truly a man none the less. He was *Emmanuel*—God with us—a truth so profound it defies an absolutely exact and precise definition in the form of a man-made creed, and can only be spiritually discerned if it is to be properly understood. So shot through with it were all the things that Jesus said and did, that the Synoptists could not adequately convey the uniqueness and the wonder of his Ministry except by applying to him words which the prophet Isaiah had applied to God Himself. "Prepare ye the way of the LORD," said Isaiah, "make straight in the desert a highway *for our God*" (Isaiah 40:3). "The beginning of the gospel of Jesus Christ, *the Son* of God", wrote Mark, "As it is written ... Prepare ye the way of the Lord, make *his* paths straight" (Mark 1:1-3; cf. Matthew 3:3; Luke 3:4), adding no explanation or excuse for so adapting the words, but leaving the rest of his record to explain why he had done so. He knew that God was in Christ and had been constrained to write on that very account, for he wished that others should realize for their eternal good that God had revealed Himself uniquely in a Son.

This was precisely what Jesus claimed the facts to be, identifying himself as none other than that Son. Here, then, was the secret of his imperiousness, his seeming arrogance, his self-assertion, his invocation of his own authority. "All things are delivered unto me of my Father", said he, adding, "and no man knoweth the Son, but the Father; neither knoweth any man the Father, save the Son, and he to whomsoever the Son will reveal him" (Matthew 11:27). Here was the reason why he had sent forth his messengers, saying, "He that receiveth you receiveth me, and he that receiveth me receiveth him that sent me" (Matthew 10:40), using those words in a sense that was truer than it had been or could have been of any of the prophets before him.

It is of such an one that we have come to enquire and learn more in this study. Only with awe and utter humility ought we to approach so exalted a task. Let us then, as it were, put off our shoes from off our feet, for the place whereon we stand is holy ground, sanctified by the revealed presence of God Himself.

JESUS—HEALER & TEACHER

2
THEN CAME JESUS FROM GALILEE
The antecedents of the ministry

B EFORE Jesus came John; not an accident of history, however, but as part of a divine plan, with the result that we cannot properly understand Jesus unless we first understand John. He came as a herald before the King, breaking the four centuries of prophetic silence since Malachi's day, as Malachi himself said he should. In the prophet's day men wearied God by asking, defiantly, "Where is the God of judgement?" (Malachi 2:17). Swiftly the answer came, "Behold, I will send my messenger, and he shall prepare the way before me: and the Lord, whom ye seek, shall suddenly come to his temple, even the messenger of the covenant, whom ye delight in". To counter their doubt, with solemn emphasis the prophet added, "Behold, he shall come, saith the LORD of hosts". Then to shake them further out of their complacency, he went on to ask, "But who may abide the day of his coming? and who shall stand when he appeareth? for he is like a refiner's fire, and like fullers' soap". There would therefore be no doubt as to whether there was a God of judgement when this Messenger of the Covenant appeared, for God Himself would appear among them in His person: "I will come near to you to judgment; and I will be a swift witness against the sorcerers, and against the adulterers, and against false swearers, and against those that oppress the hireling in his wages, the widow and the fatherless, and that turn aside the stranger from his right, and fear not me, saith the LORD of hosts" (Malachi 3:1-5).

This is Elias
Clearly a sinful nation could not hope to abide the day of this Messenger's coming, nor to stand when he appeared, unless first it had prepared to meet its God. So to precede

the Messenger of the Covenant there would come another, according to the promise, "Behold, I will send my messenger, and he shall prepare the way before me" (verse 1). "Before *me*", said God, hinting at that closeness of identity between the Messenger and Himself which would characterise His drawing nigh to Israel in judgement in this unique way. And in so hinting, God made all the more evident the nation's need of one to recall it to the way of righteousness. Malachi therefore concluded his own message, and with it the testimony of all the prophets, by announcing, "Behold, I will send you Elijah the prophet before the coming of the great and dreadful day of the LORD: and he shall turn the heart of the fathers to the children, and the heart of the children to their fathers, lest I come and smite the earth with a curse" (Malachi 4:5,6).

Here several important factors should be noted: the preparatory messenger is designated Elijah, and styled a prophet; his ministry is to usher in the "day of the LORD", and so to be almost coincident with it; and his task is to reform the chosen people lest, refusing to mend their ways, they bring down penal judgement upon themselves. With the assistance of the New Testament the full significance of these facts emerges; and, in turn, a careful re-reading of the Old helps towards the proper understanding of what is to some extent obscure in the New.

From the point of view of chronology the first New Testament reference to Malachi's message, and the first details of its fulfilment, are to be found in Luke's Gospel. The priest Zacharias and his wife Elisabeth were to have a son whose name was to be John. Breaking the news to Zacharias, the angel Gabriel announced, "And thou shalt have joy and gladness; and many shall rejoice at his birth". John's birth was therefore to be a cause of rejoicing not only to his hitherto childless parents but equally to the nation at large, and the reason for this was that he, like the holy men of old, would speak under the Spirit's influence, being nothing less than a prophet. "For he shall be great in the sight of the Lord, and shall drink neither wine nor strong drink; and he shall be filled with the Holy Spirit, even from his mother's womb". Even from birth, that is, he was to be subject to the prophetic impulse. The reason for this lay in his distinctive mission: "And many of the children of Israel shall he turn to the Lord their God. And he shall go before him in the spirit and power of Elias, to turn the hearts of the fathers to the children, and the disobedient to the wisdom of the just; to make ready a people prepared for the Lord" (Luke 1:13-17).

The angel's words were a tissue of Old Testament allusions, both indicating that Malachi's prophecy would find an incipient fulfilment in the mission of John, and serving in the process to elucidate that prophecy. They made it clear that the "Elijah" of Malachi 4:5 was a title, not a personal name: John was to be "Elijah" inasmuch as he was to perform his mission "in the spirit and power of Elias". Subsequent events made it clear that this "spirit and power" referred to Elijah's work as a *reformer*, not as one who did miracles (for the Synoptists attribute no miracle to him); but Gabriel's words made this clear at the time, stressing as they did that John would turn many of his fellow Israelites to God by turning "the disobedient to the wisdom of the just" ("the just" being "the fathers" of old, i.e. Abraham, Isaac and Jacob). Implicit in the application of Malachi's words to John there was also a censure of the nation in Zacharias' day, for had not Israel been wholly given to idolatry, except for a faithful remnant, when Elijah the Tishbite began his ministry? John's appointed task was therefore to recall the nation from apostasy to righteousness. Yet not only in a prophetic capacity, like all his predecessors, was he to do this: the uniqueness of his task lay in the fact that he was to be so in order "to make ready a people prepared for the Lord"—"the Lord whom ye seek, the messenger of the covenant", as Malachi called him; that is, "the God of judgement". Zacharias, himself filled with the Holy Spirit, prophesied also of this (Luke 1:67), saying, "Thou, child, shalt be called the prophet of the Highest: for thou shalt go before the face of the Lord to prepare his ways; to give knowledge of salvation unto his people by the remission of their sins" (verses 76,77).

From these words it is plain that John was to introduce men to salvation, but would not himself be able to confer it upon them. It would come only "through the tender mercy of our God", a mercy which would send it to men in the person of One of higher origin than John, "whereby the dayspring from on high hath visited us, to give light to them that sit in darkness and in the shadow of death, to guide our feet into the way of peace" (verses 78,79). Like the angel's words, those of Zacharias were shot through with allusions to the Scriptures, and were a commentary on them. They indicated how immeasurably superior to John would be the One who would succeed him. "Prepare ye the way of the LORD ... make a highway for our God", were Isaiah's words (Isaiah 40:3); "Thou, child, shalt go before the face of the Lord to prepare his ways", was the inspired commentary of Zacharias. "The glory of the LORD shall be *revealed*, and all flesh shall *see* it together", was Isaiah's promise (Isaiah 40:5); "The dayspring from on high hath *visited* us", was Zacharias' explanation of the means of its fulfilment. That is, a theophany—and that the greatest ever—was about to take place in Israel, and John's was the supreme, the unique, privilege of preparing Israel for it.

John, then, his thinking conditioned by the instruction of his father, and the guidance of the Holy Spirit, developed physically and mentally ("grew, and waxed strong in spirit") in preparation for his great work. That work was to have a decisive beginning, for "he was in the deserts", says Luke, "till the day of his showing unto Israel" (Luke 1:80). Before that "showing", his life as a recluse afforded him ample opportunity of acquainting himself with the testimony of Scripture. Nothing would be more natural than for him to pore over the pages of the prophets, for the guidance of the Spirit would not supersede these but rather serve him as a help to their elucidation. His recorded words, in fact, bear plainly the impress of those Old Testament passages which dealt with his own mission and that of his illustrious successor. What is more, as we shall now proceed to find, he came more powerfully under the influence of some of them than of others.

John, like all God's servants, was "a chosen vessel", God utilising his temperament for His own purposes. He was, it would seem, abstemious and ascetic by nature. Not only did he, for conscience' sake, as a Nazarite, eschew the excitement of drinking wine and strong drink the better to experience the potent influence of the Holy Spirit (Luke 1:15), but he also found the life of a recluse in the stillness of the wilderness congenial to his nature. His diet was of the most austere kind, and like Elijah's his clothing of the most rugged (2 Kings 1:8; Mark 1:6). In fact malicious and self-righteous men made his asceticism a matter of reproach against him; "for", as Jesus said, "John came neither eating nor drinking, and they say, He hath a devil" (Matthew 11:18). John, however, was supremely sane: he clearly considered an abstemious way of life to be the only one befitting his mission as an uncompromising reformer calling upon sinners to repent in preparation for the revelation of God's glory in their midst. So, in literal conformity with Isaiah's words, which bore so closely on his mission, he began his preaching in the barren wastes surrounding the fords of lower Jordan, directing his message principally to the crowds of wayfarers traversing the highways bent on their personal business.

For all three Synoptists this commencement of John's ministry is a signal event. For Matthew it is as significant as the decision of Moses to champion the cause of his oppressed brethren, as his use of the formula, "In those days", quietly hints (Exodus 2:11, cf. verse 23). "*In those days* came John the Baptist, preaching in the wilderness of Judæa, and saying, Repent ye, for the kingdom of heaven is at hand" (Matthew 3:1,2). Mark, with an abruptness that commands notice, and a terseness that directs his readers' attention to essentials only, actually makes the preaching of John "the beginning of the gospel of Jesus Christ, the Son of God" (Mark 1:1-4). As for Luke, whereas he attaches only a vague note of time ("Jesus himself began to be about thirty years of age") to the occasion of the baptism of Jesus (Luke 3:23), yet he dates with the most precise care the year when "the word of God came unto John the son of Zacharias in the wilderness", as though that was an even more important event (Luke 3:1-3).

From one point of view it was indeed more important, for it set in motion a train of events that led logically to the commencement of Jesus' Ministry. Once the herald appeared, the King could not be far behind. The appearance of the herald was therefore vitally important as a signal to men that the advent of the King was almost upon them—as Matthew has it, once again, "In those days came John the Baptist ... saying, Repent ye, for the *kingdom* of heaven is *at hand*". More important still, however, is the fact that it was as much a signal to the King himself as to the people, for clearly the King would know his herald, and be ready to follow closely after him.

Now we have already most decisively demonstrated that Jesus was sublimely conscious of his own standing before God. He, too, like John, came under three most potent influences—firstly, the instruction of his mother (and it is hard to believe that Joseph, his foster-father, did not confide in him also); secondly, the witness of the prophets; and, thirdly, and above all, the guidance of the Holy Spirit, that guidance assuming in his case the unique form of a Father's influence upon his Son. It is futile for us to attempt to decide the relation of these three influences or the manner of their interplay. Of one thing we can be certain, however, and that is that for Jesus, as for John, his course of action was determined for him in advance by the revelation of the prophets. Time and again Jesus indicated that what he did was done to conform to, and to fulfil, the Scriptures which spoke of him. It was an axiom with them that "all things which are written" could not help but be fulfilled (e.g. Luke 21:22). Thus he relied on Scripture even for predicting the treachery of Judas: "Behold, the hand of him that betrayeth me is with me on the table. And truly the Son of man goeth, as it was determined" (Luke 22:21-22). He likewise saw himself as the sufferer of Isaiah chapter 53, and his experiences as fulfilling it in every detail, telling his disciples, "For I say unto you, that this that is written must yet be accomplished in me, And he was reckoned among the transgressors" (verse 37). So we could proceed with everything that befell him; as Matthew puts it, in words that are general, as well as particular, in their application, "All this was done, that the scriptures of the prophets might be fulfilled" (Matthew 26:56).

We can thus see that John and Jesus, their births being separated by a few months only, both grew to maturity during the same period, though in regions widely separated from each other; simultaneously but independently they decided on the nature of their respective missions (and of the other's also) with the aid of the Scriptures before setting out to fulfil their vocations. Jesus had an advantage in his search which was denied John, the very experience of which served as one of the most convincing confirmations of his Messianic consciousness, for it was written of the King to come, "The spirit of the Lord shall rest upon him, the spirit of wisdom and understanding, the spirit of counsel and might, the spirit of knowledge and of the fear of the LORD; and shall make him of quick understanding in the fear of the LORD" (Isaiah 11:1-3). John was, it is true, "filled with the Holy Spirit, even from his mother's womb", but Isaiah's words nevertheless did not apply to him as forerunner but only to his successor. And John realized that this was true of other passages besides this one, and there was in consequence no doubt in his mind of his own inferiority to the One to come. Indeed that consciousness of inferiority was the thing which was uppermost in his mind, as Mark, with an eye once again to essentials, has made plain in his concise account of John's preaching. John "preached, saying, There cometh one mightier than I after me, the latchet of whose shoes I am not worthy to stoop down and unloose" (Mark 1:7). Moreover it was clear to John that that inferiority was much more than moral. He said, unashamedly, "I indeed have baptized you with water: but he shall baptize you with the Holy Spirit" (verse 8). In every way, in fact—in personal worth, in status, in endowments and in power—Jesus was superior to him, and he knew it. We can therefore confidently conclude that, inspired prophet though John was, he had not the same penetrating insight into the meaning of Scripture that Jesus had. For him, as for the long line of prophets before him, there was much that remained an enigma in the divine revelation of Messiah's work (1 Peter 1:11).

Yet John would have been no prophet had he erroneously construed the Scriptures which spoke of him—for inspiration is not compatible with error. To say that his knowledge was incomplete is quite a different thing from saying that it was incorrect, and the distinction here is vital. John rightly and properly understood himself to be in one sense the Elijah messenger of Malachi's prophecy. He therefore strenuously and uncompromisingly applied himself to the task of persuading his contemporaries of their guilt. The first thing that Mark says of him is that "John came, who baptized in the wilderness and preached the baptism of *repentance* unto *remission of sins*" (Mark 1:4, RV). All who came to him, therefore, were "baptized of him in the river Jordan, *confessing their sins*" (verse 5). Luke, in what he admits to be only a summary and selection of John's teaching (Luke 3:18), shows how urgently John stressed to men the need for bringing forth "fruits worthy of repentance" (Luke 3:8). A more terrified readiness to confess one's personal unworthiness was for him no better than the fright of a desert snake fleeing before a bush fire. It was no use the serpent remaining a serpent, and John called upon those who came to him to become no less than changed men. The "God of judgement" was about to appear in their midst, and it was pointless for them to rely upon their lineal descent from Abraham. It would be their spiritual kinship to Abraham—their readiness to be turned from their past disobedience to his wisdom and justness before God (Luke 1:17)—which alone would give them acceptance before the coming Judge. "Begin not to say within yourselves, We have Abraham to our father: for I say unto you, That God is able of these stones to raise up children unto Abraham" (Luke 3:8). No, it was not sons, just for the sake of having sons, of Abraham that God wanted, but rather children who were truly his spiritual seed. Not upon the grand figures of the past, then, but upon themselves ought their gaze to be directed. What fruits were they actually purposing there and then to produce for God? That was the urgent question. *"Now"*, said John, stressing the immediacy of their peril, "Now also the axe is laid unto the root of the trees: every tree therefore which bringeth not forth good fruit is hewn down, and cast into the fire" (verse 9).

John's manifest preoccupation with impending judgement is only too understandable. His role was plainly laid out for him in Malachi: for it was therefore his inescapable duty to warn men of "the coming of the great and dreadful day of the Lord" which his ministry was (according to Malachi's inspired forecast) to precede. Even the metaphors which enlivened his preaching lay ready to hand for him in the very same context. "For, behold, the day cometh, that shall burn as an oven; and all the proud, yea, and all that do wickedly, shall be stubble: and the day that cometh shall burn them up, saith the LORD of Hosts, that it shall leave them neither root nor branch" (Malachi 4:1). Useless stubble and unproductive trees were destined to serve as fuel for the divine fire of judgement, as the Scriptures said, and none but those who truly feared God's name (Malachi 4:2)—the precious seed, as it were of the divine harvest-field—could hope to escape that fire. So of the coming Judge John said, his "fan is in his hand, and he will throughly purge his floor, and will gather the wheat into his garner; but the chaff he will burn with fire unquenchable" (Luke 3:17).

The fierceness of John's preaching was in keeping with his own rugged temperament: he was just the man to deliver such a sombre call to repentance. But he would have had no right to deliver it unless it had also been in keeping with Scripture, and this it certainly was. Yet one thing was unrevealed in Scripture, namely, "what manner of time" it would be when the appointed judgement would be visited upon the proud and wicked. John clearly thought that as the advent of the Coming One was imminent—as every sign so manifestly indicated—so also was the Day that would "burn as an oven". In one sense he was right— the advent of the Coming One, by the very fact that it made salvation available to men, was also a stroke of judgement for all who would reject that salvation. Yet, in another sense, he was mistaken. True, Jesus took up John's very words to warn men how the offer of salvation could thus become to them a cause of judgement: "Every tree that bringeth not forth good fruit is hewn down, and cast into the fire" (Matthew 7:19). And what is more, as we have already seen, Jesus made it clear (again in conformity with John's testimony) that he himself would be the one to kindle the fire of judgement—that he was, in effect, the "God of judgement" spoken of in Malachi's prophecy. In contradistinction to John, however, Jesus also intimated that "that day" (i.e. "the day that shall burn as an oven", "the great and dreadful day of the LORD") was not to be there and then but lay in the future. He understood the Scriptures as John did not. He perceived the significance in full of God's promise to the righteous through Malachi. "Ye shall tread down the wicked; for they shall be ashes under the soles of your feet in the day *that I shall do this*, saith the LORD of hosts" (Malachi 4:3). But John perceived that significance, as did all the men of that generation— the Apostles of Jesus among them—in part only. Those words—"in the day that I shall do this"—signified that the time of actual judgement was still a long way off, but their meaning was hidden from the eyes of all but him who was "of quick understanding".

It was this error—albeit understandable—of John's own unaided judgement that made Jesus an enigma even to him, the forerunner. John had been aware that the Coming One would have God's Spirit "put upon" him in a unique sense, according to Isaiah's prophecy (Isaiah 42:1). That prophecy fulfilled itself before his very eyes. Like Jesus himself, John "saw the heavens opened, and the Spirit like a dove descending upon him; and there came a voice from heaven, saying, Thou art my beloved Son, in whom I am well pleased" (Mark 1:11). For John, therefore, there could from this moment forward be no doubt that the King had come and his identity been revealed. Yet the time came when "he sent two of his disciples" to ask Jesus, "Art thou he that should come, or do we look for another?" Both Matthew (11:2,3) and Luke (7:17-19) are careful, however, in recording this, to indicate what the circumstances were which led to the asking of such a question. John was at the time in prison, the helpless captive of two evildoers— Herod and Herodias—whose waywardness, *in keeping with his divine commission*, he had fearlessly denounced; and the question was prompted by the news brought to John of the marvellous works of Jesus. Both these facts shed light on the question, and Matthew in reporting it also draws out its irony. Preoccupied here, as always, with the Kingship of Jesus, he writes, "Now when John had heard in prison the works of Christ, he sent two of his disciples, and said unto him, Art thou he that should come, or do we look for another?" Let us note the words—"the works of *Christ*". This is a confession of faith by Matthew called forth by the implications of John's question, namely, that Jesus was not, after all, the Anointed. We judge John harshly and unfairly, however, if we accuse him of rank unbelief for asking such a question—a thing incredible in view of his own witnessing of the anointing of Jesus. No, not unbelief, but bewilderment, was what the question expressed. First the anointing, then the works. Yes, Jesus was the Coming One, and had actually "come", of that there could be no doubt; and exactly as Isaiah had predicted, it had been reported to John that Jesus had been able "to open the blind eyes" (Isaiah 42:7) and given other tokens of his identity as the One who would "set judgement in the earth" (Isaiah 42:4). But why did he not also proceed "to bring out the prisoners from the prison, and them that sit in darkness out of the prison house" (Isaiah 42:7)? That was what baffled John.

We miss the pathos of the situation completely unless we bear in mind that "John had heard *in the prison* the works of Christ". He knew that Jesus had been anointed with the Spirit expressly "to bind up the brokenhearted, to proclaim liberty to the captives, and the opening of the prison to them that are bound" (Isaiah 61:1). Yet he himself still lay languishing in prison! It seemed to him that something was amiss—and so there was, but only in his own understanding, both of the mission of Jesus, and of his own. The reply which Jesus sent was purposely enigmatic, and constituted an invitation to John to ponder the Scriptures afresh. "In that same hour he cured many of their infirmities and plagues, and of evil spirits; and unto many that were blind he gave sight. Then Jesus answering said unto them. Go your way, and tell John what things ye have seen and heard; how that the blind see, the lame walk, the lepers are cleansed, the deaf hear, the dead are raised", and, finally (and paradoxically as the culminating sign) "to the poor the gospel is preached". Then came the gentle rebuke, "And blessed is he, whosoever shall not be offended in me" (Luke 7:21-23).

The cures were purposely performed to lend point to the answer which Jesus sent to John. They demonstrated beyond doubt that Jesus was indeed the Coming One. The fact was that John had missed the distinction between "the acceptable year of the LORD, and the day of vengeance of our God" (Isaiah 61:2): the one had to precede the other, but he, engrossed with the work of the Anointed in bringing forth judgement unto truth, had not taken into account that it was also first written, "A bruised reed shall he not break, and the smoking flax shall he not quench" (Isaiah 42:3). That is, Jesus intimated to John that it was not his own mission *at that time* to bring physical deliverance by coercive methods (cf. Matthew 12:14-21), nor John's privilege to be excused from suffering for righteousness' sake. On the contrary it was part of John's work so to suffer, for Jesus himself was destined so to suffer also, and *in this respect as in every other, John was destined to be the forerunner.*

This great fact, here implicit only, was stated explicitly by Jesus on a later occasion. The disciples shared John's bewilderment at the unexpected course of events, and they "asked him, saying, Why then say the scribes that Elias must first come? And Jesus answered and said unto them, Elias truly shall first come, and restore all things. But I say unto you, That Elias is come already and they knew him not". Then Jesus added (for by this time John had died a victim of Herodias' hatred): "But they have done unto him whatsoever they listed. Likewise shall also the Son of man suffer of them". Matthew's comment is, "Then the disciples understood that he spake unto them of John the Baptist" (Matthew 17:10-13). Mark's report of Christ's words has a significant addition: "But I say unto you, that Elias is indeed come, and they have done unto him whatsoever they listed, *as it is written of him*" (Mark 9:13). John, manifestly, had not seen things that way. There was place in his thinking for the sufferings of Christ, for not otherwise could he visualize the Anointed becoming "a covenant of the people" (Isaiah 42:6), or pouring out "his soul unto death" (53:12) so that sinners might be healed by his stripes (Isaiah 53:5). But the foremost place in his thinking was, it is evident from his preaching, occupied by the glory, rather than the sufferings, of the Anointed, and the precise relationship between the two proved to be beyond his ken. It had escaped him therefore that in fulfilment of his vocation he would be called upon to precede the Anointed also along the way of martyrdom, and that far from treading down the wicked (such as Herod and Herodias) like ashes under the soles of their feet (Malachi 4:3) he would first have to be trodden down under the soles of their feet. Would he—or, for that matter, any one else— shrink from following the path of duty? That for him was the operative question, not whether Jesus was the Coming One. So, said Jesus, in mingled rebuke and encouragement, "Blessed is he, whosoever shall not be offended in me" (Matthew 11:6).

So John died beneath the executioner's sword, a true forerunner of the Coming One, his dearest longings and expectations unfulfilled—as yet. As Jesus said to the people when his two disciples had set off back to the prison with the answer to John's enquiry, "All the prophets and the law prophesied until John. And if ye will receive it, this is Elias, which was for to come". There was a profundity in those words as great as in his enigmatic message to John. The wise would seek it out, and he invited them to do so, adding, "He that hath ears to hear let him hear" (Matthew 11:13-15). John, though none but Jesus realized it, had not only to prepare the way of the Lord, but had also in one respect himself to traverse it to the end—even to death.

The messenger of the covenant

"This", said Jesus weightily, "is Elias, which was for to come". This of necessity meant that another was to come close behind him. More, it meant that that other had actually come, and was in fact the speaker who addressed these very words to the people. If John was conscious of his vocation, Jesus was immeasurably more so. The gospels convey no other impression but that Jesus was aware of his appointed work down to the minutest detail. Time and again as we proceed we shall find that this was so, but already we have discovered the secret of Jesus' self-possession and have sufficient warrant for assuming that when he began his Ministry he knew the time to be propitious. Thanks to Luke, we know that at the tender age of twelve he was aware of his relationship to God, and by virtue of that relationship had an astounding grasp of the Scriptures. His sorrowing and anxious parents "found him in the temple, sitting in the midst of the doctors, both hearing them and asking them questions. And all that heard him were astonished at his understanding and answers" (Luke 2:46,47). We gather from this that Jesus sat as a pupil before the Rabbis. But never had there been a pupil before like this, so exacting were his enquiries and so penetrating was his insight into the meaning of Scripture. Yet the fact that he felt the urge to make enquiries of the authorities of those days is proof that his knowledge was still expanding and as yet incomplete. All that was so far fully developed was his sense of mission. When Mary and Joseph chided him for causing them such concern for his safety, with an ingenuousness that was perfectly natural to one who was aware that he was uniquely related to God, he replied, "How is it that ye sought me?" By that he meant that they should have known that there was one place only where he would be bound to be found— the Temple. It was they, not he, who merited reproach; "Wist ye not that I must be about my Father's business?" he asked (Luke 2:42-49). That is, already he conceived of himself as a Levite, under the obligation to minister full-time in the service of God, but with this difference, that, for him, God was also Father. So profound a consciousness was beyond the power of Mary and Joseph to understand; he was undergoing an experience which they could never hope to share, and, inevitably, "they understood not the saying which he spake unto them" (verse 50), though Mary in particular continued to brood enquiringly over all that had happened on this memorable occasion. Not yet, however, had Jesus reached the stage of experience where his divine sonship had to assert itself to the exclusion of the human; almost twenty years had still to elapse before that took place. So "he went down with them and came to Nazareth, and was subject unto them" (verse 51). Thus the years passed with the mental and physical development of Jesus, for all their distinctiveness, following a natural course. "Jesus", says Luke, "increased in wisdom and stature, and in favour with God and man" (verse 52).

Then something happened which transformed the situation. "The word of God came unto John the son of Zacharias in the wilderness" (Luke 3:2). God Himself took the initiative, as it were, and the day of John's "showing unto Israel" had arrived. At once a great stir was caused, "and there went out unto him all the land of Judæa, and they of Jerusalem" (Mark 1:5), plus (as Matthew tells us) "all the region round about Jordan" (Matthew 3:5). Men were agog with expectancy and the authorities were obliged to take note of what was happening (3:7), for the question on everyone's lips was whether this remarkable person was the long awaited Messiah, or no (Luke 3:15). John's answer was categorical. He was not, could not, be the Messiah, for Elijah had first to come, and no one had preceded him, their excitement being witness. For himself he claimed no higher rank than that of the messenger destined to go before Messiah's face—"One mightier than I cometh" (Luke 3:16; cf. Mark 1:2). His chosen place of witness—the wilderness—announced to men that he was merely "the voice of one crying in the wilderness, Prepare ye the way of the Lord", and that he was not himself the Lord who would manifest God's glory before all flesh (Mark 1:3; Isaiah 40:3,5).

Then who was that Lord? Clearly someone yet to be revealed—and soon. But who, in fact, was he? None knew the answer, not even John, but only the One concerned. And for him also the day of his showing to Israel had now likewise come. His Messianic consciousness had now at last come to the full, and the decisive hour to break with all earthly ties had arrived. This meant that John's work was finished; the herald had to give place to the King, but this he could not do unless first he knew who the King was.

For John the knowledge came in startling fashion. It would be a routine matter for him to seek, by private interview, to assure himself that each candidate for baptism was sincere, and a discourse on repentance would on such occasions be axiomatic, the baptismal act also in many cases, doubtless, being performed in private. Finally the day came for Jesus to set out along the appointed path of duty. As Matthew has it, "Then cometh Jesus from Galilee to Jordan unto John, to be baptized of him". John quickly perceived what manner of man stood before him. This man had no sin to confess or be forgiven. So, naturally, there was no place in John's thinking for the baptism of such a one. "John forbad him, saying, I have need to be baptized of thee, and comest thou to me?" Yet it was pointless for John to protest: it had to be. "Jesus answering said unto him, Suffer it to be so now: for thus it becometh us to fulfil all righteousness". The words of Jesus were carefully chosen, "Suffer it to be so *now*." The time would come when such a procedure would be indeed out of the question; but there and then it was essential, indispensable, part and parcel of Jesus' work. John could not help but acquiesce: "then he suffered him", and plunged Jesus beneath the waters of Jordan. The very uniqueness of the circumstances is evidence enough that if any baptism was held in private this one was. None but John and Jesus were present, we can be sure, for had there been others we should have had some mention of them.

The sequel was staggering. As Jesus emerged from the water, "Lo, the heavens were opened unto him". That is, in symbol, it was indicated that his access to God (and that access to God which he would offer to others also) was *direct*. "And he saw the Spirit of God descending like a dove, and lighting upon him". Before his very eyes, John saw Isaiah's words fulfil themselves and simultaneously heard them quoted and explained. Isaiah, speaking for

God, had said, "Behold my servant, whom I uphold; mine elect, in whom my soul delighteth; I have put my spirit upon him" (Isaiah 42:1): and here, in his very presence, "lo a voice from heaven, saying, This is my beloved Son, in whom I am well pleased" (Matthew 3:13-17).

The whole incident was of enormous significance for John; but for Jesus it was of incomparably greater meaning still, for it was he who was the subject of the Spirit endowment, not John, and it was to him that the words from heaven were directly addressed. They came as an evident vindication of the claim to sinlessness which he had only just made (Luke 3:22) to John: "In thee I am well pleased", said God. But they came, more especially, as a vindication of his own self-consciousness. From infancy he had assumed himself to be the Son of God: here was clinching objective proof of the fact—"Thou art my Son, my Beloved" (Luke 3:22). Increasingly he had come to think himself to be the Messiah, marked out to be God's Anointed Servant, and he had come to John in the fullness of that conviction—and not in vain, for the Anointing itself had quickly followed.

Yet what is so significant is that none of these remarkable occurrences took place until *after* the act of baptism. Those words of endorsement of his past manner of life—"In thee I am well pleased"—therefore embraced with it the baptism which he had just undergone, expressing divine approval of it—as indeed was inevitable, for Jesus had submitted himself to it as *an act of obedience*. This at once prompts the query, Why? Why had he, a sinless man, to be baptized as part of his fulfilment of all righteousness?

The question is crucial. One answer suggests itself at once. Baptism for sinners was a break with the past, and the beginning of a new existence. So it was for Jesus, sinless though he was; that is indeed true. For him it was a decisive event: it began his Ministry, and henceforth there was no turning back, God endowing him right at the outset with all the powers necessary for the performance of his appointed work. But this answer merely begs the still more serious question, why had he to break with the past as decisively as any sinner? The vital clue lies in the fact that he broke with it *in precisely the same way as sinners themselves.* This can only mean that there was some radical connection between them and him. There was: like them he sprang from Adam, as Luke is at pains to emphasize by deliberately appending the genealogy of Christ to his account of his baptism (Luke 3:21,22,23-38), tracing it back to the very beginning of the human family. Now no child was born to Adam *until after sin had entered into the world.* With sin came death, passing like a congenital malady to every one of his descendants, even to Jesus, partaker as he was of our human nature. Here then, in an act which so aptly symbolized death, Jesus identified himself with sinners, so anticipating that literal death in which he would, in due course, be "numbered with the transgressors" and so "bear their iniquities" (Isaiah 53:11,12). It would not have been consonant with the justice of God for Jesus to have been "numbered with transgressors", and for God to lay their iniquities upon him (Isaiah 53:6), unless in one respect he and they had something in common; unless there were some nexus uniting them. There was such a nexus: it was their common human nature with all its frailty and proneness to wrongdoing. It was therefore dramatically fitting that, no sooner had Jesus so identified himself with sinners than he himself came to experience the sorest temptation imaginable to do wrong, a temptation more intense than anything he had yet endured because it resulted directly from his unique experience after emerging from the waters of the Jordan.

The temptation in the wilderness

All three Synoptists stress the connection between Christ's endowment with the Spirit and his Temptation, Mark doing so with especial vigour (weaker though his language may be than it sounds in our English translation). "There came a voice from heaven, saying, Thou art my beloved Son, in whom I am well pleased. And immediately the Spirit driveth him into the wilderness. And he was there in the wilderness forty days, tempted of Satan" (Mark 1:11-13; cf. Matthew 4:1; Luke 4:1). The Spirit, as it were, deliberately subjected Jesus to a special test.

To put matters thus is to talk in metaphor. The plain fact is that the receipt of the Spirit brought unprecedented experiences to Jesus which were fraught with the greatest dangers—for his Anointing put illimitable power at his disposal. He was given such power expressly for the furtherance of his work for God. But how was he to use it in pursuit of that object? There, in a nutshell, was the simple issue at stake in the Temptation—simple, yet enormously complex in its implications, both for Jesus and for those on whose behalf he had set out on his divinely appointed mission.

The awfulness of the Temptation lay in its uniqueness. It befell—and could only have befallen—one man. Suddenly, at Jordan, Jesus—a flesh and blood man like ourselves, one tempted like as we are (Hebrews 4:15) because physically he was as we are (Hebrews 2:14)— became aware that he possessed the ability to accomplish anything he chose to do. Command of the Spirit's energy had been entrusted to him. The access of power which he experienced as a result is beyond the capacity of our imagination fully to understand, for we cannot ourselves get to know it experimentally. Neither on that account can we fully enter into the mental struggle that ensued for Jesus. But that such a struggle did ensue the record of the Temptation bears out only too plainly. Jesus had risen from the waters of Jordan to begin his mission, but in a flash, he who had come to Jordan so serenely composed in mind, had the problem of how that mission was to be discharged thrust upon him in a wholly novel form. It must have been in a mood of almost terrifying elation that Jesus at once sought to escape the company of men to think the matter out and recover his composure and consolidate his knowledge of his true duty. Solitude was now his greatest need; only prolonged meditation far from all distraction could enable him to decide how to utilize his newly-gotten power aright, so overwhelming was its first effect upon him.

The mingled experience of limitless power and of the fearful responsibility accompanying it absorbed Jesus to the exclusion of all concern for his bodily needs, "and he did eat nothing in those (forty) days" (Luke 4:2, RV). Throughout that long fast his Temptation continued without respite for he could not again join the company of men until he had first settled his course of action absolutely. He had come to Jordan rightly convinced that he was the Christ, and understanding precisely what manner of Christ he had to be—one who would have first to suffer and who only after suffering would enter into glory—because that understanding of the Scriptures which his disciples later acquired with his assistance was his from the outset (Luke 24:25-27,44-47). By the time he left Jordan, however, this new circumstance had arisen which at once put his clearly formulated conception of his Messiahship to the most formidable test—his Anointing with the Spirit. The Anointing itself had been no surprise to him: understanding the Scriptures as he did he had come to Jordan prepared for it. But for its tremendous impact on his experience he could not in the nature of things prepare himself in advance. Not until he had actually felt it could he even begin to react to it—and feel it he did, to the uttermost; and, feeling it, experienced a mental struggle of fearful intensity, which is pictorially represented for us in the Synoptic accounts of the Temptation.

No details are given by the Synoptists of its earliest stages. All they reveal is that it was uninterrupted: "he was in the wilderness forty days tempted of Satan" (Mark 1:13). The culmination of the crisis did not come until the very end, but, throughout, the crisis was one and the same for no sensation that Jesus experienced during those days was in essence different from those which he came to experience at their close. They all revolved around the same centre and the final trial was clearly the epitome and intensified re-enactment of all that had gone before. It began in a very natural way. His bodily needs could be denied no longer; seek the company of men he must, lest he perish of hunger. But here lay the rub: on the one hand, unless he had finally resolved the problems which his access of power had created for him he was not ready to come once more into the society of his fellows; and on the other, unless he procured bread from somewhere he would die there in solitude, and his Anointing would have been in vain (for his mission would then not even have been begun, far less completed). Clearly, not for a moment longer could the supreme decision be deferred. What was it to be?

A lump of limestone suggested the wrong answer. Resembling powerfully the loaves of bread, powdered with grey ash, which Jesus had seen come out of the grass ovens of those days, it stood as a challenge to his newly-gotten power. Surely his Father had not given that power to him only to leave it to perish with him unused? How reasonable it seemed, therefore, that his very first use of it should be on his own behalf, and for the sustenance of his own physical life: "And the devil said unto him, If thou be the Son of God, command this stone that it be made bread". Yet attractive though the suggestion was, it was utterly incongruous. Was the *Spirit* to be regarded as expressly given for merely *carnal* ends? The idea was unthinkable. Then, perish any notion of living in defiance of the will of God, for in that way lay death not life. "And Jesus answered him, saying, It is written, That men shall not live by bread alone, but by every word of God" (Luke 4:3,4). He would leave it to God to see that he did not starve, and would commit himself wholly to His keeping, knowing that as God had fed Israel, His Son, in the wilderness long ago, so He would feed him, His Beloved, and that the very hunger which he was permitted thus to suffer had an ulterior purpose for him as for Israel before (Deuteronomy 8:2,3).

When we penetrate the parabolic exterior of the Temptation record we catch glimpses of a struggle between two interpretations of Scripture for possession of a man's will. That man knew himself to be the Son of God: he had heard himself so acclaimed (Matthew 3:17). What was more, *it was written* in Scripture that God would put His own Spirit at his disposal; "I have put *my* spirit upon *him*" (Isaiah 42:1). When temptation to abuse his gift assailed him, however, his persuasion of the authority and inviolability of Scripture sustained him, and what was written elsewhere revealed to him the limits which he had himself to impose upon his use of that same gift. Reconciling Scripture with Scripture he simultaneously reconciled his own will with God's. Not for his own ends, then, but only for ends conformable to the will of God was he to use the Spirit of God entrusted to him.

Yet the struggle was not over. In repudiating all thought of using his Spirit endowment in his own interest he was at the same time repudiating popular notions of the Messiah. Nothing would have more readily endeared Jesus to his own people than for him to assert himself as a secular leader and proceed to satisfy their material wants; nor—in view of the invincible power at his command—would anything have been easier for him to accomplish. The whole nation was chafing under a tyrannous foreign yoke and the Jews could conceive of Messiah only as a militant figure who would come to liberate them and forthwith found a material kingdom with Jerusalem as its centre, and themselves as the head of the nations. For this conception they had the warrant of Scripture, as John had the warrant of Scripture for his preoccupation with a Messiah who was above all a dispenser of fiery judgement. But not of *all* Scripture: they were blind to the teaching of the prophets concerning the prior *sufferings* of Christ.

Now, as we have already seen, the solemn decision of Jesus to be baptized—to submit symbolically to death with, and for, sinners—in Jordan was proof of the fullness of his understanding of his role as Messiah; proof that he saw the fallacy of the popular view; proof, too, that he was resigned to the tragic outcome of the clash which would ensue between that view and his own. But to reject the popular conception before his baptism was one thing: to reject it *after* was an altogether different matter. In any crisis he had now only to ask for help and all opposition to him would be blasted out of existence by the hosts of heaven. Jesus made that plain to Peter in the final crisis of the Ministry. "Thinkest thou that I cannot now pray to my Father, and he shall presently give me more than twelve legions of angels?" These were not empty words: they were true—and they meant that Jesus could have used the power of God to frustrate the will of God! For him, however, that will was supreme: "But how then", he asked, "shall the scriptures be fulfilled that *thus it must be?*" (Matthew 26:53,54). The self-restraint of Jesus in Gethsemane was of a piece with his self-restraint during the Temptation, and the later trial but an earlier one in a different guise, though the weaker for having been triumphantly endured at the outset of the Ministry. It is Jesus' use of the word "angels" that provides the crucial nexus between the two occasions.

In the wilderness, Jesus, knowing himself to be the Son of God, knew also that it was written of himself, "He shall give his angels charge concerning thee: and in their hands they shall bear thee up, lest at any time thou dash thy foot against a stone". Unlike the idea of using divine power for purely selfish ends, this scripture (Psalm 91:11,12) bore directly upon his mission, and the immunity from harm which attended it. To implement this promise seemed, therefore, a reasonable way of furthering that mission, and the more conspicuously it was implemented the more effectively would men be persuaded of his Messiahship. Herein lay the subtlety of the temptation, but there was one consideration which laid bare that subtlety—Moses' rebuke to Israel for likewise seeking to force God's hand (Deuteronomy 6:16). So when the devil invoked the promise of divine protection as yet another inducement to abuse his divine power, Jesus said unto him, "It is written again, Thou shalt not tempt the Lord thy God" (Matthew 4:5-7). To have thrown himself down from the top of the Temple colonnade into the abyss of the Kidron valley below and there to land unharmed would have been proof irrefutable of his Sonship, but one that was also incompatible with it. The true Messiah was to be no mere wonder worker.

The enemies of Jesus repeatedly urged him to vindicate his Messiahship in just this way, each time they did so renewing for Jesus the conflict of the wilderness. Pharisees and Sadducees joined forces to demand of him "a sign from heaven" (Matthew 16:1). Matthew, perceiving once more the irony of the situation, said they did so "tempting" Jesus. The irony lay in the fact that their request was

deliberately designed to discredit him. They were sure no
sign would come because they took him for an impostor.
Yet Jesus could, upon the instant, have utterly discredited
them! He had the power at his command—but not the
right—to tempt the Lord his God as they were tempting
him. So he forbore—but with what a strain upon his mastery of his human feelings we can barely hope to understand. There is no indignation greater, or harder to keep in
check, than that which is aroused by wrongful victimisation: and when it has the power immediately to hand to
justify the innocent and condemn the guilty its pressure
upon the will is intolerable. If this is true of normal
humans, how much truer was it of the sinless Son of God
as his malicious foes thus taunted him. But he had fought
and won this battle right at the beginning: he was the
master of every situation that arose during his Ministry
because he had become master both of himself and of his
miraculous powers before embarking upon it. The strug-
gles of the wilderness Temptation comprehended all that
were to follow, and as the final crisis of the wilderness was
the epitome and intensification of the travail of the forty
days that had gone before, so was it an anticipation of the
travail of the three odd years that lay ahead for Jesus.

Herein lay the significance of the Temptation. It was the
key to the Ministry. Jesus had to be prepared for every
contingency that would assail his constancy thereafter, so
he was expressly "led up of the spirit into the wilderness to
be tempted of the devil". In the most subtle and unexpected forms the principle of evil would be ever ready to lure
him from the path of duty, so he was made to equip himself
in advance to resist its enticements. And necessarily so,
not only for himself but for the very world itself. It was to
be his one day—all of it. To the Son, God had said prophet-
ically, "Ask of me, and I shall give thee the heathen for
thine inheritance, and the uttermost parts of the earth for
thy possession" (Psalm 2:8). Before his mind's eye Jesus
saw "all the kingdoms of world, and the glory of them".
And he saw them knowing that he had—if he chose to act
illicitly—the power to seize possession of them there and
then. To dazzle his eyes, and bemuse his will, he saw not

only the kingdoms themselves but also "the *glory* of them". Before him, in contrast, lay the *shame* of the Cross, if he was faithful to his vocation.

Who, being human, would fail in such circumstances to feel the desirability of the short and effortless way to dominion over the world? His was a unique position, for none but he was ever thus able, quite literally, to gain the whole world at the cost of forfeiting his own soul. And not his own soul only, but all hope of salvation for those for whom he had come to die that they might live.

Thus in these moments of Christ's agony the future of the entire world stood in jeopardy. If he gained the whole world by false means, then the whole world would be lost, and he with it. His mission was of truly cosmic significance, for it lay in his power to wreck the purpose of God— a fact which doubtless explains the peculiar dramatic form which the presentation of his Temptation assumes in the records of Matthew and Luke. Would his own desires or his Father's prevail? Was God or man to be the master of his will, the spirit or the flesh? The devil said, "All these things will I give thee, if thou wilt fall down and worship me". We thank God that Jesus was equal to the crisis. "Then saith Jesus unto him, Get thee hence, Satan: for it is written, Thou shalt worship the Lord thy God, and him only shalt thou serve" (Matthew 4:8-10). "Then", adds Matthew significantly, "the devil leaveth him", and, in contrast, God drew near in approbation of his constancy and in vindication of his utter faith and obedience: "Behold, angels came and ministered unto him". "Angels", we note. Yes, they were indeed to be his ministers, and God's promise would not fail. Before, he was alone "with the wild beasts", "the lion and the adder"—symbols of the evil force of sin that was assailing him. But metaphorically he had trampled them under his feet and would continue steadfastly so to do (Psalm 91:13; Mark 1:13). So the Scripture stood firm, "Because he hath set his love upon me; therefore will I deliver him; I will set him on high, because he hath known my name. He shall call upon me, and I will answer him: I will be with him in trouble. I will deliver him, and honour him. With long life will I satisfy him, and show him my salvation" (Psalm 91:14-16).

So forth Jesus went, fully armed and equipped now for the strife, assured of ultimate victory, and unflinching before the prospect of the Cross which would terminate the Ministry about to begin. He was master both of himself and of the world's destiny, for God was still master of him. He now stepped forth on to the stage of history to invite men, for their own eternal good, to allow him in turn to become master of them.

3
WHO WENT ABOUT DOING GOOD
The character and significance
of the miracles

THE gospels were written not to gratify the curiosity of the antiquarian but to satisfy men's hopes and longings for the future; not to interest, but rather to convince and convert. This they did not through any subtle argumentation of their own but by a calm appeal to incontrovertible historical facts; facts which, for their writers, were charged with momentous ulterior significance. For this significance no better name is available than the term, 'Christology'. The more is the pity that this word has by destructive critics been more often used to belittle the Evangelists than to exalt Christ. Such critics affirm that the meaning which the facts recorded in the gospels undoubtedly bear, is not intrinsic to these facts but has been imposed upon them by writers dominated by a theological prepossession of their own. When faced by words of Jesus in which he himself attached the very same significance to all his activities, rather than abandon their untenable position, many of these critics do not shrink from accusing the gospel writers of fathering fictitious sayings upon Jesus to impart verisimilitude to the subjective conception of him which they present in their records. They allege, that is, that the historical Jesus was merely a moral teacher whose features have been submerged beneath a mass of doctrinal interpretation which has been imposed upon the original memory of him by the Evangelists.

Such teaching is belied by the continued power of the living Christ, and is utterly self-stultifying. Provoked as it is by the uniqueness and abiding influence of the gospels it leads to the absurd conclusion that the writers of them merely wasted their time after all! The truth is that it is the critics who waste their time. No logical reason has yet been advanced—nor can be—for believing that Christianity is founded upon a fiction; such a view just does not make sense either of Christianity or of life itself. Jesus, on the other hand, claimed to have the key to the meaning of both—and proved it by his miracles. They, as we have already summarily stated, were the authentication of all his stupendous claims. We must now proceed to verify that fact.

He could not have performed any of them had he not received the necessary Spirit endowment from God, and it was the fact that he did receive it which imparted to the Temptation all its poignancy and horror. His Anointing and his Temptation were complementary experiences, as we have seen. Indeed it is no exaggeration to say that if the gospels be fictions, then the inclusion of the Temptation record at the very commencement of the account of the Ministry is a stroke of literary and dramatic genius of the highest order. That fact, however, is further proof that, far from being fictions, they were (as they manifestly claim to be by their very sobriety) faithful transcripts from life, and that Jesus did indeed receive power from on high. Witnesses of his works were obliged to admit as much. For the cure of the palsied man we read that the onlookers "glorified God" saying, "We have seen strange things today" (Luke 5:26), while Luke anticipated their reaction by the comment with which he introduced the miracle, "the power of the Lord was with him to heal" (verse 17, RV). Likewise not only did a once blind man upon receiving his sight, follow Jesus, "glorifying God", but "all the people, when they saw it, gave praise unto God" as well (Luke 18:43). We gather that the multitudes who followed Jesus from Tyre and Sidon to Decapolis were mostly Gentile from the fact that when they saw "the dumb to speak, the maimed to be whole, the lame to walk, and the blind to see, they glorified *the God of Israel*" (Matthew 15:31). Matthew—a Jew to the core—would not have us miss the significance of their acclamations.

The Lord hath anointed me

The inference is obvious: when Jesus worked miracles God was at work through him. Jesus claimed no less. When he came to preach in the synagogue at Nazareth the fame of his works of healing in Capernaum had gone before him. His own words make that clear, for "he said unto them, Ye will surely say unto me this proverb, Physician heal thyself: whatsoever we have heard done in Capernaum, do also here in thy country" (Luke 4:23). There was no doubt therefore of his motive in reading the words of Isaiah's prophecy to this particular congregation, and then with solemn deliberation adding, "This day is this scripture fulfilled in your ears". The words ran, "The Spirit of the Lord is upon me, because he hath anointed me to preach the gospel to the poor; he hath sent me to heal the broken-hearted, to preach deliverance to the captives, and recovering of sight to the blind, to set at liberty them that are bruised, to preach the acceptable year of the Lord" (Luke 4:17-21). And there he stopped, omitting the words, "and the day of vengeance of our God" (Isaiah 61:2). The time for that had not yet come, as John the Baptist had later to learn. Thus far his errand was one of mercy only. And it was a divine errand. Normal though he appeared outwardly, he had been anointed with the Spirit, and his works were evidence of the fact: what he did was proof that he was Messiah, the long-awaited King.

The Christology of the miracle stories, therefore, was not something foisted upon the actions of Jesus by misguided disciples, but a property of the miracles themselves, for they were all Messianic acts deliberately performed by Jesus to authenticate his Messiahship. "I have put my spirit upon him", was the promise made by God; and in fulfilment of it Jesus was able to do as God did (Isaiah 42:1). "Strengthen ye the weak hands and confirm the feeble knees", was the summons of Isaiah (35:3). Mark pointedly draws our attention to its fulfilment, first in the healing of the palsied man (Mark 2:3-12), and then in the cure of the man with the withered hand (Mark 3:1-6). Did it not follow from this that the prophet's next words were applicable to the one who could do such mighty works?

"Say to them that are of a fearful heart, Be strong, fear not: behold your God will come with vengeance, even God with a recompence; he will come and save you" (Isaiah 35:4). The inspired commentary of Zacharias on this and kindred scriptures was, "Blessed be the Lord God of Israel; for he hath visited and redeemed his people, and hath raised up an horn of salvation for us in the house of his servant David; as he spake by the mouth of his holy prophets, which have been since the world began" (Luke 1:68-70). A divine visitation in the person of David's Son (Messiah) for the salvation of God's people—that was the subject of Zacharias' utterance and the secret of the meaning of Isaiah's words and, with them, of the healings which Jesus performed. *"Then"*, said Isaiah (that is, when God thus comes to save His people), "the eyes of the blind shall be opened, and the ears of the deaf shall be unstopped. *Then* shall the lame man leap as an hart and the tongue of the dumb shall sing". Jesus did all these things, says Mark in effect. Twice he records the restoration of sight to the blind (Mark 8:22-25; 10:46-52), on the second occasion making it obvious, by the very words he uses, that he has this very passage of Scripture in mind. "Go thy way", said Jesus to Bartimaeus, "thy faith hath made thee whole." Mark adds, "And immediately he received his sight and followed Jesus in the way." "In the way"—that is, along the road to Jerusalem; but the words implied more than that, meaning also that the believing, once-blind man whose faith had *saved* him, also followed Jesus in *the way to life*, for Isaiah had said, "And an highway shall be there, and *a way*, and it shall be called, The way of holiness ... the redeemed shall walk there: and the ransomed of the LORD shall return, and come to Zion with songs and everlasting joy upon their heads" (Isaiah 35:8,10). In following Jesus on the road to Zion (Mark 11:1) Bartimaeus unconsciously fulfilled this prophecy in both senses, the literal and the metaphorical, as Mark (his mind saturated with Old Testament teaching) delicately hints.

The influence of this particular prophecy upon Mark emerges in more ways than this. He also records the healing of a deaf man with a degree of circumstantial detail which makes it virtually certain that he had these same words of Isaiah in mind. Jesus, Mark says, "put his fingers into his ears" to cure him, as though quite literally removing some obstruction. And further, to clinch matters, the same man had also "an impediment in his speech". That is, he was a *stammerer*—a sample of the type of men that Isaiah spoke of, according to the Septuagint rendering of his words, for precisely the same word is used (and used only here) in that version as the one employed by Mark to describe this man (Isaiah 35:6; Mark 7:32-35). In exultation at Christ's fulfilment of the prophecy, Mark concludes, "And straightway his ears were opened, and the string of his tongue was loosed, and he spake plain".

The gospel of the kingdom

Thus what Mark saw in this incident was none other than what Jesus designed that men should see in all his works: Messianic fulfilment of Old Testament prophecy. His preaching and healing were merely different aspects of his mission, "Jesus went about all Galilee, teaching in their synagogues, and preaching the gospel of the kingdom, and healing all manner of sickness and all manner of disease among the people" (Matthew 4:23; cf. 9:35). We note the conjunction of ideas—"preaching the gospel of the kingdom", and "healing all manner of sickness". It recurs everywhere. Sending out his Apostles, Jesus said, "As ye go, preach, saying, The kingdom of heaven is at hand. Heal the sick, cleanse the lepers, raise the dead, cast out devils: freely ye have received, freely give" (Matthew 10:7,8). "And they departed", says Luke, "and went through the towns, preaching the gospel, and healing every where" (Luke 9:6). It was the same with the Seventy who were sent out later (Luke 10:9), and similarly the news which John's two messengers were to bear back to him in prison was "how that the blind see, the lame walk, the lepers are cleansed, the deaf hear, the dead are raised", and then, finally, that "to the poor the gospel is preached" (Luke 7:22). Jesus' cures were the good news come to reality, a present foretaste of the coming kingdom.

I beheld Satan fall

His enemies roundly denied this. When on one occasion he healed a dumb demoniac, "the multitudes marvelled, saying, It was never so seen in Israel. But the Pharisees said, He casteth out devils through the prince of devils" (Matthew 9:32-34). Nor was this the only time that they attributed his actions to the power of the devil. Later, when he had cured a similar demoniac, who was also blind, they renewed this infamous charge, in muttered undertones this time because the crowds construed the cure as a Messianic act. "All the people were amazed and said, Is not this the son of David?" 'The son of the devil, more like', was in effect the retort of the Pharisees; or, to quote Matthew, "But when the Pharisees heard it, they said, This fellow doth not cast out devils, but by Beelzebub the prince of the devils". "And Jesus knew their thoughts", adds Matthew, who next proceeds to show how Jesus swept aside their false reasoning (Matthew 12:22-27).

Their charge was the grossest blasphemy and also the negation of common sense. If, as they alleged, Jesus was effecting his cures "by Beelzebub" then Beelzebub was doing God's work for Him and stultifying his own! "If Satan cast out Satan, he is divided against himself'; how shall then his kingdom stand?" asked Jesus with devastating logic, leaving them next to reconcile their approval of their own relatives' attempts at exorcism with the false construction which they put upon his own incontrovertible cures. No, the truth was that Satan's kingdom was being invaded by God's Kingdom in the person of the King: God, through him, was putting Satan to rout.

Here, once again, if we are to appreciate the true drama of the situation and the full power of Jesus' reasoning we need to note to what extent his language was penetrated by the phraseology of the Old Testament prophecies. As in Mark's accounts of his cures, here, too, there is a palpable allusion to Isaiah's thirty-fifth chapter. "Your God will come ... and save you. *Then* the eyes of the blind shall be opened and the tongue of the dumb sing", had been the prophet's promise (Isaiah 35:4-6). In their very presence a once blind and dumb demoniac man had just been cured by Jesus so that he "both spake and saw". The conclusion was therefore inevitable: Isaiah's "then" had become "now"; therefore God had actually "come to save" in the person of Jesus. As Peter put it later, "God anointed Jesus of Nazareth with the Holy Spirit and with power: who went about doing good, and healing all that were oppressed of the devil; *for God was with him*" (Acts 10:38). Or, as Jesus put it at the time, "If I cast out devils by the Spirit of God, then the kingdom of God is come unto you" (Matthew 12:28). If only they could see it, the assurances of God were taking effect before their very eyes. When Israel were in exile the captives' plight would seem hopeless, their servitude interminable. "Shall the prey be taken from the mighty, or the lawful captive delivered?" they would despairingly ask (Isaiah 49:24). But their despair, as the prophet proceeded to make plain, would result only from a forgetfulness and underestimation of God's power, for He was stronger than any earthly monarch who might downtread them: "But thus saith the LORD, Even the captives of the mighty shall be taken away, and the prey of the terrible shall be delivered: for I will contend with him that contendeth with thee, and I will save thy children ... and all flesh shall know that I the LORD am thy Saviour and thy Redeemer, the mighty One of Jacob" (Isaiah 49:25,26). Jesus, knowing himself to have been expressly anointed "to proclaim liberty to the captives" (Isaiah 61:1), at once took up the prophet's words, and applied them allegorically to his own power over disease. "Or else how can one enter into a strong man's house, and spoil his goods, except he first bind the strong man? and then he will spoil his house" (Matthew 12:29). Far from working as Satan's subordinate, each time he performed his cures he was on the contrary asserting his power over Satan and demonstrating God's sovereignty over all things, the forces of evil included. Then followed the stern words, "He that is not with me is against me; and he that gathereth not with me scattereth abroad" (verse 30).

These words were tinged with dramatic irony. Self-righteous men had accused him of being one of Satan's agents. The tragic truth was that thereby they merely proved that they were no more than that themselves, and actually in conflict with the goodness of God as made manifest in Jesus. "O generation of vipers, how can ye, being evil, speak good things?" asked Jesus, castigating them for their hypocrisy (verse 34). He was on God's side: so, if they were not on his side, they were inevitably on Satan's, for no neutrality is possible in the struggle between good and evil.

The claims implicit in these words of Jesus here were stupendous. But his cures authenticated them to the uttermost; and not his own only, but also those performed by his messengers whom he had endowed with his own power. The Seventy, their twin task of preaching and healing done, "returned again with joy, saying, Lord, even the devils are subject unto us through thy name". Jesus saw a prophetic significance in their work—the final triumph of good over evil—and acclaimed it exultantly, saying, "I beheld Satan as lightning fall from heaven" (Luke 10:17,18), using for that purpose the same pictorial form of language as he used to predict the ruin of wicked Capernaum (verse 15).

The prison house

This moral issue which Jesus presented the Pharisees in concluding his altercation with them interprets his otherwise enigmatic language for us. He was obviously speaking metaphorically throughout, for in claiming to be "stronger" than Satan it was not physical strength that he had in mind, and in drawing a parallel between the bondage of exiled Israel and the plight of the diseased he likewise made it clear that he was speaking parabolically. The mistake that John the Baptist made was to attach a literal meaning to the work allotted to the Coming One of bringing "the prisoners from the prison, and them that sit in darkness out of the prison house" at a time when a figurative meaning only was required. Having stated that, however, we are still left with the task of deciding what was the actual literal truth which Jesus was expressing in this parabolic way. What was the prison house, and who were the captives, and what manner of person was he who could deliver and release them? The answer to all these questions lay implicit in Isaiah's promise, "God ... will come and *save* you". Salvation has to do with sin and all its baneful consequences. Each act of healing was therefore an enacted parable of salvation from sin and its effects.

At this truth Jesus hinted expressly on frequent occasions. To the penitent sinner who anointed his feet, as to the woman with the issue of blood, he said, "Thy faith hath made thee whole" (Luke 7:50; 8:48; cf. Mark 10:52, AV and RV margin). In the one case the woman's unwholesome condition was moral; in the other physical. No matter; for Jesus that condition was a symptom of the same disability in them both—the infection of sin; and he made it obvious on the first occasion in particular that he conceived of sin as the disease at the root of all diseases. "Thy sins are forgiven", and, "Thy faith hath saved thee" (i.e. made thee whole) were, for him, but two different ways of effecting the same 'cure' (Luke 7:48,50).

The most convincing proof, however, that Jesus attributed all man's physical disabilities ultimately to sin is in the record of the healing of the palsied man. The obtrusive factor for all the onlookers was that the man was physically paralysed: Jesus, however, treated his physical condition as a spiritual parable. "Jesus, seeing their faith, said unto the sick of the palsy; Son, be of good cheer; thy sins be forgiven thee". To suggest that in this man's case his helplessness was the direct result of his own excesses may be true; but that does not alter the basic principle that disease originated with sin, but rather serves all the better as a particular illustration of that general law (provided it is not used to prove that sin has always an automatic physical effect of some kind upon the sinner). Jesus clearly intended his forgiveness of the man's sins to be understood as guaranteeing his cure. It was an odd way of effecting a cure—superficially; but its ulterior purpose was not hard to detect, particularly as fault-finding men were present to construe it as blasphemy rather than oddity. He was in the prison house, a helpless captive of Satan: Jesus could release him—and did, to the utter confusion of his critics (Matthew 9:2-6).

Thus, as on so many other occasions, he demonstrated that his cures were tokens of the true purpose of his coming—to save men from sin—and of his power to do so to the uttermost. They were concrete realizations of the gospel. Not without good reason, as we have seen, Jesus sent back John's messengers to report firstly that he had performed miraculous cures, and lastly that "to the poor the gospel is preached" (Luke 7:22). Less spectacular though the conversion of a sinner is than the miraculous cure of a diseased person, yet it is no less a miracle on the spiritual plane; no less an act of God.

The gospels are clearly dessigned to emphasize this fact, and so to stress the radical oneness of Christ's use of the Spirit both to heal and to preach. Thus the catalogue of miracles beginning at Matthew 8:1 recounts a series of six events demonstrating Jesus' complete power over disease and the forces of nature and then proceeds without a break to record the conversion of Matthew the publican. The last of the six miracles is that of the healing of the palsied man which we have just examined. As we have seen, it authenticated Jesus' claim to be able to forgive sins in his own right. On seeing that to be so the multitudes praised God, says Matthew, "which had given such power (i.e. authority) unto men" (Matthew 9:8). He then goes on to record his own conversion, intending it obviously to serve as a further example of Jesus' use of this same power—one further 'cure' of sin. The sequel proves this: "It came to pass, as Jesus sat at meat in the house, behold, many publicans and sinners came and sat down with him and his disciples". With this the Pharisees found fault, "but when Jesus heard that, he said unto them, They that be whole need not a physician, but they that are sick" (Matthew 9:10-12). He himself explained what he meant, "I am not come to call the righteous, but sinners to repentance" (verse 13). There was no mistaking the parallelism: he was the Physician, and sinners were the patients. He had come expressly to call them to repentance, i.e. (to extend the metaphor) to 'heal' them. Once again his language could only mean that he regarded sin as a disease, and treated it as such (as he had treated disease as a symptom of sin a little earlier) because sin and disease are as cause and effect. Sin is the tyrant who lords it over men, making them all its captives—or, to put the matter picturesquely, sinners are Satan's prisoners in bondage to him, their physical infirmities being only an outward proof of their inner state.

Who then can release them from Satan's grip? Clearly, as Jesus argued, only one more powerful than he. Once again we must strip down the metaphor and lay bare the literal facts. What Jesus was really saying to his enemies was that only one who was sinless could save men from sin: the Physician is not true to his calling if he is himself in need of healing. So in claiming to be stronger than Satan he was in fact claiming to be sinless—and (glorious irony!) they were actually accusing him of being Satan's agent! The situation was truly ludicrous—but also pathetic. In rejecting him they were rejecting escape from the thraldom of sin, rejecting the salvation of God, blasphemously spurning the Spirit's work to their own eternal ruin (Matthew 12:31,32), as we shall see in more detail later.

Himself took on our infirmities

Nothing was a hindrance to the healing power of Jesus except men's unbelief (Mark 6:5,6), and the speed and completeness of his healings staggered the onlookers. They were accustomed to seeing charlatans employ incantations and weird gesticulations in an attempt to heal the sick, particularly the mentally inflicted. But when he encountered a demoniac in the synagogue at Capernaum he summarily commended the unclean spirit, "Be muzzled (AV, "hold thy peace") and come out of him"; "and," says Mark with dramatic sobriety, "he came out of him". The effect upon the congregation was overwhelming. They could merely blurt out in bewilderment, "What thing is this? what new doctrine is this? for with authority commandeth he even the unclean spirits, and they do obey him". Small wonder that "his fame spread abroad throughout all the region about Galilee" (Mark 1:23-28). But, as Mark proceeds to show, physical, as well as mental, disorders yielded with the same promptitude to his healing power. Entering Simon's house after leaving the synagogue Jesus learned that "Simon's wife's mother lay sick of a fever". The low-lying regions surrounding the Lake of Galilee were malaria infested, and the victims of fever were numerous. Of those who recovered, all, debilitated by the terrible effects of the disease, took a long time to recuperate. This was not the case this time, however. Jesus "came and took her by the hand, and lifted her up; and immediately the fever left her, *and she ministered unto them*" (Mark 1:29-31). So it was too in the case of the cure of a leper which occurred later, "Jesus put forth his hand, and touched him, and saith ... Be thou clean. And *as soon as he had spoken*, immediately the leprosy departed from him, and he was cleansed" (Mark 1:41,42). And, naturally, in no case was the immediateness of the cure more remarkable than when Jesus raised the dead. To Jairus' daughter, and to the widow's son, he gave the simple peremptory summons, "Arise", and his word took instant effect (Mark 5:35-43; Luke 7:11-15).

Power, super-human and irresistible, was at work before their eyes—such was the impression bound to be created on all but the fanatically prejudiced. And each time what they witnessed would recall the words of Scripture to their minds, "Fools because of their transgression, and because of their iniquities, are afflicted. Their soul abhorreth all manner of meat; and they draw near to the gates of death. Then they cry unto the LORD in their trouble, and he saveth them out of their distresses. *He sent his word, and healed them*, and delivered them from their destructions" (Psalm 107:17-20). To none would these words come home with greater force than to those who heard Jesus' assurance to the centurion who had asked, "Speak the word only, and my servant shall be healed". Jesus did in fact, in response to the man's transcendent faith, so act—speaking the word only. "He sent his word", and the centurion's servant "was healed in the selfsame hour" (Matthew 8:5-13).

All the more singular by contrast with this is the fact that Jesus did not generally confine his manner of healing to the use of the spoken word only. If we look closely at some of the miracles we have just reviewed we shall find that he took Simon's wife's mother "by the hand, and lifted her up" (Mark 1:31); that "he put forth his hand and touched" the leper (verse 41); that as a step towards reviving Jairus' daughter "he took the damsel by the hand" (Mark 5:41), and before restoring the widow's son "came and touched the bier" (Luke 7:14). The deliberateness of the manual act in all these cases is beyond doubt; and we find it recurring on other occasions. When they brought a blind man to him at Bethsaida, the people besought him to touch him — a fact which is significant for the light it throws on his normal procedure as the people had observed it. Jesus complied: first "he took the blind man by the hand", and secondly put saliva on his eyes and touched them (touching them twice in all, as the healing was this time performed in stages) (Mark 8:22-25).

It is understandable, in view of all this, that the sick sought at all costs to come into physical contact with him. One reason why he arranged to preach off-shore was lest the crowds should throng him: "For he had healed many; insomuch that they pressed upon him for to touch him, as many as had plagues" (Mark 3:9,10). In the land of Gennesaret, learning of his arrival, the inhabitants "sent out into all the country round about, and brought unto him all that were diseased; and besought him that they might only touch the hem of his garment: and as many as touched were made perfectly whole" (Matthew 14:34-36). They had the same conviction as the woman with the issue who said, "If I may touch but his clothes, I shall be whole" (Mark 5:28). Contact with him tapped divine power, as it were; as Luke puts it, "The whole multitude sought to touch him: for there went virtue out of him, and healed them all" (Luke 6:19). The saving hand which he had so often proffered, they were only too eager to receive.

Why did he so deliberately extend it, seeing that the spoken word would have sufficed? And the question becomes doubly urgent when we realize that, outwardly, certain actions of Jesus (e.g. the use of saliva; the asking of the Gadarene demoniac, "What is thy name?"; even, it seems, the use of the words, "Be muzzled") suggest that he was no more than just another wonder-worker, like so many others who adopted these devices to reinforce their fictitious power. As by now we might expect, the explanation lay in Scripture. He came both "to bind up the brokenhearted" and, conversely "to bring out the prisoners from the prison". This "binding" and "bringing" were made manifest by outward physical acts, his acts of healing. But if they were parabolic, so also, we can be sure, was the physical contact between the diseased and himself which normally accompanied the performance of them. Like his baptism, it hinted at the necessity for some radical connection between him and them before he (the sinless) could save them (the sinful). It did not suffice that he should be sinless, indispensable though that was. Somehow contact had to be established between his spotlessness and their defilement before one could become efficacious for the removal of the other.

Isaiah had declared this very truth long before, and (most significantly) had done so by the use of the very same metaphor of disease and healing (Isaiah 53). Jesus was destined to be "a man of sorrows and acquainted with grief ("sickness", RV margin)". Yet not without some ulterior purpose, but expressly for the healing of the afflicted, as the prophet explained, "Surely he hath borne *our* griefs and carried *our* sorrows ("sickness", RV margin)". This very experience would bring him into reproach because seemingly he was no better than those for whom he underwent it—"yet we did esteem him stricken, smitten of God, and afflicted". The term "stricken" here was lifted from the Law; it meant "plagued" like the leper (Leviticus 13; 14), and signified that the one so "stricken" would suffer the uncleanness of death. But his affliction would be undeserved, and be undergone graciously for the good of those who properly deserved it, as the prophet indicated with mingled literal and metaphorical language, stating, "But he was wounded for our transgressions, he was bruised for our iniquities: the chastisement of our peace was upon him; and with his stripes we are healed". "Healed", said the prophet, in the same breath as his mention of "transgressions" and "iniquities". And Matthew's comment is,

"He cast out the spirits with his word, and healed all that were sick: *that it might be fulfilled which was spoken by Esaias the prophet*, saying, Himself took our infirmities, and bare our sicknesses" (Matthew 8:16,17). That is, each act of healing was an act of redemption, but also an anticipation of the means of redemption—the death of the Sinless One upon the Cross. There (in becoming one with sinners through the experience of death which was the outcome of *their common mortality*) Jesus would restore the morally unclean to God, as the trespass-offering had restored the leper under the Law: that is, God would "make his soul an offering for sin" (Isaiah 53:10; Leviticus 14:12, etc.). "All we like sheep have gone astray; we have turned every one to his own way; and the LORD hath laid on him the iniquity of us all." When sick men and women thronged Jesus, touched him, and obtained immediate healing as a result, they unconsciously fulfilled that prophecy. The only difference, when Jesus himself took the initiative in coming into physical contact with them, was that *he* fulfilled the prophecy *consciously* and with full understanding of its awful physical—not to mention spiritual—implications for himself. Only by himself suffering could he restore sufferers to soundness in the ultimate and complete sense: for those who benefited from his miracles their cure was a cause of joy, but for him it was a cause of foreboding, for in the final issue none could be "healed" except at the cost of "his stripes".

Jesus was sent to lead back to God the "sheep" which had "gone astray". Properly speaking these were only the lost sheep of the house of Israel, so in sending out the Twelve he expressly said, "Go not into the way of the Gentiles, and into any city of the Samaritans enter ye not. But go rather to the lost sheep of the house of Israel" (Matthew 10:5,6). The malady of sin, however, has never been confined to Jews: it is universal, and of necessity the healing work of Jesus had eventually to be extended also to Gentiles, "for mine eyes", said Simeon on beholding him, "have seen thy salvation, which thou hast prepared before the face of all people" (Luke 2:30,31). Simeon's next words betrayed the influence—in this case also—of the Old

Testament Scriptures: Jesus was to be "a light to lighten the Gentiles, and the glory of thy people Israel" (verse 32). Jesus himself was perfectly aware of this. He knew that it was written specifically of himself, "It is a light thing that thou shouldest be my servant to raise up the tribes of Jacob, and to restore the preserved of Israel: I will also give thee for a light to the Gentiles, that thou mayest be my salvation *unto the end of the earth*" (Isaiah 49:6). Indeed it was in that very conviction that he had taken upon himself always to speak so commandingly, as though declaiming the prophet's words, "Listen, *O isles*, unto me, and hearken ye people, *from far*" (verse 1).

As we might expect, therefore, Jesus gave enigmatic hints, even in his working of miracles, that he was not only King of Israel, but also the eventual possessor of the uttermost parts of the earth. The healing of the centurion's servant is an obvious example (Matthew 8:5-13). The man's confidence in him astonished Jesus, who made it a matter of reproach, and also of prophetic warning, to those who complacently relied on their Israelitish ancestry. "When Jesus heard it, he marvelled, and said to them that followed, Verily I say unto you, I have not found so great faith, no, not in Israel. And I say unto you, That many shall come from the east and west, and shall sit down with Abraham, and Isaac and Jacob in the kingdom of heaven. But the children of the kingdom shall be cast out into outer darkness: there shall be weeping and gnashing of teeth". He then gave the centurion the reward of his faith by sending forth his word to heal.

The circumstances were totally different when Jesus encountered the Syrophenician woman. The opposition of his foes in Galilee called a temporary halt to his ministry in these parts and he retired for privacy and refreshment to the borders of Tyre and Sidon. He did so in vain, "for a certain woman whose young daughter had an unclean spirit, heard of him and came and fell at his feet" (Mark 7:25). Matthew, with characteristic interest in Jesus as Messiah, explains the reason for her prostration: she "cried unto him, saying, Have mercy on me, O Lord, thou son of David". This was an odd salutation from a heathen and

Jesus met her request with silence. She, however, would not be outdone, and her cries led the disciples, with more respect for their own tranquillity and convenience than for principle, to beseech him to comply with her wishes. To this Jesus replied by saying, "I am not sent but unto the lost sheep of the house of Israel". The woman was distraught on grasping the implications of that remark, and in desperation "worshipped him, saying, Lord, help me". To her his reply was cast in different terms, at once less technical (in keeping with her background) and also more suggestive (in keeping with her need); he answered and said, "It is not meet to take the children's bread, and to cast it to dogs". Her preoccupations hitherto had been wholly selfish; did she appreciate to what extent the favour she asked was a participation in Israel's divinely given privileges? She acknowledged him as King: but would she be one of his subjects? Her reply was proof sufficient that she had rightly appraised the situation. Taking her cue from Jesus' words she answered, "Truth, Lord, yet the dogs eat of the crumbs which fall from their masters' table". She had her reward. Once again Jesus sent forth his word to heal, as a further token that he had come to bring salvation to Gentiles also, on the basis of faith in him. "Then Jesus answered and said unto her, O woman, great is thy faith: be it unto thee even as thou wilt. And her daughter was made whole from that very hour" (Matthew 15:21-28).

A return to the east side of the Sea of Galilee duly followed, with crowds from those heathen parts attending him (Mark 7:31; Matthew 15:29). It was these who witnessed and acclaimed the many works of healing which he performed upon his return, and who presumably were honoured with the second miraculous feeding in the wilderness; for the record of this, following so closely on the incident of the Syrophenician woman, is, it would seem, intended by Matthew to be a further example of the dogs eating the crumbs which fell from the masters' table (Matthew 15:21-31,32-38). Unlike the first occasion, when the fragments were gathered up in food-wallets used exclusively by Jews, this time they were collected in baskets of wholly Gentile origin and name (Matthew 14:15-31) and the location of the miracle in Decapolis, as well as the timing of it, would make it virtually certain that the four thousand people fed were largely, if not entirely, Gentile (N.B. Mark 8:3, RV,—"some of them are come from far"; cf. Psalm 107:1–6). The presumption is, therefore, that as the first incident demonstrated Jesus to be the bringer of life to the Jews, so the second proved him to be such to Gentiles also. But noteworthy on both occasions is the prophetic significance of one act: "He gave the loaves to his disciples, and the disciples to the multitude" (Matthew 14:19, cf. 15:36). That is, the task of declaring him to be the Saviour of both Jew and Gentile, and of ministering the word of life, would fall to *them*. And, as the incident of the Walking on the Sea likewise implied (again without their perceiving the lesson at the time) this work would have to be undertaken by them, with all its stress and strain, in his bodily absence—though none the less in his real, even if unseen, presence (Matthew 14:22-33). Let us thank God that they were loyal to their trust, and duly went forth preaching repentance and remission of sins in his name, "among all nations" (Luke 24:47). Not otherwise would we have come to learn that the LORD laid on him the iniquity of us all and that with his stripes we have been healed of a sickness which is unto death.

4

WHAT IS A MAN PROFITED?

Christ's evaluation of human life

THE record of the altercation between Jesus and those who attributed his works to Beelzebub has yielded us precious guidance as to the meaning of the miracles. Yet no less important is the light it throws on his attitude to human conduct. Jesus was not content to confute his critics: he would have them know the peril in which their hostility to him had placed them. "Wherefore I say unto you, All manner of sin and blasphemy shall be forgiven unto men: but the blasphemy against the Holy Spirit shall not be forgiven unto men ... neither in this world, neither in the world to come" (Matthew 12:31,32). The words are so important because they imply the certainty both of "the world to come", and of a divine scrutiny of human conduct as the prelude to it. Jesus never argued about these matters: for him they were axiomatic, and upon them he predicated all his moral teaching. He did so here, pressing home upon his foes an urgent appeal for a change of heart ere it was too late. They had just placed upon a good deed which he had performed the most sinister of constructions. This could only mean that, though outwardly good, they were inwardly evil. Their hypocrisy would not, and could not, deceive God, so he urged them to be done with it: "Either make the tree good and his fruit good; or else make the tree corrupt, and his fruit corrupt: for the tree is known by his fruit" (verse 33).

"The tree is known by his fruit". By that fundamental moral law they stood condemned. They had ignored and flouted it by suggesting that his own good works were the fruit of a corrupt tree—a palpable absurdity. So that absurdity was, in its turn, an evidently evil fruit, one which by its very nature betrayed what manner of trees they really were! Therefore like a fiery bolt came the words of castigation, "O generation of vipers, how can ye, being evil, speak good things? for out of the abundance of the heart the mouth speaketh. A good man out of the good treasure of the heart bringeth forth good things: and an evil man out of the evil treasure of his heart bringeth forth evil things". There they stood face to face—he, manifestly a good man; they, manifestly evil. But one day, did they but realize it, they could stand face to face again! So with measured emphasis he added, with all the force of his own moral goodness to lend weight to what he said, "But I say unto you, That every idle (i.e. evil, malicious) word that men shall speak, they shall give account thereof in the day of judgement. For by thy words thou shalt be justified, and by thy words thou shalt be condemned" (verses 34-37).

At this juncture allies of these wicked men chose to intervene with a request for "a sign from heaven" (Luke 11:16). Such a request, in view of the circumstances, seems scarcely credible to us, and wholly irrelevant. To witness a patent miracle—the healing of a man infirm in mind and also blind and dumb—and at once to ask for a sign seems to make no sense; but it does so only if we miss the point of those two crucial words, "from heaven". They speak volumes. The prevailing view was that Messiah would make himself manifest to Israel to the accompaniment of some celestial prodigy. It was this that these men were demanding of him, dismissing his works hitherto—this last miracle among them as merely signs *on earth*, and insisting that they had to authenticate his claims in what they adjudged to be the only valid way or else stand condemned as an impostor! So their request was neither nonsensical nor irrelevant, but consummately cunning. Where their brethren had been repulsed in their frontal attack upon Jesus, these latter would assail his position from the flank. As we have already had occasion to note, no trial could have been harder for him to endure than this one. To know himself capable of producing just such a sign, and yet to desist when to desist meant exposing himself further as the butt of their gibes—this, truly, was greatness which, if only they could have appreciated it, shamed them utterly.

But alas, their cheaply won victory (as they thought) merely emboldened them in their impudence.

As they stood there gloating, Jesus pursued his train of thought, interrupting it only to declare the very nature of their request to be a moral judgement upon themselves, and then resuming it with all the more sombre emphasis as a result of that digression. "He answered and said unto them, An evil and adulterous generation seeketh after a sign, and there shall no sign be given to it, but the sign of the prophet Jonas; for as Jonas was three days and three nights in the whale's belly; so shall the Son of man be three days and three nights in the heart of the earth" (Matthew 12:39,40). The irony of the situation was terrific. They were asking *him* for a sign—in heaven; and he, by way of reply, was telling them that there would be a sign all right, but that they themselves would create the conditions for its manifestation, and that this would be not in heaven, but in the heart of the earth! Absorbed with the spectacular and the sensational they had lost sight of the relevance of Messiah's advent for themselves. What they ought to have concerned themselves with was whether they personally would be able to abide the day of his coming, and stand when he appeared. Their complacency was blinding them to their need to repent, and Messiah's coming—*his* coming!—had caught them unawares and found them stubbornly unwilling to amend their ways. Knowing themselves to be the chosen of God they blandly forgot their sinfulness before Him. So aliens would be their judges as the outcome: "The men of Nineveh shall rise in judgement with this generation and shall condemn it; because they repented at the preaching of Jonas; and behold a greater than Jonas is here" (verse 41). It was the realization that the day would assuredly come when these men would be brought inexorably face to face with reality that helped to sustain Jesus under this immense strain on his forbearance: he calmly committed himself to Him that judgeth righteously. He manifestly spoke with the wisdom of God: but they flatly denied the fact. So for this too, an alien would be their judge: "The queen of the south shall rise up in the judgement with this generation and shall condemn it: for she came from the uttermost parts of the earth to hear the wisdom of Solomon; and, behold, a greater than Solomon is here" (verse 42).

Such, as Jesus pointed out to them, was the significance of his coming for them: it had related them to an eternal Judgement. And what he said to them he said to all. He was forever trying to bring men face to face with moral realities. His healing work was an essential attestation of his mission, but it could so easily lead men to miss the character of that mission and overlook their profoundest need. Men were only too eager to be healed in body, but they were by no means so anxious to be reformed in soul. It was as much to afford the sick an opportunity to ponder the moral implications of their cure as to discourage popular enthusiasm to make him a secular king, that he so often issued the command (alas, all too frequently ignored), "See that no man know it" (e.g. Matthew 9:30; cf. 8:4; Luke 8:56, etc.). Again his first words to the paralytic (so significant by their abruptness) were, "Son, be of good cheer; thy sins be forgiven thee" (Matthew 9:2). Jesus did not want the man's absorption with his physical plight to make him unmindful of his more serious spiritual need. For Christ the transformation of publicans and sinners constituted him more effectively a Physician than any of his physical cures, as it fulfilled and bore witness to the immediate purpose of his coming, "For I am not come," said he, "to call the righteous but sinners to repentance" (Matthew 9:12,13).

Except ye repent

There was therefore a continuity between John's work and that of Jesus, as Matthew (with intentional repetition) makes plain for us. "Repent ye; for the kingdom of heaven is at hand", said John (Matthew 3:2); and likewise Jesus, "Repent: for the kingdom of heaven is at hand" (Matthew 4:12-17). Their messages were thus the same in this respect: only the different emphasis which each attached to the words "at hand", distinguished them (for Jesus actually brought the Kingdom with him). He, as strenuously as John, taught that only those who began life afresh could qualify to enter the Kingdom. The folly of the Pharisees lay in their considering themselves as automatically qualified to enter it without need of amendment of life. Jesus sternly disabused them, condemning them out of their own mouths. "But what think ye?" he asked. "A certain man had two sons; and he came to the first, and said, Son, go work to day in my vineyard. He answered and said, I will not: but afterward he repented, and went. And he came to the second, and said likewise, And he answered and said, I go, sir: and went not. Whether of them twain did the will of his father? They say unto him, The first". They could give no other answer, and Jesus receiving it, then pointed out to them that "the first" was also "the penitent". And he did more: he also drew a parallel between the second son and themselves—and this in two respects. Like the second, not only had they belied their pretensions by failing to do God's will, but had also been content to let matters stay like that and to ignore his own call to repentance as completely as they did John's. "Verily I say unto you, That the publicans and the harlots go into the Kingdom of God before you. For John came unto you in the way of righteousness, and ye believed him not: but the publicans and harlots believed him: and ye, when ye had seen it, repented not afterward, that ye might believe him" (Matthew 21:28-32). They stood aloof from these "publicans and sinners" and made it a matter of reproach to Jesus that he should fraternise with them, but the truth was that they should have been doing the same as he. Instead they made it a matter of pride that they did not! Though "sick" they spurned the Physician on the false assumption that they were "whole". That he condemned them—them, the only truly virtuous!—was sufficient in their judgement to condemn him absolutely.

Thus it was that the situation could—and did—arise where with diabolical cunning they demanded of him a sign from heaven. And they did so repeatedly because it was so cheap a way of scoring a victory at his expense. Once, as we have noted, they even joined forces with the Sadducees to do so (Matthew 16:1). Jesus' rejoinder on that occasion was equally significant. "He answered and said unto them, When it is evening, ye say, It will be fair weather: for the sky is red. And in the morning, It will be foul weather today: for the sky is red and lowering. O ye hypocrites, ye can discern the face of the sky; but can ye not discern the signs of the times?" (verses 2,3). They had their material interests very much at heart and took heed to nature's warnings to protect these interests. How lamentable in contrast was their neglect to safeguard their real interests—the spiritual. They clamoured for a sign: yet signs were everywhere about them; and they merely blind to them, else they would never have clamoured!

Now Jesus did not confine his rebuke to such men as these. As Luke reveals it was his general censure on the age. "He said also to the people. When ye see a cloud rise out of the west, straightway ye say, There cometh a shower; and so it is. And when ye see the south wind blow, ye say, There will be heat; and it cometh to pass. Ye hypocrites, ye can discern the face of the sky and of the earth; but how is it that ye do not discern this time? Yea, and why even of yourselves judge ye not what is right?" (Luke 12:54-57). If the people thought that, in thus suspending judgement upon themselves or upon the nature of the time, they were obviating all forms of judgement, they were victims of the greatest fallacy. They were, in fact, proceeding along the road to judgement, and, as Jesus in parable warned them, time was desperately short for every one of them. "When thou goest with thine adversary to the magistrate, as thou art in the way, give diligence that thou mayest be delivered from him; lest he hale thee to the judge, and the judge deliver thee to the officer, and the officer cast thee into prison. I tell thee, thou shalt not depart thence, till thou hast paid the very last mite" (verses 58,59).

The metaphor which he here employed, and which was based on legal procedure at the time, served its purpose excellently as an exhortation to prompt action in coming to terms with God. The nature of their peril, however, and the extremity of punishment which disobedience would entail, needed more explicit definition so that there should be no room for misunderstanding. The opportunity for this arose almost immediately and in a most natural way. "There were present at that season some that told him of the Galilæans whose blood Pilate had mingled with their sacrifices". Their motive in informing him of this outrage may have been to cast aspersions on the victims, but it is more probable that, here again, they were subtly urging him to begin, as King, a holy war against their tyrannical Roman masters. Whichever it was, his reply was equally pertinent: it brought them face to face with their own sin and emphasized the proper nature of his Messianic mission. "Jesus answering said unto them, Suppose ye that these Galilæans were sinners above all the Galilæans, because they suffered such things? I tell you, Nay: but except ye repent, ye shall all likewise perish". Their standing before God had to become a matter of consuming interest to them and lead to a complete moral reformation without delay; if not, they too would perish. To bring this sombre fact home to them with the vigour which the situation demanded, Jesus promptly enlisted another item of gossip to illustrate the point. "Or those eighteen, upon whom the tower of Siloam fell, and slew them, think ye that they were sinners above all men that dwelt in Jerusalem? I tell you, Nay: but except ye repent, ye shall all likewise perish" (Luke 13:1-5).

The warning was comprehensive: it admitted of no exceptions; and it was delivered with a tone of authority and with an air of finality that left men with no illusions as to the peril which assailed them. They had either to repent, or perish! Yes, *perish!*

Saving the lost

Both these aspects of Jesus' warning need careful note. Its comprehensiveness reveals plainly what was his estimate of man's natural condition. For him all were sinners, and that without question. So none was exempt from the obligation to repent, no, not one. And as for those who shirked that obligation, their doom was equally beyond dispute: they would perish under the Judgement of God.

These two axioms of Christ's were not popular then, and have never been popular since, with the mass of men. Yet, clearly, no theology is entitled to the name, "Christian" which either discards or nullifies them. Jesus saw eternal death to be the certain doom of all in the natural course— and any system of theology which has the inherent immortality of the human soul as one of its fundamental postulates is manifestly irreconcilable with his teaching, and utterly subversive of it, however Christian it may claim to be. So far as he was concerned it was precisely this tragic helplessness of men which gave point to his advent and determined the nature of his mission. That men—all men—were lost was for him axiomatic. The folly of the Pharisees lay in their bland and misguided assumption that they were exceptions to this rule. But there was only one exception—himself. Therefore one only was capable of rescuing the helpless—again himself. So his duty was plain—it was to rescue them from certain extinction, to offer them release from the prison-house of the grave—life in place of death.

This the prophecies made plain in advance. It was written of him, "Thus saith the LORD ... I will preserve thee and give thee for a covenant of the people, to establish the earth, to cause to inherit the desolate heritages; that thou mayest say to the prisoners, Go forth; to them that are in darkness, Show yourselves" (Isaiah 49:8,9). Here, then, even though it meant that the self-righteous (blind to their own sinfulness and so to their peril) would deride him for it, was full warrant for his mingling with publicans and sinners. Not that this mingling was to be undertaken for its own sake; it would have no other purpose than that of saving them from their grim, and otherwise inexorable, fate. Rash disciples wished that fire should be brought down there and then upon Samaritans who had rejected him. "They said, Lord, wilt thou that we command fire to come down from heaven, and consume them, even as Elias did?" Their request betrayed a similar sad lack of comprehension. It was precisely because men were doomed, anyway, that he had come into the world: to hasten their doom would be to undo his work, not further it. So "he turned, and rebuked them, and said, Ye know not what manner of spirit ye are of. For the Son of man is not come to destroy men's lives, but to save them" (Luke 9:51-56). It was enough that sin should be doing its silent irresistible work of destruction: his mission was to undo that work, not to hasten and abet it.

In what sense did Jesus claim to be saving men's lives? That is the question which now presses for an answer. Our consideration of his miracles has already provided it for us. He had not come to *exempt* men from the actual experience of death, but to make it possible for them to live despite it. Indeed, for many of his followers death would be hastened, not postponed (far less circumvented) as a result of their attachment to him. "The brother shall deliver up the brother to death, and the father the child: and the children shall rise up against their parents, and cause them to be put to death. And ye shall be hated of all men for my name's sake". Yet, notwithstanding, there was every incentive for them so to prove their loyalty to him—"he that endureth to the end *shall be saved*" (Matthew 10:21,22). They would be saved therefore in the sense that though death intervened—and even did so earlier than nature demanded—they would be eventually rescued from it. In short, they would be raised again. In that confidence they could be bold to endure; so Jesus added, "Fear not them which kill the body, but are not able to kill the soul: but rather fear him which is able to destroy both soul and body in hell" (verse 28).

Here, at first blush, it might be inferred that Jesus was talking as though something which they possessed—"the soul"—was immune from the extinction which death spells. But his next comment obviated such a false conclusion—there is One who can *destroy* the soul, which means that it has no inherent indestructibility. What, then, did he mean by saying that there were some who could not "kill" it? The context provides the answer. Though obliged to submit to death at the hands of their foes, they would nevertheless be "saved" from it: that is, the experience of death would deprive them of life (in the immediate and physical sense) but it would not cheat them of it absolutely, for their restoration to life would be the reward of their faithfulness. He meant, that is, that what they would thus lose should be given back to them, and, in that sense, would be preserved from destruction. He was thus using the word "soul" (i.e. life) as a technical term, but no notion was further from his mind than that of some immaterial entity inherent in man which, owing to the subtle influence of those Greek notions of man's nature which later adulterated the Christianity of Christ, the term "soul" connotes for so many in these days. His message was to the effect that he, by his saving work, conferred on men there and then the right to live eternally, free from the trammels of a mortal nature and so free from sin. Thus by freeing men symbolically from sin (in the act of freeing them from the disease which is sin's consequence) he provided proof of his ultimate saving power, and gave men a foretaste of the life to come. But no more than a foretaste. Only the Day of Judgement would decide whether that foretaste would become fulness of joy—whether the right to live eternally would be finally realized, or whether it would be taken from them by Him "who is able to destroy both soul and body in hell".

Jesus thus assumed men to be "lost" without him. But did this signify that his advent conferred this right to life upon them automatically? Not in the least. Acceptance of him was the prerequisite condition of salvation. There could be no hope of life without self-committal to the Saviour: "Whosoever therefore shall confess me before men, him will I confess also before my Father which is in heaven". The guarantee was in one sense indiscriminate— any man could qualify; yet, in another, it was rigidly exclusive—only confession made qualification effective. This at once begs the question, Could men then please themselves how they responded to him? To answer, "Yes", would be to make mockery of his teaching on repentance. His was no mere benevolent invitation to men to avail themselves of a boon which it would be foolish for them to refuse. In his view refusal would be as criminal as it was foolish. His teaching, therefore, took the form of an imperious summons (rather than a mild appeal) to repent. Far from men being able to ignore that summons with impunity, he declared, "Whosoever shall deny me before men, him will I also deny before my Father which is in heaven" (Matthew 10:32,33), The men of Nineveh would rise in judgement with that generation because *they had repented* and *these had not*; added to which, the fact that he was greater than Jonah rendered their culpability proportionately greater than that of the Ninevites, and this act of judgement all the more inevitable and condign on that account (Matthew 12:41). His mighty works were a standing reproach against many of their cities, *"because they repented not"*. Therefore if even heathen Tyre and Sidon had been judged by God, how much more proper it was that these cities should be punished too! And in that respect the fate of impenitent Sodom was a warning to them also (Matthew 11:20-24). God is not mocked, and will not (despite His saving love) tolerate the flagrant choice of sin in preference to Himself—such was the stern teaching which Jesus addressed to the impenitent.

Take heed!
We thus see how Jesus regarded grace and judgement as complementary, the first being the ground of the second. But if he brought this solemnly home to the impenitent, he did so no less to the penitent also. He taught his disciples that in whatsoever way it be done, for man to stultify the saving work of God is a monstrous crime incurring certain punishment. Making repentance his starting point Jesus had pointed out to them the folly of pride and rivalry. He had "called a little child unto him and set him in the midst of them, and said, Verily I say unto you, Except ye be converted, and become as little children, ye shall not enter into the kingdom of heaven" (Matthew 18:4). It is the ingenuousness of a young child, its utter reliance upon its parents, its unquestioning confidence that they can answer all its questions and supply all its needs—these are the qualities which render a grown-up person acceptable to God. Only if a man divests himself of his pride can he begin to manifest such a disposition, and an immediate practical outcome of such a change in himself is an unconcern with his own prestige and standing in the sight of men. He is great in the sight of God in proportion to his

self-effacement, not to his accomplishments or his self-assertion; "whosoever therefore", added Jesus, "shall humble himself as this little child, the same is the greatest in the kingdom of heaven" (verse 4).

Here was a complete inversion of human standards. What Jesus would call trust, men despise as naïveté; what Jesus would call true strength of character, the world construes as timidity. The call to repentance demands of a person the surrender of what he values most—his manliness (as the world with all its arrogance and materialistic preoccupation conceives as manliness). If he answers that call aright he is a "little child" again, and only the spiritually minded will pay respect to his greatness as a result. Those who pay such respect therefore honour Jesus as much as they do the man himself for "whoso shall receive one such little child in my name receiveth me" (verse 5). Such discerning people have an assured reward, said Jesus, for "whosoever shall give to drink unto one of these little ones a cup of cold water only in the name of a disciple, verily I say unto you, he shall in no wise lose his reward" (Matthew 10:42).

It is clear that in developing this brief exhortation to humility and self-effacement Jesus moved on in thought from the literal little child before him to the conception of true disciples as being also "little ones". The truly humble disposition which constitutes men acceptable to God in this way is all too rare, for it runs counter to nature. But it follows that since the transformation which it effects is so rare it is all the more precious to God, and that to destroy it is one of the most criminal acts that a man can perform. If to receive such a little child is to receive Christ, it follows that to discourage such a child is likewise to insult Christ himself. More serious still, it may undo God's work in that disciple for he may be led to abandon the faith and so become once more "lost". Not only, therefore, for their intrinsic wrongness did Jesus denounce pride and the spirit of rivalry, but also for their potential tragic effects upon another. He did so with a sternness befitting the crime: uncharity which drives another back into the way of death must of necessity be itself visited with the punishment of death. "Whoso shall offend one of these little ones which believe in me, it were better for him that a millstone were hanged about his neck, and that he were drowned in the depth of the sea" (Matthew 18:6).

For the disciples there would be a terrifying literalness about these words. They would all have heard of cases where condemned criminals—and they the worst of their kind—had been so done to death in the Sea of Galilee. They would therefore have no illusions as to the awfulness of the crime of offending a fellow-believer, or as to the certainty of its punishment by God. Their minds would thus be prepared for the advice which followed—advice which had the double purpose of reminding them not only of their brother's preciousness in God's sight, but also of their own. As they could, by their misdeeds and wrongful desires, jeopardize the salvation of others, so they could jeopardize their own as well.

First came the reiterated warning: "Woe unto the world because of offences! for it must needs be that offences come; but woe to that man by whom the offence cometh!" (Matthew 18:7). Then came the prescription for avoiding all forms of offence, namely, esteeming the attainment of one's ultimate and eternal salvation an incomparably more urgent and worthwhile pursuit than any form of self-expression or self-indulgence, for all the present satisfaction which these may give. "Wherefore if thy hand or thy foot offend thee, cut them off, and cast them from thee: it is better for thee to enter into life halt or maimed, rather than having two hands or two feet to be cast into everlasting fire. And if thine eye offend thee, pluck it out, and cast it from thee: it is better for thee to enter into life with one eye, rather than having two eyes to be cast into hell fire" (verses 8,9). This counsel was next reinforced by a further reminder to the individual of his social responsibility: "Take heed that ye despise not one of these little ones". And lastly came the factor which made sense of all that had gone before; "For I say unto you, That in heaven their angels do always behold the face of my Father which is in heaven. For the Son of man is come to save that which was lost" (verses 10,11).

Nowhere is Christ's evaluation of human life revealed more clearly than in this saying, and its importance is capital (cf. Matthew 5:29,30). Fundamental throughout is the certainty that, left to their natural fate, men perish, for it is this tragedy which calls forth the merciful intervention of God on their behalf through Jesus. But while this intervention testifies to the greatness of God's *mercy* it signifies no less assuredly that men are precious in God's sight *merely for being men*: it presupposes that man, as man, has an eternal worth for God, otherwise He would not have gone to such lengths to offer him life. To bring this fact home to men, and so to throw into relief the heinousness of frustrating (whether wittingly or unwittingly) God's saving work, Jesus deemed it essential to append a parable to his warning. It ran thus, "How think ye? if a man have an hundred sheep, and one of them be gone astray, doth he not leave the ninety and nine, and goeth into the mountains, and seeketh after that which is gone astray?" Jesus was drawing on his listeners' own experience: each of his sheep is valuable to the shepherd, and is no less (but, in a sense, is even more) precious when it is lost from the fold; to secure its safe return is the shepherd's first concern, and he will go to the greatest lengths to trace it. But Jesus was also drawing on their knowledge of the Old Testament: other "sheep" had "gone astray", too, and not one only, but "all" (Isaiah 53:6), as they well knew—and they had gone astray from God. But the fact that they had strayed—the fact that men are sinners—did not minimise but rather accentuate His care for them. He, being intrinsically loving, could not help but go forth to restore them to His fold, so fitting was it that they should be *within* and *not outside* it. Such is manifestly the burden of the parable thus far; and it bespeaks the exceeding preciousness of men, though sinners, in God's sight.

God, then, said Jesus, takes the initiative in seeking to save men. But all sinners do not consent to be saved—all straying sheep cannot be found—but some only. Precious beyond compare therefore are those who, having been lost, are actually retrieved. As Jesus puts it, "And *if so be* that he find it, verily I say unto you, he rejoiceth more of that sheep than of the ninety and nine which went not astray" (Matthew 18:13). The stage has now been reached in the parable where the "lost" one is back within the fold, or, to use the language with which Jesus began, a sinner has been converted and become a "little one" believing in him (verses 3,6). Now it is at this stage (the stage where a convert's very conversion bears palpable witness to the extremity of God's grace and the greatness of its victory over sin) that human self-will—both in the convert himself and in his fellow-converts—can undo the effect of grace. A lost sheep's return to the fold is proof that the divine Shepherd *wants* it within the fold, i.e. *desires* a sinner "to enter into life", for life is the goal that God deems solely fitting for man if He be true to the purpose of His creation. To quote Jesus again (in conclusion of the parable, and in explanation of its relevance in the sequence of his thoughts), "Even so it is not the will of your Father which is in heaven, that one of these little ones should perish" (verse 14). This verse can only signify that apart from grace men do in fact *perish*; and it can only be relevant in the reasoning of Jesus if a convert who abandons the faith is likewise doomed to *perish*; and can only be pertinent as a warning (for the statement is not gratuitous) if a convert whose actions cause another to forsake Christ is also doomed to *perish*. Metaphor must not blind us to reality: the choice for the convert is either "to enter into life" or "to be cast into everlasting fire" (verse 8)—otherwise, "Gehenna fire" (verse 9). For the disciples there would again be a terrifying literalness about these words. As they would perceive the point of the drowning of Galilæan criminals with millstones, so they would see the significance of Christ's allusion to Gehenna. There, upon this refuse dump, forever burning outside Jerusalem, the bodies of Judæan criminals were consigned to the flame as a fitting end to their evil lives. The illustration was different, but its moral the same. We can safely conclude that there can be no contrast whatsoever involved in the convert's choice unless "everlasting fire" here connotes extinction; nor can there be any topical connection with these two sombre warnings unless the offender's fate is as final and inexorable as the criminal's who meets his merited end in a watery or fiery grave. The converse of everlasting life is, and must be, everlasting death.

It is by now obvious that for Jesus the one (everlasting death) was the normal and natural end, and the other (everlasting life) the divinely intended end, of human existence. To that divinely intended end only God's merciful work in Jesus, gladly accepted by the perishing, can men relate. Henceforward it is the wise convert's consuming aim both to attain to the realization of that end himself and also to induce the perishing to seek it as well: when God offers it is folly to refuse. Thus, for Jesus, life as a "little one" believing in him was essentially a probation for eternity, with the Judgement succeeding it to decide the final issue—eternal life or eternal death.

Rich toward God

Death terminates life, and deep down men know it, whatever illusions they may cherish to the contrary. It is not without good reason that the philosophy of the mass of men, in practice even if not in theory, is, "Let us eat, drink and be merry, for tomorrow we die". Such a creed is a crude recognition not only of the brevity of human life, but also of its intrinsic vanity when lived as an end in itself. But once human life is conceived of as a means to a higher and nobler end, the situation is transformed. The Christian call is essentially a call to regard life as something more than a futile animal existence, a call predicated on the fact that, in the mercy of God, death need not terminate life after all. Jesus had given man the *opportunity* to live for ever, and in responding to his call they give assent to that fundamental doctrinal truth: it is for them the essence of the Gospel. Thus the first thing which Christianity offers men is hope in a hopeless situation. The second, as is inevitable, is a statement of the conditions upon which this hope can be realized.

The life to come, which Jesus came to make attainable to men, is no mere continuation of the present life. By its very nature it is life on an altogether different plane of existence. Continuity between both forms of life is indeed assured by the fact that it is the same individual who experiences them both, but their character and conditions are utterly different. Jesus made this plain in his clash with the Sadducees. They merely betrayed the deficiency of their own understanding when they attempted to measure a life to come in terms of this present life in order to prove the absurdity of belief both in a life to come and in a bodily resurrection as the essential prelude to it. They posed the question to Jesus of a woman who had had seven brothers in succession as husbands, bearing children to none. "Therefore", they asked, "in the resurrection whose wife of them is she? for seven had her to wife?" Jesus at once pointed out the fallacy lying at the root of their question—the notion that the world to come is merely an extension of the world that is. Marriage is an institution necessitated by the very limitations of human life. Because men die they must reproduce themselves, otherwise their own extinction in death must spell the extinction within a brief period of the human race as a whole. But from this it follows that no such device to offset the effects of death is necessary in a life which knows no death. "Jesus answering said unto them, The children of this world marry, and are given in marriage: but they which shall be accounted worthy to obtain that world, and the resurrection from the dead, neither marry, nor are given in marriage; neither can they die any more: for they are equal unto the angels; and are the children of God being the children of the resurrection" (Luke 20:27-36). Paul merely extended this argument to another aspect of experience which has its origin in the physical conditions of the present life when he declared that the need to eat to live must lapse in an eternal order: "meats for the belly and the belly for meats" is a physical law of life today, but it will automatically cease to operate when the conditions and character of life are both simultaneously transformed (1 Corinthians 6:13).

What both Jesus and Paul were saying, then, is that a man's purely physical functions are as temporal as the man himself: they possess no eternal worth-whileness. Yet both insisted with the utmost emphasis on the eternal worth-whileness in God's sight of the man, as a man. Jesus did so on this occasion by at once proceeding to confute with the aid of the Pentateuch the Sadducees' belief that the doctrine of the Resurrection was incompatible with the teaching of the Pentateuch.

This seeming paradox of man's position before God clamours for an explanation. In what did Jesus and Paul judge his worth-whileness to consist? This question is vital, for the answer to it is the key to their conception of the proper manner of living this present life. That answer, said Jesus, lies in man's capacity for *spiritual* experience and activities. An animal has purely animal interests: man has these too, for they are fundamental to his survival, but he can also have other and higher interests which distinguish him from the brute creation with which he has so much in common, and which endear him to God on that account. That is, man has unique qualities which if properly exercised can, in the mercy of God, relate him to a new life transcending the limitations of the present life and these qualities are therefore both his glory, *and his responsibility.*

That they are man's responsibility has emerged from Christ's teaching on Judgement: when men spurn God's offer of life they do more than exercise their free will; they also flout the will of God, and must accept the consequences. That these qualities do not, on the other hand, automatically relate a man either to the hope of an afterlife, or to the Judgement is again equally evident from Christ's consciousness of his mission: man's natural destiny, due to his sinfulness, is to perish and only the saving work of the Son of man can rescue him from it or condemn him for resting content with it. But that they are nevertheless man's true glory is also without question, for it is they that explain God's yearning to save men (and man alone among all things that He has created) from eternal death. Jesus clearly regarded the Creation story as affording the key to the value of human life: only man has been made in the image and after the likeness of God, and so he alone is capable of becoming one with God (Genesis 1:26,27). It is this capability which has prompted God to invite man, though man is sinful, to partake of His own immortality. Having physically no pre-eminence above the beasts, man is nevertheless in a class apart from them by virtue of his moral faculties and his spiritual potentialities. Which is to be his final end—death with the beasts or life with God? To decide this, said Jesus, is the true purpose of man's life on earth. The way he lives it is fraught with eternal consequences one way or the other. In the final reckoning men either build a house on rock, which like the rock endures, or on sand which like the sand has no stability or permanence (Matthew 7:24-27). Or to change the metaphor, it might equally be said that before every man who learns of Christ there stand two doors. Which he chooses will determine where he will end life's journey. "Enter ye in at the strait gate", said he, "for wide is the gate, and broad is the way, that leadeth to destruction, and many there be which go in thereat: because strait is the gate, and narrow is the way, that leadeth unto life, and few there be that find it" (Matthew 7:13,14). The figure, we note, is different but the essential lesson the same—men's present choice settles inexorably their future fate.

What is tragic, as Jesus notes, is that so few make the correct and the sensible choice, whereas many take the wrong and suicidal decision to follow the broad way to destruction. Nor is this tragedy confined to the unconverted: disciples can all too easily be guilty of the same crass folly. At first it seems unaccountable that this should be so. Who, in his senses, seeing what is best in his own interests wantonly forgoes it? It might be argued in reply that, as far as the unconverted are concerned, the wrong choice is made for lack of conviction that it is in fact the wrong one, they being unpersuaded that the narrow way actually does lead to life. This, however, makes the false choice by the converted seem all the more senseless by contrast: they above all should realize where it leads, and should follow it relentlessly to the ultimate goal of blessedness. That is true enough: viewed dispassionately, their choice, if wrong, is sheer madness. Yet it is in this very respect that a Christian's true standard of values betrays itself. What commends—and alone can commend—him to God is his spirituality, his evaluation of entry "into life" as of such surpassing worth that it secures his unfailing devotion to the things of God. But that spirituality has to be manifested in the same material body as was his before conversion, and the demands of the new life and the habits of the old clash from the outset, and contend for mastery of his will. That in him which distinguishes him from the beasts tells him that it is only the unseen things of the world to come which are ultimately real and should be the sole object of concern to him; but that in him which he shares in common with the beasts also asserts itself, bidding him pursue his immediate material good to the exclusion of all else. The spirit indeed is willing, but the flesh, alas, is weak— that is why so few choose the way which leads to life unending.

The fact is that the cares of this life can so easily oust all concern for the next. The things which are seen possess an almost hypnotic power over the human will, so capturing men's affections and setting their standards that the spiritual man quickly languishes and dies. Upon every convenient opportunity Jesus sought to counter this inherent materialism of the human outlook. As we have noted, he reproached the age for its aptitude in conserving its physical interests and in reading the signs in earth and sky, because that aptitude was not matched by a corresponding moral sensitivity. On one occasion a motherly soul, in an understandable burst of commendation, "lifted up her voice, and said unto him, Blessed is the womb that bare thee, and the paps which thou hast sucked". The implied compliment was obvious, but Jesus, his mind set solely on divine and spiritual matters, sought to transmute her legitimate enthusiasm into something nobler and finer. "Yea rather", he replied, "blessed are they that hear the word of God and keep it" (Luke 11:27,28). When his exultant disciples "returned again with joy, saying, Lord even the devils are subject unto us through thy name", he likewise tempered their enthusiasm with the comment, "Notwithstanding in this rejoice not, that the spirits are subject unto you; but rather rejoice, because your names are written in heaven" (Luke 10:17-20). He was forever trying to raise men's outlook to heavenly heights. Martha, aggrieved at Mary's unconcern for the preparation of a meal for Jesus, was reminded by him of the much greater importance of Mary's concern for spiritual things. "Martha was cumbered about much serving, and came to him, and said, Lord, dost thou not care that my sister hath left me to serve alone? bid her therefore that she help me. And Jesus answered and said unto her, Martha, Martha, thou art careful and troubled about many things: but one thing is needful: and Mary hath chosen that good part, which shall not be taken away from her" (Luke 10:38-42). And, again, when well-intentioned people wished him to interrupt his spiritual activity of preaching out of deference for those who were physically related to him—his mother and brothers—and who were standing on the outer edge of the crowd, he asked, "Who is my mother? and who are my brethren? And he stretched forth his hand toward his disciples, and said, Behold my mother and my brethren! For whosoever shall do the will of my Father which is in heaven, the same is my brother, and sister, and mother" (Matthew 12:46-50).

Always with Jesus the spiritual took precedence over the physical. When asked to adjudicate in a case of a disputed will, he took advantage of the situation to bring home to men that "a man's life consisteth not in the abundance of the things which he possesseth". To drive home this truth "he spake a parable unto them, saying, The ground of a certain rich man brought forth plentifully; and he thought within himself, saying, What shall I do, because I have no room where to bestow my fruits? And he said, This will I do: I will pull down my barns, and build greater; and there will I bestow all my fruits and my goods. And I will say to my soul, Soul, thou hast much goods laid up for many years; take thine ease, eat, drink, and be merry" (Luke 12:13-19). Here was the typical materialist, self-centred, and engrossed with his possessions— *my* barns, *my* fruits. But in his short-sightedness he laid claim to something which was not properly his—his life. He had not reckoned with losing that, and glibly assumed it to be his own unquestionable possession. But, even as he hatched his selfish plans, "God said unto him, Thou fool, this night thy soul shall be required of thee: then whose shall those things be, which thou hast provided?" (verse 20). Without life to sustain him this man would be incapable of retaining possession of any of those things which he had so thoughtlessly assumed to be his: they would pass to another. What purpose then would his life have served by the time that his material possessions had thus become another's? None whatsoever; it would have proved itself to have been utterly futile, worthy of no perpetuation, for no spirituality remained as the condition of its perpetuation. The man's doom was therefore certain. And not his only, for Jesus used this particular example to illustrate a general law—"So is he that layeth up treasure for himself, and is not rich toward God" (Luke 12:21).

By this he meant that materialism merely spells its own ruin; that to make the living of life an end in itself is to waste life and, at last, to lose it. Not what a man has at death but what he is; not what material possessions, but what spiritual treasure, he has amassed—this alone is what will enable him to vanquish death. As Jesus put it on another occasion, "If any man will come after me, let him deny himself, and take up his cross, and follow me. For whosoever will save his life shall lose it: and whosoever will lose his life for my sake shall find it" (Matthew 16:25). The short-term view of life—the natural habit of putting self first and making the most of the present—can give a man no more than a short-term existence. But if he wishes to live life to the full, and for ever, he must be prepared here and now to deny himself much that seems essential to life. That is, the life to come can only be secured at the expense of this present life. Instinct clamours in the cause of this present life only, and self-preservation is its first law, but instinct must be curbed and present advantage must, if necessary, be forgone in favour of one's ultimate good. Jesus himself found that to be a fundamental spiritual law in the course of his wilderness trial. He therefore spoke straight from his own experience when he posed the question, "What is a man profited if he shall gain the whole world, and lose his own soul?" (verse 26). The term "soul" here, though it literally means "life", clearly stands for more than just the possession of animal life: it connotes rather that stake in the life to come which is vouchsafed to a man through his relationship to Christ as a believer. He cannot simultaneously retain that, and acquire possession of all that this life affords as well. One or the other must be relinquished: he cannot serve God and Mammon, but must give to the one an undivided loyalty which excludes all possibility of service to the other (Luke 16:13).

The fascination of present advantage may be such as to prevail over a believer's faith and better judgement to the detriment of his eternal salvation. If so, the day of reckoning will expose his own folly to him. Then he will realize that his preoccupation with mere temporal things will have cost him the forfeiture of his title to things eternal. "What shall a man give in exchange for his soul?" asks Jesus poignantly with such a person in mind (Matthew 16:26). Clearly the man will then be prepared to relinquish all his coveted possessions—the entire world itself if it be his—in order that he shall at all costs survive, for unless he does survive, all these things will have lost their value for him anyway. But such a readiness to put things eternal before things temporal will be too late in the Day of Judgement. That readiness must be evinced *now* not then, "for the Son of man shall come in the glory of his Father with his angels; and then shall he reward every man according to his works" (verse 27). Those works, performed during his days of probation, will have already settled his fate long before the Judgement makes it manifest. The wise will have decided that "it is better" to suffer present pain and deprivation, and thus to "enter into life", than to refuse to undergo these distasteful rigours only to find themselves cast into Gehenna at the last. As Jesus saw it, a life which is not lived in service to God but in the interests of self is a life wasted, a wanton frustration of the grace of God and a slight upon his own saving mission. That only can become a Spirit-sustained existence in the future which is so already in the present. Men's best and only fitting rule for everyday life is, "Seek ye first the kingdom of God, and his righteousness", for this is also the way to life more abundant in the presence of God. And if men observe it they will find that God is not unmindful of their present, any more than of their future, needs; for all His children are precious in His sight and recipients of His providential care. If they are rich toward Him He will be surpassingly rich toward them, for the purpose of human life is not being realized by any man unless God reigns supreme in his heart. And if God does so reign, that man's place in His Kingdom is assured, for he is one of those once-lost sheep who, having returned to the Shepherd of their souls, receive the comforting counsel, "Fear not, little flock; for it is the Father's good pleasure to give you the kingdom" (Luke 12:32). Believing that promise, true Christians have no difficulty in relegating the things of this life to their proper place, thus losing life to save it. Having been converted and become little children once more, they are true to their conversion, and in fact as well as theory, live a new life here and now, a new life which, in God's mercy, is a foretaste of that newness of life to be enjoyed in the Age to come.

5
EXCEPT YOUR RIGHTEOUSNESS EXCEED ...
The rigours of the Christian way

SO many in these days say to the Christian, "I am willing to accept the moral teaching of Jesus, but you can
keep your dogma—it just doesn't interest me". This
attitude is largely a reaction against the shortcomings of
Christians on the one hand, and their irreconcilable differences over doctrine on the other, and on first encounter it
sounds impressive. It bespeaks a commendable moral
earnestness and concern for essentials. Yet it is at heart
fallacious, as closer examination all too quickly proves, for
it fails to take into account that the facts which persuade
men to become believing Christians do not cease to be facts
just because certain happen to bring discredit upon belief
in them. What Jesus said, he said; and only that can claim
to be true Christianity which originates in him. He laid
down as law that "except ye be converted and become as
little children, ye shall not enter into the kingdom of heav-
en" (Matthew 18:3). Many may find it repugnant to accept
this dictum because it smacks too strongly of what they
despise as "theology" and "dogma" in its mention of "the
kingdom of heaven", and its insistence that men must be
"converted". No matter; the fact remains that Jesus said it.
So such men must either accept it and the doctrinal implications which go with it, or, if they reject it, be honest and
cease to claim Jesus as their moral guide. His moral teaching is what it is, not what misguided zealots, out of regard
for their own prejudices and preconceptions, think it
should be. This particular saying is, in fact, but one of
many which bring this truth sternly home to them.
Another is the warning, "Not every one that saith unto me,
Lord, Lord, shall enter into the kingdom of heaven, but he
that doeth the will of my Father which is in heaven"

(Matthew 7:21). It is futile for a man to protest against the notion of eternal Judgement which forms the basis of this warning just because it is repugnant to him, and at the same time to present himself as an admirer of Christ's moral teaching. This *is* Christ's moral teaching, or at least a sample of it, and it cannot be trimmed to conform to men's personal tastes and inclinations without being destroyed in the process.

False and true

Always the case is the same with the sayings of Jesus. They are everywhere too subtly penetrated with theological claims and dogmatical instruction for the distinction commonly drawn between Christian "ethics" and Christian "dogma" to be other than forced and artificial. The sad truth is that those who adopt this cavalier attitude toward Christian belief, ostensibly out of zeal for true Christian morality, do so from ignorance, not from knowledge, of what Jesus actually taught. They airily assume that they are familiar with the substance of his discourses, whereas, if the truth be told, they are acquainted with no more than a snatch or two of them. So naturally, when its real nature is brought to their attention they are quite nonplussed to find it based on a clearly formulated doctrine of judgement for which there is no room whatever in their thinking.

It is by now evident that those who thus so rashly discard Christian "dogma" (as they call it) are not so zealous for the moral teaching of Christ as at first they so impressively seem: they relish parts of it, but are as eager to jettison the remainder as they are to jettison doctrine, when once they see where it leads them. Even when they limit their acceptance of his teaching to the twin precepts, "Love God", and, "Love your neighbour as yourself", their case is no better, for these precepts are meaningless unless all the emphasis in each instance falls on "love", and none can truthfully claim them as their rule in life who have not made an honest attempt to grasp the far-reaching implications of that word. They are indeed the essence of all true morality and for that reason naturally assume a central position in the moral code laid down by Jesus, but they do not cease to have the gravest doctrinal import on that account. In fact it is just this doctrinal import which gives them their unique importance. Those who have no relish for it need to realize that the question, "Why call ye me, Lord, Lord, and do not the things which I say?" (Luke 6:46), is one that can be addressed as much to the moral zealot who fastidiously picks and chooses among the sayings of Christ, as to those against whose hypocrisy that zealot's attitude to doctrine is a kind of indignant protest.

The fact remains therefore that right belief and right conduct are indistinguishable: one is but the other in action. If the tree is good, so is its fruit. Jesus demanded perfect obedience to his precepts precisely because they were the moral corollary of those fundamental and unalterable facts concerning God, concerning man, and concerning the relation between God and man, which he came into the world expressly to reveal. Acceptance of his precepts, then (a full, uncompromising acceptance, that is), presupposes acceptance also of those facts divorced from which they would have had neither meaning nor authority. So firmly were they set into the context of his saving mission that they cannot be dislodged from that context without suffering irreparable damage as a result.

Life through death

Jesus laid down the criterion of true discipleship for all time when he declared, "If any man will come after me, let him deny himself, and take up his cross, and follow me" (Matthew 16:24). Here clearly was no prescription for success in this present life, but the very opposite. From the world's point of view it was the road to material suicide. None knew this better than Jesus himself. It was an axiom with him that "the disciple is not above his master, nor the servant above his lord", and he clearly intended this to be as true of his suffering for righteousness' sake (Matthew 10:24; see verses 22,23) as of his example of perfect benevolence toward all men (Luke 6:40; see verses 35-39). His was a call, then, not to present gain but to sacrifice and loss. But it did not make sense and could not have made sense, apart from the solemn truth on which it was based—"For whosoever," he added, "will save his life shall lose it: and whosoever will lose his life for my sake shall find it" (Matthew 16:25). This was no pious hope which he was expressing, but sober fact. He knew that men could have life through himself—and through himself alone. But he knew equally that they could by no means have it if they were obsessed with the temporal things of this life. So he made both truths known at once, and did so expressly that men should realize where their true self-interest lay. He declared all forms of conduct which are congenial to sinful human nature to be disastrous to the spiritual life, the very negation of successful living. That only, said he, is the proper, the truly successful, way to live this present life, which assures one a place in the world to come, for this future world, though unseen, is in fact more real than the material order in which men's present life is lived. Jesus' call to action was thus in essence a challenge to *faith*—a challenge to flesh and blood to acknowledge the transcendence of the spirit over itself, an insistence that men should face up to the ultimate facts of life and act in the only way compatible with them.

This cannot be too greatly stressed. Some, it is true, wishing to excuse themselves from the irksomeness of discipleship, protest that Jesus was making a cynical appeal to men's grasping nature and making base use of the incentive of an eternal reward to bribe them to live virtuous lives. Such reasoning is specious but entirely misrepresents the situation. Only if the eternal reward were a fiction could it be true. But that reward is *not* a fiction, *not* an illusion—it is an assured fact, and it conditioned Jesus' presentation of his challenge on that account. He did not conceive of the Christian's other-worldliness as mere sublimated self-interest, nor did he wish the Christian to conceive of it as such, either. He was simply proclaiming the intrinsic rightness of virtue, even when it militates against a man's manifest self-interest, and appealing, in order to prove it, to a fundamental and immutable law that right must eventually prevail over wrong, good over evil, God's holiness over sin. He was bearing witness to the great fact that human life has an ultimate purpose which it is man's

duty before God
to further, and on that basis pledging that if men would co-
operate with God in furthering that purpose by surrender-
ing their wills to His, He would for His part be true to
Himself and bring it to fulfilment in them.

It was therefore not ignoble, but inevitable, that Jesus
should insist that there would be an ultimate reward for
present virtue which is performed out of respect for the
essential sanctity of human life. Not otherwise can life
make sense. So indispensable to man is their animal life (if
it can be so termed) that they do everything conceivable to
preserve and prolong it. If that entails being self-assertive
then they have no hesitation in being self-assertive. But
Jesus calmly points out the gross short-sightedness of such
a reflex action: "Blessed", said he, "are the *meek*, for *they*
shall inherit the earth". The sad fact that, in the ordinary
course, the meek emphatically do not inherit the earth, but
are victimised, exploited, and even swept helplessly off the
surface of the earth by their powerful and ruthless
brethren, needs no argument to support it. No matter: it is
not the powerful and ruthless but their self-effacing
victims who will prove to be its ultimate heirs. That is
incontrovertible fact, fact which necessitates an after-life
and a final assessment of human worth, but is true for all
that. In the face of it, to suggest that Jesus was corrupting
men's motive for right-doing by invoking it as a sanction to
his moral teaching is utterly ludicrous. Rather was he
purifying and ennobling their motive by convincing them
as to what is the ultimate reality and what is the true
purpose of man's life.

The Pharisaic mentality *

The Pharisees acknowledged the transcendence of the life
to come, but in theory only. Their practice belied their pro-
fessions of godliness, for they tried to make the best of
both worlds in defiance of the fact that such a course is, in

---

* The Pharisaic teaching concerning the afterlife will be found fully set
out in Whiston's translation of *The Works of Josephus*, in the section
headed *An extract out of Josephus' discourse to the Greeks concerning
Hades*.

the nature of things, impossible. "They were covetous", is Luke's pregnant comment on them, meaning by that, not only that they were as human as all other men, but that they exposed the hollowness of their profession of spirituality by giving success in this life a religious sanction (Luke 16:14). They construed their own prosperity as a token of divine favour: so, incredible though it seems, they measured their preciousness to God in terms of cash—the spiritual by the material! It was for this reason that they derided Jesus when he announced to them that the interests of this life and those of the next are mutually exclusive and irreconcilable (Luke 16:13,14). His retort was significant. "He said unto them, Ye are they which justify yourselves before men; but God knoweth your hearts; for that which is highly esteemed among men is abomination in the sight of God" (verse 15). With withering irony he then went on to recount the parable of Dives and Lazarus, warning them, in terms of their own fantastic beliefs concerning the afterlife, that the eternal reward which they so blandly expected would not in fact be theirs but would fall to others, to those whom they despised as spiritually unacceptable to God just because they happened to be financially destitute! (verses 19-31). With biting satire Jesus made Abraham say to complaining Dives, in terms ominous in their finality, "Son, remember that thou in thy lifetime receivedst thy good things" (verse 25).

"Thou *receivedst* thy good things", said Abraham—that is, what Dives had really set his heart on he had received. And that was all he would receive, moreover—"Thou in thy *lifetime* receivedst thy good things". If his recompence had come to him in his lifetime, there remained nothing else for him to enjoy beyond it. His preoccupation with things material, having inevitably made him recklessly neglectful of things spiritual, had brought its own automatic punishment. As he had sowed so he would reap. He had lived in defiance of the testimony of Moses and of all the prophets that it is the interest which captures a man's heart which determines his ultimate fate; having made temporal things his aim and object, no eternal reward awaited him, nor could. What a man is, not has, is what concerns God—and, alas, what a man has all too often determines what he is, for his possessions all too readily consume his interest to the exclusion of the things of God.

So it proved to be with the Pharisees. Their acquisitiveness destroyed their spiritual sensitivity. "Woe unto you, scribes and Pharisees, hypocrites!", said Jesus to them, "for ye devour widows' houses, and for a pretence make long prayer" (Matthew 23:14). Not without good reason were those two vices conjoined: they were symptoms of the same materialistic outlook. In their love of money the Pharisees became so rapacious that even from the impoverished they accepted gifts offered out of respect for their status and dignity as religious teachers, with never a thought for the unfairness and inhumanity involved in thus exploiting those who were in such desperate need. In fact they indirectly encouraged such unworthy transactions by their calculated attempts to raise their prestige in the eyes of men. They saw to it, for example, that at the traditional hours of prayer they were not merely out of doors, but also standing on prominent street corners where they would be sure of an audience (and this the largest possible), and they there in full view of all, unblushingly offered long prayers with the sole object of impressing others with their devoutness (Matthew 6:5). All this, said Jesus fiercely, was a prostitution of religion in the cause of present self-interest. Not the reward which they expected, therefore, but rather "greater damnation" was all which they deserved or would receive.

All their interests were in fact earth-bound. They were fanatically scrupulous in the precautions which they took to ensure that their crockery and plate were free from defilement, but their scrupulosity did not carry over into the moral sphere. It did not occur to them that the rapacity and dishonesty with which they had acquired the resources to buy their food and drink were defilements more real, and incomparably more hateful, than anything that dirt could cause, because such vices *stained their souls.* "Woe unto you, scribes and Pharisees, hypocrites! for ye make clean the outside of the cup and of the platter, but within they are full of extortion and excess", said Jesus to them, adding, in blazing indignation, "Thou blind Pharisee, cleanse first that which is within the cup and platter, that the outside of them may be clean also" (Matthew 23:25,26).

There was a double significance to these words; though they were primarily applied to literal cups and platters they had their relevance also for the Pharisees as men, as an earlier use by Jesus of the same metaphor makes plain. On that occasion Jesus had been invited to dine with a Pharisee. Upon his arrival he proceeded without formality to his couch alongside the table. "And when the Pharisee saw it, he marvelled that he had not first washed before dinner". Jesus promptly accepted the challenge and administered the stinging rebuke which his materially-minded host deserved. It was a rebuke which brought the man abruptly face to face with moral realities. Why was he so bland as to condemn Jesus for not performing the ablutions which the tradition of the elders prescribed when he himself was defiled by the evil practices which were the source of his wealth? "And the Lord said unto him, Now do ye Pharisees make clean the outside of the cup and the platter; but your inward part is full of ravening and wickedness". Finally, to drive the lesson home, Jesus gave a twist to the metaphor which presented the Pharisee with a more startling challenge still: "Ye fools, did not he that made that which is without make that which is within also?" (Luke 11:37-40).

Jesus meant the man to see himself as a cup fashioned by God. That part of him which was "without" was clearly his physical, animal constitution. But there was something "within" also—that is, that capacity for moral resemblance to God which it is man's unique privilege to possess and his unique responsibility to develop in fulfilment of the purpose of his existence. Why had the Pharisee thwarted and debased his spiritual powers instead of allowing them to motivate his actions and dominate his outlook? The question was charged with the direst warning. The Pharisee had not reckoned with either the holiness or the moral requirements of God, so consumed was he with concern for his reputation both in his own sight and in others.

"God knoweth your hearts", was the simple but stern comment with which Jesus jolted this man, and all like him, out of their complacency (Luke 16:15). By it Jesus meant that God, though unseen, was aware of that inward rottenness which vitiated all their pious acts and which was so cunningly concealed from the eyes of their fellows. God, said Jesus, is the great Reality in every human situation, and if the Pharisees had been wise they would never have engaged in so futile a course of action as to leave God out of account.

The Pharisees did so because they were, in their own estimate, self-sufficient. The parable of the Pharisee and the Publican praying in the Temple was designed to expose the heinousness to God of such an attitude. It was spoken expressly "unto certain which *trusted in themselves* that they were righteous, and despised others". The Pharisee depicted in the parable was guilty, like all his class, of the folly of exalting himself instead of leaving his exaltation to the only One qualified to effect it. In effect, as Jesus indicated with such delicate satire, the man though ostensibly addressing God, was really praying "with himself" (Luke 18:9-14). He was his own god, guilty of that besetting fault of human nature of being so engrossed with things material and mundane as to lose sight of things spiritual and eternal. That is, the typical Pharisee was merely the typical materialist dressed up in pious garb, but his outlook was a hundred-fold more damnable on that account. There is little enough excuse for the materialist: for the Pharisee there could be none whatever—he was just a wolf in sheep's clothing, not even hesitating to trim and attenuate the very commandments of God Himself to subserve his own immediate financial advantage or to excuse himself from irksome acts of service (Mark 7:9-13).

There, for the time being, we must leave the Pharisee, postponing further consideration of the fundamental misconceptions responsible for his moral bankruptcy until later. We must now turn our gaze to the Christian—as Christ defined him.

The Christian attitude

It goes without saying that the Christian, to be true to his calling must differ radically in his outlook from the Pharisee. "For I say unto you", said Jesus, "That except your righteousness exceed the righteousness of the scribes and Pharisees, ye shall in no case enter into the kingdom of heaven" (Matthew 5:20). Such a stipulation, so categorically made, must have left his listeners stunned. The Pharisees were paragons of punctiliousness! What then was this righteousness which was to exceed even theirs? The rest of the Sermon made its nature plain. It was not after all to be an intensification of Pharisaic scrupulosity and formalism, a burden even more grievous to be borne than that which they laid upon men's shoulders. Yet its demands would not for that reason be any the less exacting, for it would necessitate the surrender by men of all their worldly ambition, and entail a complete reorientation of their outlook.

How painful the process of reorientation was in the case of the disciples the gospel writers reveal with unreserved candour. Later we shall follow that process out in detail, but in this present context it will be helpful to note one telling example of its impact on their established ways of thought. The occasion in question followed on the clash between Jesus and the confederacy of Pharisees and Sadducees who, materially-minded as always, had demanded of him a visible sign from heaven (Matthew 16:1-4). The incident was fresh in their minds as they crossed the Lake in their boat, but Jesus saw that something else of a material nature would shortly engross them, too, to the exclusion of all spiritual realities. They had neglected to bring provisions with them (verse 5). Jesus seized the opportunity, and purposely spoke in enigmatic vein. Seemingly 'apropos' of nothing, he broke the silence with the bald remark, "Take heed and beware of the leaven of the Pharisees and of the Sadducees" (verse 6). At once the disciples "reasoned among themselves" as to what he could mean. Then it struck them that they had "taken no bread" (verse 7). So he was cautioning them, it seemed, against buying their provisions from men like the

Pharisees and Sadducees. Once again the irony of the situation was pathetic—pathetic because it exposed their lack of faith, a lack which always betrays itself in an obsession with the visible and tangible things. "When Jesus perceived" what conclusion they had drawn, "he said unto them, O ye of little faith, why reason ye among yourselves because ye have brought no bread?" The two miraculous feedings were proof that he could make good their lack of literal bread. So he asked, "How is it that ye do not understand that I spake it not to you concerning bread, that ye should beware of the leaven of the Pharisees and of the Sadducees?" (verses 8-11). Crestfallen they saw light at last: "Then understood they how that he bade them not beware of the leaven of bread, but of the doctrine of the Pharisees and Sadducees" (verse 12). That "doctrine" was clearly something more than the formal teaching of the Pharisees and Sadducees: it comprehended their fundamental outlook—their fixed habit of conducting their lives as though God did not exist, or was powerless to call them to account.

It was against this arch-heresy that Jesus was constantly protesting—a heresy so monstrous because so insidious in its power over men, even the best of them. The Christian is not worthy of the name except his life and outlook be motivated by the consciousness of God's near presence, unless the unseen is for him both an immediate, and the ultimate, reality. In the hearing of a vast crowd Jesus made a point of repeating his caution to his disciples, "Beware ye of the leaven of the Pharisees". It was doubtless for the enlightenment of the huge accompanying audience that he also this time defined that leaven as "hypocrisy". He added a reason for the warning, "For there is nothing covered, that shall not be revealed; neither hid that shall not be known" (Luke 12:1,2). This was another concrete allusion to the Day of ultimate reckoning, that Day of final and inexorable Judgement when all shams will be exposed and divine approval or disapproval of men's worth will be openly declared. Jesus was here, as always, calling on men to face up to what God is, and to adjust their lives to that unalterable fact. And in so doing he was making demands upon their faith, their sincerity and their resolution to which the observances of the Pharisees were as mere chaff to wheat. That was why he stressed from the very outset that a righteousness which was no advance upon that of the Pharisees had no abiding worth, and therefore could not relate men to the life which he had expressly come to bring. Or, to express the matter differently (and, in a sense, more exactly), unless men rated as most important the attainment of that life which he had come to win for them, they could not begin to be truly righteous, for not otherwise could they give practical proof that God was an ever-present, ever-near Reality to them.

This emerges from his teaching on the true Christian attitude to the material things of this life—food, clothing, etc. They are indispensable to man; Jesus admitted that, and never once did he suggest that the use of them was in the slightest degree incompatible with the living of a spiritual life. But the more important fact which he wished men to realize, was that God *knows* that they are indispensable to man, and that, knowing this, God (He being what He is) will see that man will not suffer from the lack of them. He therefore called upon men to entrust the care for their bodily wants to God, and to concentrate upon the far more important and urgent task of fulfilling the spiritual purpose of their existence. The first process, declared Jesus, is the absolute prerequisite of the other.

God cares

Jesus thus made the Reality of God his starting point and was merely drawing out its implications when he gave men specific precepts to carry out as acts of obedience to God. Thus, as we have cursorily noticed earlier, he told his disciples, "Fear not, little flock; for it is your Father's good pleasure to give you the kingdom" (Luke 12:31). He said this, as we have seen, not for the mere sake of saying it, far less to make them feel proud or complacent, but rather as an inducement to absolute trust in God for the necessities of life. That trust, that other-worldliness and detachment which he was demanding of them, would, he knew, demand the utmost of their spirituality. It was therefore both becoming and considerate that he should remind them of God's goodness toward them. It would be the easier for them to meet the arduous task which he was setting before them if they conceived of it as one which it was as much their privilege as their duty to perform. With masterly skill he had just recounted the parable of the Rich Fool to illustrate his dictum that "a man's life consisteth not in the abundance of the things which he possesseth" (Luke 12:15-21). But then, like the great teacher that he was, he had also proceeded to point out what this entailed in terms of everyday life, using a significant "therefore" to show the connection between principle and precept— "Therefore I say unto you, Take no thought for your life, what ye shall eat, neither yet for your body what ye shall put on. The life is more than meat, and the body than raiment" (verses 22,23).

Jesus regarded life as man's greatest possession, the very gift of God, and man's body as the crown of all God's creative work. If God then gave man these, would He not just as assuredly provide the wherewithal to sustain them? The case needed no arguing on those grounds alone. But, moreover, God's care for His handiwork is evident throughout Nature, and that should satisfy the doubting as to God's willingness, let alone His ability, to satisfy their merely animal needs (verses 24-27). But there is yet another, and an immeasurably greater, factor which demands trust, as Jesus, by a felicitous choice of language, delicately indicated. "If God so clothe the grass", he added, "which is today in the field and tomorrow is cast into the oven; how much more will he clothe you, O ye of little faith?" (verse 28). Why, "how much more"? Is it because man is automatically better than a raven, or superior to the grass? By no means: man has no physical pre-eminence over the beasts, and all flesh is all too evidently grass, for it has no permanence, but like the grass is here today pulsating with life, and tomorrow is gone, dead and inert. Why then the "how much more"? Because flesh *need* not be like grass—for man is capable, through Jesus, of living for ever. And, if so capable, says Jesus, then he should

make the business of living for ever bulk largest in his present life and leave to God the problem of his immediate
survival. But, clearly, only those will so act who are convinced that they are in fact thus capable of living for ever.
For them the rule is absolute, "Seek not ye what ye shall
eat, or what ye shall drink, neither be ye of doubtful mind.
For all these things do the nations of the world seek after:
and your Father knoweth that ye have need of these
things" (verses 28-30).

"The nations of the world seek these things ... Your
Father knoweth that ye have need of these things". The
contrast is pregnant with meaning. There is a sharp division of mankind into two groups—"the nations" and "ye";
those who belong to this world and those who are related,
as God's sons, to the next. Worldlings naturally seek the
things of the world: therefore those who are God's ought in
their turn just as naturally and spontaneously to seek the
things of the world to come! That, said Jesus, is the logic of
faith. "All *these* things do the nations seek ... but rather
seek *ye* the kingdom of God." And apart from the exalted
responsibility which is implicit in this contrast there
comes the reassurance that the Christian life is not after
all destined to be one of present privation and soul-
destroying want, as instinct suggest it must be. Says
Jesus, "Seek ye the kingdom of God; and all these things
shall be *added* unto you" (verse 31). In fact neither for the
present nor the future need men of faith be anxious as his
culminating reassurance proves—"Fear not, little flock, for
it is your Father's good pleasure to give you the kingdom"
(verse 32). To believe that is to act on it, for faith always
proves itself by outward action, and outward action is
always an index to inward faith—or the lack of it. Half
belief is no belief: it is devoid of power—it is "the leaven of
the Pharisees".

God sees

Nothing is so difficult to acquire, let alone to maintain as a
fixed attitude of mind, as that detachment from worldly
anxiety which Jesus thus insisted to be the only valid proof
of true faith in God. There is not a Christian who does not

from time to time long to enjoy his good things during his lifetime, and the more intense that longing is the more worldly his conception of "good things" becomes. At the lowest end of the scale comes preoccupation with one's physical security, not only in the immediate present, but in the foreseeable future also. This, as we might expect, Jesus condemns—condemns for its futility and danger to the spiritual life. It is futile because the very uncertainties of life against which it is intended to be a safeguard can wreck every carefully made plan: moth and rust corrupt and thieves break through and steal. And it is dangerous because abiding treasure, real security against the uncertainties of mortal human life, can only be laid up in heaven, a truth to which concern for earthly treasure can so easily blind men, "for where your treasure is, there will your heart be also" (Matthew 6:19-21).

Acquisitiveness is thus a man's spiritual undoing, and this not only in the ultimate, but also in the immediate, sense. For engrossment with one's personal possessions breeds indifference to the needs of others: a man thus becomes mean and niggardly, and his spiritual vision is darkened. On the other hand generosity is the natural fruit of the Christian attitude to material things, and brings joy both to the receiver and to the giver (Matthew 6:22,23).

Are all generous men therefore good? and have they automatically the proper attitude to material things? Alas, no. Even the Pharisees, acquisitive though they were, regularly made lavish gifts to others. But such generosity did not commend them to God: it merely damned them, for it was performed not out of love for the recipient (far less for God), but out of love for themselves alone, for they took pains to bring their munificence to others' notice lest their sacrifice should fail to bring them in immediate compensating recompence. Thus, even in their spiritual exercises, as we have noted, the Pharisees betrayed their inveterate material-mindedness. This form of temptation, to enjoy his good things in his present lifetime, the Christian however must also at all costs resist. His alms, his prayers, his fasting, all are to be performed in secret, as unto God alone.

The man who performs them openly, has his reward—the praise and esteem of men; but his reward stops there. The man who performs them secretly has his reward also—but not yet. He acts in faith, not in calculated self-interest, leaving it to God, who sees in secret, to reward him openly in the Day when all that is covered shall be revealed (Matthew 6:1-18). He stakes all on his conviction that God is aware of him and of all he does for his brethren and for God Himself.

That awareness however is total not partial. It is not confined to men's virtues: it also searches out their vices. If a man feels inward hatred for his brother, even though unexpressed or never betrayed in outward acts of enmity, it does not escape God's notice (Matthew 5:21-23). If he nurses adulterous desires, however outwardly correct and proper his conduct may be, God knows for what he secretly longs (Matthew 5:27,28). The Sermon on the Mount is founded on the conviction that God knows men's downsitting and their uprising, understands their thoughts afar off and is acquainted with all their ways (Psalm 139:2,3), and is in effect the translation of that conviction into terms of everyday conduct. A Christian who is guilty of deceit or dishonesty is a man who—at least for the period of wrong-doing—has ceased to be a Christian because he has ceased to believe that God has him under constant scrutiny. Each time he acts as a man-pleaser his faith that God sees in secret, and will eventually reward his virtue openly, fails him, and he is no better than the unconverted. It is his faith—his vital unquenchable conviction that God is the supreme Reality—and that alone, which distinguishes him or can transform him.

God loves

Is man's consciousness of God therefore to be dominated by fear? Fear is certainly not to be absent, as Jesus stressed more than once, particularly in his caution to his "friends" against "the leaven of the Pharisees" (Luke 12:4,5). But never is that healthy and truly humble respect for God's power which Christ meant by fear to degenerate into slavish terror. God's benevolence is writ large in Nature and on that score alone men ought to conceive of Him as their merciful and considerate heavenly Father rather than as an impersonal force or a censorious judge. Not otherwise can the Christian entrust his physical security to God's keeping, as Jesus urges him to do (verses 24-30). But the testimony of Nature is meant to inculcate into man more than a sense of dependence upon God, difficult enough as that alone is to acquire. It should also induce him to go out to emulate God's goodness and emulating it, to reflect His forbearance with human waywardness to the extent of submitting to wrong and eschewing all forms of retaliation against maltreatment at the hands of others.

The Law of Moses conceded rights of redress and compensation to the victim of another's violence or fraudulence, rights which are indispensable to any properly constituted society if evil is to be restrained and law to be upheld. Jesus called upon all who would follow him to relinquish such rights and by silent submission to victimisation to oppose evil by no other weapon than goodness. Implicit in such a call was a demand that the victim should be willing, if need be, to suffer unto death. Now clearly, only the certainty of eternal recompense for the loss of one's life under such circumstances can make sense of such a call to sacrifice in the cause of goodness. So once again we are driven back to the same fundamental truth as before, namely, that it is the as yet unseen world of the future which is the true reality. And clearly, too, none but those who truly believe that truth can be impelled by it to act as Jesus required, and turn the other cheek to those who wrong or persecute them (Matthew 5:38-42).

Jesus, however, intended non-resistance to evil to be the beginning only. Love is only love when it is active, positive, constructive. It is so with God's love: He confers benefits on those who do not deserve them, Nature being once more witness, "for he maketh his sun to rise on the evil and on the good, and sendeth rain on the just and on the unjust". To emulate His goodness, therefore, men too must do good to them that hate them. For men to love those that love them is natural, and in no way meritorious, and so can bring no eternal recompense for any loss which it happens to entail (Matthew 5:43-48). In fact men find it so attractive a course of action precisely because it costs them so little sacrifice. But Jesus calls upon men to pursue the course which is incompatible with instinct and immediate self-interest, because only that way can they become like God, which is their appointed duty and privilege as beings made in His image. "Sinners also lend to sinners, to receive as much again. But love ye your enemies, and do good, and lend, hoping for nothing again; and your reward shall be great, and ye shall be the children of the Highest: for he is kind unto the unthankful and to the evil. Be ye therefore merciful, as your Father also is merciful" (Luke 6:34-36).

God's self-disclosure

Thus for Jesus the Reality of God was synonymous with His love. God is the fount of all goodness, therefore men can only truly seek their own good by seeking God—there in a nutshell was his philosophy. For him what God is, must determine for men how they should act. He was qualified to tell men of God, and what God is, because he *knew* God: "No man knoweth the Father, save the Son, and he to whomsoever the Son will reveal him" (Matthew 11:27). By the very act of revealing God, then—revealing His care, His compassion, His goodness and His hatred of evil—he laid down man's duty for them. And no duty could be more comprehensive or more exacting: it demanded no less than the utter surrender of themselves to the service of God, and pressed home that demand upon them relentlessly in the person and teaching of Jesus. In Jesus' own picturesque language, "From the days of John the Baptist until now the kingdom of heaven takes men by storm". Then, inverting the metaphor, he added, "and the violent take it by force" (Matthew 11:12). That is, the demands of the Christian ethic must be matched by moral (and, if need be, physical) courage and spiritual steadfastness in the Christian disciple. Only on that condition can he hope to storm his way into the most secure, and also the most desirable citadel of all—the Kingdom of heaven.

6
I WILL HAVE MERCY AND NOT SACRIFICE
The essentials of true worship

IT is time we took stock of our findings. Firstly, so far as the gospels themselves are concerned, it is by now abundantly evident that each is an artistic whole.

Faithful witnesses

All three writers had selected their material according to a predetermined plan and produced a portrait that is life-like and consistent with itself. Let any of that material be discarded, and at once the portrait becomes distorted and unconvincing. The Temptation, for example, is meaning-less unless the subject of it had the power to work stupen-dous miracles. And, again, the moral teaching of Jesus loses all its distinctiveness and relevance if the doctrinal beliefs and eschatology on which it is based are adjudged to be the Evangelists' and not his own. As for Jesus him-self, he is either what he claims to be, the Christ, and the Son of God, in which case men must accept the gospels as they stand, or he is some phantom figure of the past whose personality and teaching can never be more than matters of conjecture and subjective reconstruction, in which case men cannot be expected to accept as authentic history any single item of the gospels which conflicts with their own predilections. That is, Jesus and the gospels stand or fall together, so that he could well have said of them, as of his disciples, "he that heareth you heareth me; and he that despiseth you despiseth me, and he that despiseth me despiseth him that sent me" (Luke 10:16). At every turn we have seen him claim, both explicitly and implicitly, that he was a man with a unique mission, and we have found him in that capacity assuming on the one hand that men are sinners and in need of saving from their sin and its effects; and on the other that they have a preciousness in

God's sight, despite their sin, because of their potential capacity to be like Him—a capacity which has excited His compassion, and moved Him to send Jesus to their rescue as their all-availing Saviour. This means that the teaching of Jesus can no more be divorced from the opening chapters of Genesis, than from the general context of the gospels into which the Evangelists have set it. Jesus and Genesis are complementary, and everywhere we have found him treating not only the opening section of Old Testament Scripture, but also every other, as a depository of divine truth concerning man, his origin and his destiny. Not without some compelling reason did he say, "Think not that I am come to destroy the law, or the prophets: I am not come to destroy but to fulfil" (Matthew 5:17).

Greater blessedness

John too, as Jesus himself insisted, was a man with a unique mission. "John *came* unto you in the way of right-eousness", was Jesus' way of convincing the Pharisees that John's baptism was in fact "from heaven" and not "of men" (Matthew 21:32,35). And there was just as careful a choice of language even in his allusion to John's abstemious-ness—"John *came* neither eating nor drinking" (Matthew 11:18). John so "came" because God "sent" him. "What went ye out for to see?" asked Jesus rhetorically. "A prophet? yea, I say unto you, and more than a prophet. For this is he, of whom it is written, Behold, I send my messen-ger before thy face, which shall prepare thy way before thee" (Matthew 11:10). Nothing could more effectively stress John's greatness and importance than the applica-tion of Malachi's prophecy to him in this way. But that in turn only stressed the transcendent greatness of the One who so applied it to him. Jesus intended his comments to serve as a form of personal acknowledgement of John's ser-vices, and they therefore amounted also to an assertion that it was to himself that John had acted as predecessor. The citation of the prophecy was thus on this occasion an authoritative interpretation of it also, and, as such, two-edged as the sequel shows, for Jesus proceeded to state further, "Verily I say unto you, Among them that are born of women there hath not risen a greater than John the Baptist".

In which sense was John the greatest among men? The word "risen" suggests that it had to do with his status and mission, rather than his personal moral worth, and Luke's variant rendering bears this out. It reads, "For I say unto you, Among those that are born of women there is not a greater *prophet* than John the Baptist" (Luke 7:28). Enoch was great, Elijah was great, Isaiah and Jeremiah and Ezra were great, but whatever debate there may have been as to their superiority or inferiority to John morally, in one respect John was unquestionably greater than all of them—he, and no other, was the one privileged to serve as herald to the King. But if such was the greatness in status of the last of the prophets how much higher must have been the status of those who were actually the King's personal companions, even down to the meanest of them? As Jesus put it, though none before had been as great in rank as John, "notwithstanding he that is *least* in the kingdom of heaven is greater than he" (Matthew 11:11).

This assertion was all the more staggering on account of what had preceded it. It was in effect a challenge to the listeners to recognise in the speaker the King himself, and in his coming the actual advent of the Kingdom so long awaited. In keeping with that fact Jesus therefore drew a sharp distinction between the preparatory work of the prophets (John himself included) and his own. *"From the days of John the Baptist until now* the kingdom of heaven is forcing itself upon men"*, he said, "for all the prophets and the law prophesied *until* John" (Matthew 11:12,13). There was no mistaking his meaning. John's message had, it is true, been in one respect an anticipation of his own: "Repent ye: for the kingdom of heaven is at hand" (Matthew 3:2). But the difference between their messages, though they were in essence the same, lay in the fact that Jesus did not begin to preach in this vein until *first* he "had heard that John was cast into prison" (Matthew 4:12). Matthew stresses the point, *"From that time Jesus began to preach* and to say, Repent: for the kingdom of heaven is at hand" (Matthew 4:17). As we have noted

117

earlier, there was a novel emphasis in Jesus' testimony: by virtue of what he did, he actually translated the prophecy of John into reality—in his person the kingdom of heaven broke into the world of men! It was (as we have noted) on account of this very fact that the miracles were so significant: they were tokens of the Kingdom, samples of its blessings, proof of its actual existence at that very time. The cautious and timid could not accept them with the necessary forthrightness, but some were sufficiently bold to appraise the situation aright and to press their way eagerly into the Kingdom *as then constituted*. They became the King's personal associates; nay, more, they in one sense actually constituted the very Kingdom itself, for they alone at that time comprised the Realm in which God was acknowledged as sovereign and His King was served with total and unreserved loyalty and devotion. They were the ones, who, even the lowliest of them, had a rank higher than John, and so were "greater" than he.

Now "John came neither eating nor drinking". Not so the Son of man. John, again, shunned the company of men, insisting that repentant sinners "went *out* unto him" (Mark 1:5). Not so, once more, the Son of man—he moved so freely among the profane and evil that it was disdainfully said by some, "Behold a man gluttonous and a winebibber, a friend of publicans and sinners" (Matthew 11:19). But what a friend, as Matthew and others found! Yet to the Pharisees, and to the disciples of John, alike, this friendship was a stumblingblock. It was capable of a sinister interpretation for the Pharisees, and was accompanied by an indifference to established fasting traditions which offended the followers of John. The former censoriously asked his disciples, "Why eateth your Master with publicans and sinners?", attacking Jesus via them. With more respect, the followers of John addressed their question directly to Jesus himself, but there was a note of grievance in it, and also a betrayal of sympathy with the Pharisees: "Why do *we and the Pharisees* fast oft, but *thy* disciples fast not?" (Matthew 9:11,14). Their choice of language spoke volumes: it signified that the way in which Jesus was a scandal to each of these respective groups was in essence one. He was a non-conformist to hoary practices which were regarded as indispensable to an acceptable religious life, and the fact not only amazed them, but also constituted an affront to their sense of piety, and almost of decency. If their queries were thus really only variations of the same question, so also must the answers which Jesus in each case gave have been in substance one. Indeed we have already had sufficient occasion to respect the editorial skill of the Evangelists in arranging their material to be justified in assuming this to be so; moreover, the manifest design in the construction of this very chapter is clinching proof that the conjunction by Matthew of these two incidents was not haphazard but deliberate, because he took the issue at stake to be the same in each case. Let us then allow each answer to help us interpret the other.

Form and Substance

"Why eateth your Master with publicans and sinners?" asked the Pharisees. "Why not?" it could be retorted. The Pharisees' response would have been one of horror. Casual contact with such folk was abhorrent enough to them because of the ceremonial defilement which that contact almost inevitably entailed. But to *eat* with such folk! The very idea was revolting on account of the closeness of friendship which eating a meal together symbolized in those days. It damned Jesus in their eyes: "Why *eateth* ...?" they asked aghast, and in indirect eulogy of their own rectitude. Jesus took up the challenge, and with it, accepted for the purposes of his argument that evaluation of themselves which it implied. "They that be whole", said he, "need not a physician, but they that are sick".

If at this point we imagine a long silent pause as the full meaning of his truism sank in we can appreciate what a furious mental questioning it must have prompted in every Pharisee present. They had no time for Jesus; but at heart that was because they felt no *need* of him—they were too righteous. But, of course, the more they based their disdainful separation of themselves from the rabble on the fact that they themselves were so righteous and the rabble so sinful, the more they insisted by implication that

119

that rabble had a need which was too desperate to be ignored or neglected by them. But what were they doing to alleviate it? Precisely nothing. Nor, what is more, did they feel the slightest obligation to do anything—a shameful state of affairs, when they came to think of it! So his fraternisation *could* bear a commendable interpretation after all: these folk were truly, as he put it, sick, and common humanity demanded that someone should do something to succour them. But who was actually qualified to do it? Who could fill the role of physician, as it were?

It would be then that the full force of his imagery would strike them. He had recently claimed to be able to cure sin, and had authenticated that claim by healing a physically sick man. So in the very act of thus mingling with the morally diseased, he was putting himself forward as the required Physician, and the reformation which he was effecting in these people was demonstrable justification of his action in so doing. As they wrestled with the challenge which he had thus posed he spoke again, "But go ye and learn what that meaneth, I will have mercy and not sacrifice", adding by way of explanation, "for I am not come to call the righteous, but sinners".

No book of the Old Testament could have served Jesus' purpose better than Hosea, for was not the notion of the compassion of God on sinners the very stuff of the book? Had not Hosea's action in seeking out his erring wife, in loving her despite her adulteries, and in restoring her to her former dignity been a parable of God's dealings with sinful Israel? Nay, the very figure of sickness had been used by the prophet to describe both Israel's waywardness and the punishment which God had visited upon it; punishment visited, however, not in anger only but also in mercy, because it was *meant to lead Israel back to God* (Hosea 5:13-15). Pursuing the same allegory of sickness the prophet had anticipated Israel's eventual return to God by depicting the nation as saying, after having vainly sought a human remedy for its sickness, "Come, and let us return unto the Lord: for he hath torn, and he will heal us: he hath smitten, and he will *bind us up*" (Hosea 6:1). That is, Hosea had represented God as essentially loving towards sinners and eager to save them, and Israel as being saved once they had thrown themselves utterly upon His mercy: "He hath torn, *and* he will heal us". 'Now', said Jesus in effect to the Pharisees, 'that is what God is like. So that is why I, the Physician sent from God, act as I do: I am not come to call the righteous, but sinners'. Thus effectively did he dispose of the Pharisees' automatic disapproval of his manner of performing his work by the mere act of referring to Hosea's prophecy. But his reference was specific not general, precise not vague. "Go ye and learn what *this* meaneth, I will have mercy and not sacrifice", said he. We look once more then at the prophecy. And there, plain for all to see, is the contrast between God and men. No sooner had the prophet depicted the people, chastened and humble, freely availing themselves of the mercy of God, than he had then to depict God reproaching them for failing to manifest the same mercy in their dealings with one another. "O Ephraim, what shall I do unto thee? O Judah, what shall I do unto thee? for your goodness (i.e. mercy, lovingkindness) is as a morning cloud, and as the early dew it goeth away".

The prophet Hosea was in his time the embodiment of his own message—the personification of God's goodness and compassion toward sinners. So was Jesus—else he would not have come. In Hosea's day, God was grieved because His lovingkindness, which is constant, was not matched by the people's. Theirs was as fleeting as the morning mist, and as unsubstantial also. The situation was no different in the days of Jesus—the attitude of the Pharisees to the publicans and sinners being witness. Hence his request, "Go ye and learn what this meaneth". And what had they to learn? The same lesson as the men of Hosea's day. These were punctilious in the performance of the ceremonial of worship, scrupulously conforming to all the ritual of the Law. This was good; but there was something far more essential, and therefore better. This contrast between good and better sounds to modern ears like a contrast between the unwanted and the wanted, but the sense of the idiom would be clear to Hebrew ears—"I desired mercy and not sacrifice". That is, God ranked mercy even higher than sacrifice, "the knowledge of God *more* than burnt offerings" (Hosea 6:6). That "knowledge of God" was defined in the very context of Hosea as the emulation of God in His exercise of mercy: "After two days will he revive us: in the third day he will raise us up, and we shall live in his sight. *Then* shall we know, if we follow on to know the LORD" (verses 2,3). The RV and other versions bring out the sense more clearly. "He will heal us ... we shall live before him. And let us know, *let us follow on to know the LORD*". Alas, that is just what Israel and Judah failed to do, as God's reproach bears out. And that, too, is precisely what the Pharisees in their turn failed to do. Like their predecessors, centuries before, they needed reminding that mercy excelled sacrifice in God's estimation, and God-likeness was more to be desired than burnt offerings. Had they known it they would not have allowed preoccupation with punctilios to blind them to men's need. They mistook the mechanics of religion for its vitalising spirit and their vaunted rectitude was in fact no more than a husk devoid of kernel. "Woe unto you, scribes and Pharisees, hypocrites! for ye pay tithe of mint and anise and cummin, and have omitted the weightier matters of the law, judgement, mercy, and faith: these ought ye to have done, *and not to leave the other undone*" (Matthew 23:23).

So spoke Jesus: he was but restating Hosea's message, and with it that of all the prophets both before (e.g. 1 Samuel 15:22) and after Hosea (Isaiah 1:10-17; Micah 6:6-8). Judgement, mercy and faith are qualities of character, the positive manifestations of piety, which cannot be measured by weight or line; ritual however can be observed with perfect regularity even where true religion is altogether absent, and has thus no *intrinsic* value. The Pharisees acted as though this were not so, and adopting a false standard to measure their spiritual worth made shipwreck of their piety. The time came when they desired sacrifice and not mercy, the material in preference to the spiritual, and found their hidebound heartlessness more congenial than Jesus, the manifestation of divine love.

The old order changeth

The clash with the Pharisees thus put matters back into true perspective: ritual was relegated to its proper place and the essential superiority of spiritual graces was upheld. The next step was inevitable. Jesus had done more than demonstrate the intrinsic limitation of ritual: he had himself dispensed with it. The question posed by the followers of John in its defence thus gave him the opportunity to state why he had done so. "Why do we and the Pharisees fast oft, but thy disciples fast not?" they asked. His reply amounted to a decree that the age of ritualistic worship was over. It was stated enigmatically, and like all his sayings bore directly on his mission. "Jesus said unto them, Can the children of the bridechamber mourn, as long as the bridegroom is with them?" The language was challenging. It meant that the Bridegroom had come; that is, that the King was in their midst, claiming his Bride (Psalm 45:11-13). So the spirit of the times had to be in keeping with the situation, especially as it was written of the Bride, "She shall be brought unto the king in raiment of needlework", and also of "the virgins her companions", that *with gladness and rejoicing* shall they be brought: they shall enter into the king's palace" (verses 14,15). It was not fitting that Jesus' disciples, the children of the bridechamber, the companions of the King, should do other than rejoice: the practice of fasting was alien to their mood, and an utter anomaly in the circumstances.

This could only mean that the situation had radically altered since John's imprisonment. It had indeed. In fact the old system of ritualistic worship of which he was the last prophetic representative was already falling to pieces—and could not be patched, least of all by an admixture of the new order which was replacing it. "No man putteth a piece of new cloth unto an old garment, for that which is put in to fill it up taketh from the garment, and the rent is made worse" (Matthew 9:16). The figurative language was all the more significant for the way in which it presupposed that the old garment was already "rent" and approaching the time to be discarded *in its entirety*. This was precisely what Jesus next went on to state with the aid of a fresh figure: "Neither do men put new wine into old bottles: else the bottles break, and the wine runneth out, and the bottles perish: but they put new wine into new bottles, and both are preserved" (Matthew 9:14-17). Jesus thus made it plain that he was deliberately discarding ritual forms because they were already outmoded. They had served their purpose, and were now of no further use for the simple reason that *he* had come to make all things new. It was on that very account that he mingled freely with publicans and sinners, and, far worse, even ate with them, heedless of the ceremonial defilement in which he technically became involved by so doing. Not that this heedlessness sprang either from ignorance of the Law or from a reckless disregard of its sanctity. On the contrary it was an authoritative overriding of the Law, one more revelation of himself as the heavenly Bridegroom.

This emerged very clearly on a later occasion. Harvest was near, and the disciples were feeling the effects of an insufficiency of food, for they were so famished that they began to pluck the ears of corn in a field through which they happened to be passing. The act in itself was innocuous: in fact the Law itself expressly sanctioned it (Deuteronomy 23:25). But what angered the Pharisees was that it was done *on the Sabbath*, and was, by definition, a form of reaping, threshing and winnowing, all of which was expressly forbidden to be done upon the Sabbath. "Six days", said the Law, "thou shalt work, but on the seventh day thou shalt rest: in earing time and in harvest thou shalt rest" (Exodus 34:21). Nothing could have been more explicit. So their protest was inevitable, "Behold, thy disciples do that which is not lawful to do upon the sabbath". The protest was intended to discredit him rather than his disciples, for his non-interference with them was a direct connivance at their action, and thus, in the Pharisees' eyes, proof positive that he could not be the Messiah.

Jesus, accepting the implicit charge of connivance, at once proceeded to expose the falsity of the conclusion which the Pharisees were drawing from it (Matthew 12:1-8). This he did in no uncertain fashion with two arguments culled from the Old Testament. He cited two instances

where certain special factors legalised what were otherwise technical infringements of the Law—the eating of the
loaves of shewbread by David and his followers, and the
offering of sacrifice by the priests on the Sabbath day. The
record of David's action in 1 Samuel 21:1-6, without in fact
specifically saying so, reads as though it took place on the
Sabbath, the day when the stale shewbread was replaced
by fresh (Leviticus 24:5-8). There was thus probably a dual
aptness to Jesus' quotation of these two cases of technical
fault which incurred no actual blame. Nor was this all;
both the eating of the shewbread and the offering of sacrifice had to do with God's house—in the one case the
Tabernacle, in the other the Temple—and that fact was for
Jesus the crux in each case. This emerges clearly if we
follow his reasoning carefully.

David had, with kingly authority, and out of regard for
his followers' desperate need of food, overridden the Law,
which restricted the privilege of eating the loaves of shewbread to the priests (Leviticus 24:9). The Pharisees took no
exception to his action. Yet they objected to a similar
breach of divine law on the part of Jesus' disciples! There
was no mistaking Jesus' intention therefore in referring to
this Old Testament incident. He was purposely drawing a
parallel between David and his warriors, and himself and
his disciples, as though that were the most natural thing
in the world for him to do. That is, whereas his critics had
utilised his disciples' offence to invalidate his claim to be
Messiah, he had promptly turned the tables on them and
used it to authenticate that claim! Their cunning thus
rebounded on them like a boomerang. What he had done in
conniving at his disciples' action he had done with the
authority which was his as the Christ, the King who was
even greater than David. That, and nothing less, was the
implication of his reference to David's technical offence.

We thus see that, here as always, Jesus' answer was
shot through with Christological meaning, and was totally
in character. To it, as double witness, he added another.
"Or have ye not read in the law, how that on the sabbath
days the priests in the temple profane the sabbath and are
blameless?" In saying this, he in fact intensified his

oblique claim to be Messiah rather than changed his
ground. For who pronounced the priests blameless even
though they worked upon the Sabbath? Not Aaron; not
Moses—none but God Himself!—He who, though the
Sanctuary was His Dwelling-Place, was infinitely greater
than the Sanctuary for without Him it had no value or
meaning. The point of Jesus' allusion this time was thus
even more staggering than before. And he would not have
men miss it either, for he added, "But I say unto you, That
in this place is one greater than the temple" (Matthew
12:5,6). He spoke, of course, of himself: that is, he laid
undisguised claim to power to exercise divine prerogatives
in his own right. His connivance at his disciples' action
was thus tantamount to nothing less than an authoritative
abolition of the Sabbath law.

Such an abolition had in due course inevitably to come.
And the Pharisees ought both to have known it, and also to
have rejoiced that that time had now at last arrived. As
Jesus put it, "But if ye had known what that meaneth, I
will have mercy and not sacrifice, ye would not have condemned the guiltless". His disciples could only have been
guiltless if they had been divinely exonerated from guilt.
That was the precise state of affairs. And the reason? "For
the Son of man is Lord even of the sabbath day".

Jesus at once proceeded to make good that claim.
Having thus abruptly terminated this clash with these
inveterate ritualists, who set sacrifice (this by metonymy
standing for the whole ceremonial system) above mercy
(i.e. the spiritual reality of which the ceremonial was but a
symbolic anticipation), he forthwith "went into their synagogue". His enemies, in their folly, there insisted on
reopening the controversy. "Behold, there was a man
which had a withered hand". Espying this man they decided to use him as a pawn. With their tongues in their
cheeks they asked Jesus, "Is it lawful to heal on the sabbath days?" Their intent was murderous. What they
sought was not information but evidence which would
incriminate him and warrant a charge of blasphemy as a
pretext for doing him to death—and this on the Sabbath!
(Matthew 12:7-10).

Jesus, with perfect command both of himself and of the situation, first, it would seem, retorted with a question of his own, one much broader in scope than theirs. "He saith unto them, Is it lawful to do good on the sabbath days, or to do evil? to save life, or to kill?" (Mark 3:4). Here was a golden opportunity for them to see in the observance of the Sabbath law something more than a ritual act. Only a little earlier Jesus had declared, "The sabbath was made for man, and not man for the sabbath". Some today construe this to mean that Jesus sanctioned the breach of the Sabbath law *by any man* who chose to regard his personal needs to be more pressing than the obligation to obey it. But nothing could be further from the truth, for the conclusion which Jesus himself expressly drew from that axiom was, "Therefore *the Son of man* is Lord also of the sabbath" (Mark 2:28). That is, he, and no other, had the right to amend the Sabbath law. What he meant by his dictum was clearly that the Sabbath was not imposed upon man for its own sake but only as a recognition of man's desperate need, and that therefore the Sabbath would automatically outlive its purpose once that need was fully met. So the very fact that Jesus dealt with the Sabbath as he did constituted a claim that the need had been fully met in him. In other words he had translated its ritual meaning into present reality. Now that the controversy had so quickly been reopened he proceeded to demonstrate that this was in fact so.

He received no answer to his enquiry from his enemies. Doubtless their consciences condemned them. They could not very well state that it was wrong either to do evil or to kill on the Sabbath for at that very moment they were wishing him dead! And, conversely, to admit that to do good and to save life were perfectly consistent with respect for the Sabbath law would be merely to play into his hands. So "they held their peace" (Mark 3:4). He then broke the silence with a parable, one which argued from their own self-interested activities his perfect right to heal the man's paralysis there and then. "He said unto them, What man shall there be among you, that shall have one sheep, and if it fall into a pit on the sabbath day, will he not lay hold on it, and lift it out?" (Matthew 12:11). Yes, they were only too alive to the needs of their sheep, and justified the rescue of an injured animal from a pit on the Sabbath in cases where to leave it to its plight until the next day would entail the loss of its life. Could they not then let their own humaneness to their beasts serve them as an allegory?

In all this lay a delicate allusion to Old Testament Scripture. There were other "sheep"; there was another "pit"; and there was another "Shepherd" who could extend his hands to lift them out of it and save them from their otherwise certain doom (Psalm 37:24; 40:1,2). No fitter day, therefore, could there be than the Sabbath for him to do his work, for the Sabbath was in fact but a foreshadowing of that work! Jesus, however, left all this to be gathered in retrospect by the reflective listener. The blunt truth there and then—one to which the Pharisees in their hide-bound formalism had become almost totally insensitive—was that man is worth infinitely greater trouble to save than is an animal, however precious it may be to its owner. "How much then", said Jesus, "is a man better than a sheep?" There could therefore be no doubt what answer his critics ought to have given to his enquiry at the outset. "Wherefore", he concluded on their behalf, and with no fear of being gainsaid, "it is lawful to do well on the sabbath days" (Matthew 12:12). And he promptly proceeded "to do well" and to prove himself to be the one qualified to save men from the pit of death itself (Psalm 88:3,4), by saying to the man, "Stretch forth thine hand". Matthew comments, "And he stretched it forth; and it was restored whole, like as the other" (Matthew 12:13).

Thus did mercy assert itself over against sacrifice, and lovingkindness and compassion for human suffering rebel against a ceremonialism which had degenerated into a callous disregard of others' needs. But nowhere, not even here, did such a disregard prove itself to be more callous, and seeming service to God in the rigidly heartless observance of the Sabbath law betray itself more as an utter disregard of God's love of mercy and tender sympathy, than on the occasion when Jesus healed a woman who had

suffered for eighteen years from spinal curvature. He did
so in a synagogue, and on a Sabbath day. With indignation
the ruler of the synagogue protested to the people. "There
are six days in which men ought to work: in them therefore come and be healed, and not on the sabbath day". The
pathos of the story once again lies in the fact that this
man's indignation was inspired by religious fervour—but
fervour which manifested itself unhappily in a heartlessness which was the negation of true religion, and a denial
of the divine decree, "I will have mercy and not sacrifice".
The man's regard for the Sabbath assumed so perverted a
form that it deprived the Sabbath of all its meaning. This
Jesus pointed out to him, arguing once again from the
man's own self-interested practice. "Thou hypocrite, doth
not each one of you on the sabbath loose his ox or his ass
from the stall, and lead him away to watering?" This man
was well able to appreciate the irksomeness for his beast
of the tether and the halter, and eager to spare it the pain
of thirst even though it was the Sabbath! How warped
then were his standards that he could not feel with the
same—let alone a greater—intensity for a suffering
human. "Ought not this woman, being a daughter of
Abraham, whom Satan hath bound, lo, these eighteen
years, be loosed from this bond on the sabbath day?" (Luke
13:11-16).

This retort pulverised opposition. The ruler was prepared to show kindness to an animal, even an unclean ass,
but here was no ass but a human being! And it was not as
though she was a Gentile either, for she was one of the
"clean", a member of the chosen race itself. Added to which
the man's inconsistency was in any case beyond excuse—
he was anxious to obviate for his beast even a few hours'
suffering, but he was obstinately willing to prolong eighteen weary years of suffering for the poor woman! And
beyond all this lay yet another factor. All that bound the
beast was a piece of rope. Not so in the woman's case. Her
bowed body, arched as though in a vice-like grip, was a living parable of sin's terrible hold over human nature. To
free her from her physical infirmity was thus also a spiritual parable. It spoke of the power of the Healer to deal

with the root malady which is the cause of all disease and suffering. It was yet another Messianic act, an epiphany of the Kingdom, a realization of the Sabbath. No day could therefore have been more appropriate than the Sabbath itself for the performance of it, and it was precisely this which rendered the synagogue ruler's scrupulosity so damnable. He gave the type greater honour than the archetype, the shadow greater honour than the substance. In brief he preferred law to love.

God is Love

In his heartless folly the synagogue ruler was, alas, not alone. He was but one of many who likewise betrayed their spiritual deficiencies by their materialistic approach to the worship of the living God, who will have mercy rather than sacrifice because He is Himself "merciful and gracious, longsuffering, and abundant in goodness and truth ... forgiving iniquity and transgression and sin" (Exodus 34:6,7). Engrossed with the externals of their God-given system of worship they forgot its inner meaning, and in practice abused it to frustrate the will of God.

It was this sad fact which Jesus solemnly emphasized in the parable of the Good Samaritan. The poor man who fell among thieves received no more than disdainful looks from both priest and Levite. Both so feared to contract defilement that they left the sufferer to languish in his distress unaided, shutting up their bowels of their compassion against him. They typified the hide-bound ritualist, scrupulous but heartless, whose conduct was outwardly correct but whose inner-self was decaying. The Samaritan however could not bear to pass by; his compassion was too strong, and his desire to shew mercy overpowering, and regardless of ceremonial consequences he rescued and succoured the helpless one. "Go thou and do likewise" said Jesus to the self-satisfied legalist who sought to evade the duties which the great commandment, "Thou shalt love thy neighbour as thyself", laid upon him. That is, Jesus intended that the parable should be taken as grounds for practising mercy even if that entailed the technical infringement of certain ritual precepts of the Law, for these could not take precedence over its moral demands. Mercy was of overriding importance in every circumstance, for it alone took account of man's most desperate need, and made some attempt to bring him succour. And in this respect as in every other, Jesus was the living embodiment of his own teaching. He was himself the counterpart of the Good Samaritan, a manifestation in flesh of the mercy and lovingkindness of God. His compassion was always easily aroused and, if anything, even more readily aroused by men's spiritual helplessness (e.g. Matthew 9:36-38; Mark 6:34), than by their physical infirmities (Matthew 14:14). He and the synagogue ruler both acted in characteristic fashion on that momentous Sabbath day, but no contrast could be starker than their respective ways of doing so. Each claimed to be serving God by the way he acted, but there is no shred of doubt as to whose claim was true and whose was false. It was Jesus who revealed God to men by what he did: the ruler merely sounded the depths of pettiness and lovelessness in his fussy zeal for the sanctity of the Sabbath.

Never did Jesus tire of reminding men of God's love for them, and on more than one occasion as his means of doing so he used the figure of the Shepherd seeking out a lost sheep. We have already seen him use it to great effect to fire his disciples with self-effacing love and compassion for one another. He did so with no less effect on yet another occasion to rebut the oft repeated slander that he was unhealthily fond of the company of publicans and sinners (Luke 15:1,2; cf. 5:30; 19:7). There was, indeed, a sense in which he found their company congenial. But this redounded to his honour rather than his shame; for, as he used the parable of the Shepherd to show, his own love for them was but an expression of the love of God Himself. God, said Jesus, is like the shepherd who, when he recovers a lost sheep, "calleth together his friends and neighbours, saying unto them, *Rejoice* with me; for I have found my sheep which was lost". "I say unto you", commented Jesus, "that likewise *joy* shall be in heaven over one sinner that repenteth, more than over ninety and nine just persons, which need no repentance" (Luke 15:3-7). So too with the woman who lost a piece of silver and, after diligent search, found it again; she also in her joy typified God and the angels exulting over every repentant sinner (verses 8-10). So, again, with the affectionate father who rejoiced that a sinful and foolish son had returned contrite and spiritually renewed to his true home, and who pleaded with the churlish elder brother, "It was meet that we should make merry, and be glad, for this thy brother was dead and is alive again; and was *lost* and is found" (verses 11-32).

Jesus did not give such teaching for its own sake. He chose to reveal God to men in this way, in order to prevail on them to emulate Him in His compassion and longsuffering, and to work as His agents in the constant strife against sin. No worship offered to Him could, for Jesus, be acceptable which was not based on the consciousness of indebtedness to God for His gracious saving purpose, and on a yearning to show appreciation of it by loving one's neighbour as oneself. What so bedevilled the Pharisaic form of religion, as he showed, was its utter neglect of the love of God, both in the sense of affection for God because of His affection for man, and of affection for others which His affection ought to have inspired. "Woe unto you, Pharisees! for ye tithe mint and rue and all manner of herbs and pass over judgement and the love of God" (Luke 11:42). They allowed the externals of religion to take precedence over its animating principle—and the outcome was spiritual degeneration and death. Yet not all of them were like this: the odd one or two saw matters in a true light, among them the scribe who said, "There is one God; and there is none other but he: and to love him with all the heart, and with all the understanding, and with all the soul, and with all the strength, and to love his neighbour as himself, is *more* than all whole burnt offerings and sacrifices". Jesus thrilled to this man's understanding, and when he saw "that he answered discreetly, he said unto him, Thou art not far from the kingdom of God" (Mark 12:32-34).

Hearken and understand

"Thou art not far"—the compliment was truly great, and it was well deserved. Yet it was two-edged for all that: the man, though not far from the Kingdom, *had still not approached near enough*. The words of approval were therefore also an invitation. The invitation was to take one further, final step. He had come to see the essential inferiority of sacrifice to lovingkindness; could he also manage to see that sacrifice (that is, the whole ritual system) could in fact be dispensed with altogether? If he could, then he would qualify to enter the Kingdom not only in the day of its ultimate setting up, but also at the very time at which he spoke, for the one to whom he spoke had made that ritual system superfluous. Of this scribe, as of any other, it could at once become true that even if he were among the least in the Kingdom of heaven he was nevertheless greater than the last and most distinguished representative of the Old Covenant—John the Baptist—if only he chose to enter it there and then at the bidding of the King himself.

The invitation was made to this man by gentle innuendo—a token of the esteem in which Jesus held him. To his colleagues also it had been presented in a similar enigmatic form, but much more bluntly in their case, in keeping with their contempt for true spiritual greatness. Jesus had witheringly denounced them for making the word of God of none effect through their tradition (Mark 7:1-13). Then, deliberately calling the attendant crowds of listeners together, he invited them to weigh with extra-special care what he was about to say, beginning, "Hearken unto me every one of you, and understand". His introduction was a claim to ultimate authority: what was to follow was not a riddle but an authoritative decree which the truly spiritual alone would be able to understand, and, understanding, to accept. "There is nothing from without a man, that entering into him can defile him: but the things which come out of him, those are they that defile the man". Then finally, to impress on them once more the tremendously far-reaching character of this simple dictum, he added, "If any man have ears to hear, let him hear". We gather from Matthew's account that the Pharisees did have ears to hear—and at once reacted in characteristic fashion. "Then came his disciples, and said unto him, Knowest thou that the Pharisees were offended, after they heard this saying?" (Matthew 15:12). The naive way in which the disciples announced this news was truly pathetic: it signified that they had themselves missed the point of Christ's dictum. The astute Pharisees had seen in it a repudiation of their elaborate hoary traditions concerning the washing of cups, and pots, and brasen vessels, and of tables (Mark 7:4). But since these traditions had originated from an excess of zeal for those ceremonial washings which were enjoined by God's Law itself, some of the Pharisees might also have seen in his words no less than a revocation of the very precepts which Moses had received from God. Small wonder that they were offended! (cf. Luke 11:41).

In puzzlement the disciples wondered why the parable had caused them such offence, and they asked Jesus to explain it to them. He did, but not without protestingly asking, "Are ye so without understanding also? Do ye not perceive, that whatsoever thing from without entereth into the man, it cannot defile him; because it entereth not into his heart, but into the belly, and goeth out into the draught?" (Mark 7:18,19). Jesus urged them to realize that ceremonial defilement had no automatic *moral* effect upon a man. To eat swine's flesh did not *make* a man a bad man. Its only significance lay in the fact that he *was* a bad man if he ate it in blatant disregard of the fact that God had forbidden him to eat it. His act was therefore an effect, and not a cause, of moral badness: the meat as meat was harmless, and the defilement involved in eating it *purely ceremonial.* But for that very reason it was also possible for men to be scrupulous in avoiding such defilement and yet still be evil men. And of this sad truth the Pharisees were a perfect illustration. Their righteousness was never more than ceremonial, and therefore utterly worthless. This was because, as we have seen, their fundamental religious outlook was unsound. Their conception of religion was wholly materialistic. They rated things which affected the body above those which affected the soul, the belly above the heart, sacrifice above mercy. They were therefore evil plants, plants which the Father had not planted, and therefore doomed to be rooted up (Matthew 15:13); or, to change the figure (as Jesus did), they were just blind leaders of the blind, themselves heading for the ditch (Matthew 15:14). What "came out" of them, proved what Jesus said of them, for it revealed the essential man in every one of them. So Jesus proceeded to show how fundamental to true worship is a converted heart. "That which cometh out of the man, that defileth the man. For from within, out of the heart of men, proceed evil thoughts, adulteries, fornications, murders, thefts, covetousness, wickedness, deceit, lasciviousness, an evil eye, blasphemy, pride, foolishness: all these evil things come from within, and defile the man" (Mark 7:20-23).

"All these *evil* things ...", said Jesus. They are "evil" because they are an offence to God, an offence outweighing all merely technical infringements of His ceremonial laws; for the converse of "I will have mercy and not sacrifice" is, in effect, something like, 'Though I choose to tolerate ritual offences yet will I never sanction moral perversity'. The Pharisees were engrossed with the former, and a prey to the latter. And yet they were the outstandingly religious people of their day! In this, therefore, lies a warning to every generation of believers. The greatest danger for all who worship God is that the outward forms of their religious life might eclipse the inner piety of which those ought to be the natural and spontaneous expression. What God loves is the man who is genuine through and through; in whom the 'without' and the 'within' are really one; whose dominant persuasion is, "Thou God seest me"; and who, knowing the boundlessness of God's mercy toward himself, allows lovingkindness to well up out of his heart and overflow toward all others. To teach this truth, and himself to embody and personify it, was fundamental to the mission which Jesus came to fulfil. To lay hold of it and guide his life by it is in turn the fundamental duty of the Christian whom Jesus came to save. Let each of us see to it that he never forgets the fact lest a worst fate than the Pharisee's befall him.

JESUS—HEALER & TEACHER

7
THAT SEEING THEY MIGHT NOT SEE!
The parabolic teaching of the Lord

IT has been truly said that Jesus thought in pictures, for his language teemed with images. He scarcely made a statement which did not contain some bold figure of speech. He disdained to apply to his faithful disciples such trite designations as "persons of true worth" or "the greatest men of their time". They were this indeed, but he preferred to describe them as "the salt of the earth", for this was a far more forceful way of stating the essential facts. Not that he strove after effect for its own sake. On the contrary, this particular choice of metaphor brought home to them a profound moral truth. It was a reminder that as the "salt" of those days could lose its true salt content through the effects of moisture and other causes, and thus become flat and insipid, useless both as a condiment and as a fertiliser for the fields, so they also could lose their goodness and usefulness in the sight of God (Matthew 5:13). The same was true when he called them "the light of the world". The description picturesquely set forth their high status and privileges before God, but in the process of so doing, it also, with telling stress, laid the most solemn obligations upon them to fulfil the purpose of their calling. This was to bear witness, both in word and deed, to the Gospel which had been entrusted to them (Matthew 5:14-16).

New and old
Thus Jesus' use of imagery had a distinct practical and instructive purpose, and was not a mere literary embellishment of simple facts: rather did it permit those facts to be expressed with a vigour and power which would not otherwise have been possible without his forsaking that economical use of words which was everywhere character-

137

istic of him. He could not again have more effectively, and at the same time more concisely, warned his followers against their prospective adversaries than by saying, "Behold, I send you forth as sheep in the midst of wolves". By this means their own duty to be guileless and harmless, and also the certainty that their opponents would be remorseless and vindictive, were each conveyed to them with a positiveness that left them with no illusions whatsoever as to the demands which their work of witness would lay upon them (Matthew 10:16). And in turn, by upbraiding those opponents to their face for being "a generation of vipers", Jesus said more (and said it with incomparably greater effect) than could have been possible in many sentences couched in plain literal language (Matthew 12:34). His, then, was not the connoisseur's love of imagery as imagery, but a sincere man's quest of the best vehicle for expressing truth. He always spoke with a forthrightness and an aptness which impressed his sayings indelibly upon his listeners' minds. A penetrating observer of human behaviour, and a man familiar with the manifold life of lakeside and country, not only did he see analogies perceptible by none but the ablest and most pious minds, but he also put them into words with a simplicity and vigour which are the hallmark of true literary genius. It was they which enabled him so effectively to enliven all his sayings and discourses, and his use of them has marked him out ever since as a teacher without peer.

Yet when all this has been said the fact still remains that his greatest storehouse of truth, and also of the forms of expression with which he clothed it, was not the world of Nature but the pages of Old Testament Scripture. His thinking was saturated with its teaching and his vocabulary with its phraseology. Time and again the figures which he used were but veiled allusions to the Scriptures, or adaptations of the proverbs and similes to be found there. Examples come readily to mind, all the more readily because we have earlier had occasion to note their allusiveness. "I am not sent but unto the lost sheep of the house of Israel"..."They that be whole need not a physician, but they that are sick"..."How can one enter into a strong man's house, and spoil his goods, except he first bind the strong man?" Many parallels can be quoted. Sometimes the allusion takes the form of a verbal quotation, and is easily detected. Thus the "treasure" which "neither moth—nor rust doth corrupt" in the New Testament is the "righteousness" which is immune to "moth" and "worm" in the Old (Matthew 6:19,20; Isaiah 51:7,8). But at other times the allusiveness of Jesus' language is much more subtle, and for that reason can easily escape notice. Thus his way of guarding the sanctity of the Gospel (which the imperative need for its world-wide propagation might cause the over-zealous to forget) was to command his disciples, "Give not that which is holy unto the dogs, neither cast your pearls before swine" (Matthew 7:6). His words were this time borrowed from the Law: "that which is holy" was flesh which only priestly families were privileged to eat (Leviticus 22:10); as for dogs, to them fell only those *un*holy carcases which had died as victims of disease or the violence of beasts of prey (Leviticus 22:8; cf. Exodus 22:31; Deuteronomy 14:21). His listeners would see the point of his language, and act with especial care on that account.

Jesus thus thought in pictures drawn as much from the limitless depository of the Old Testament as from the store which his own observation and experience had painted for him. In fact, scarcely any of the statements which he made were not, to a greater or lesser extent, in the nature of parables, whether drawn from Scripture or from life. Few of them, certainly, were plain statements of fact, for his habit was to speak enigmatically in order to provoke careful reflection on their part. For example, to induce a worshipper who had offended his brother to make peace with that brother before attempting to offer worship to God, Jesus used an illustration which was almost pure parable. "Agree with thine adversary quickly, whiles thou art in the way with him", he said, "lest at any time the adversary deliver thee to the judge, and the judge deliver thee to the officer, and thou be cast into prison. Verily I say unto thee, Thou shalt by no means come out thence till thou hast paid the uttermost farthing" (Matthew 5:23-26). By this means he reminded them that law-cases in those days, having once begun, could not be settled out of court and that justice had perforce to take its course when once invoked, with the result that wise men came to terms with their creditors by private treaty while they had the opportunity. Jesus intended his disciples to realize from this that divine judgement will assuredly punish all unbrotherly conduct in the future unless it is undone while the opportunity is available in the present. The allegory is not perfect, but it is clear enough in its outlines. The court is the Judgement; the judge is God; one's creditor is an offended brother; the officer is the agent of ultimate judgement; the prison is the grave, a return to which cannot be evaded unless the foolish "debtor" has some compensating virtue with which to make good his bankruptcy in this respect—a truly doubtful contingency. The parable thus drew a telling analogy between the financial and the moral debtor, and emphasized that for the latter, as for the former, time is truly precious. It was precisely this effectiveness of the parable as an illustration of the fact that a sinner's opportunity to escape certain judgement is of but short duration which led Jesus to make further use of it on a later occasion. This second use (which we have noted earlier in our study) was intended to stress a closely related, but broader, truth that all who hear the Gospel must either repent, or perish under the judgement of God.

The mystery of the kingdom

We can now state with confidence that Jesus made consistent use of the parabolic method from the outset of the ministry. "Why, then", we are compelled to ask, "did his use of parables on one occasion constrain his disciples to ask him, Why speakest thou unto them in parables?" There must obviously have been something quite peculiar about his preaching on that particular day to prompt their enquiry. There was indeed. Both Mark and Matthew tell us what it was: "With many such parables spake he the word unto them, as they were able to hear it. *But without a parable spake he not unto them*" (Mark 4:33,34; cf. Matthew 13:34). This, then, was the new feature. Many a time before, as is now evident, both when he had been speaking to them and also to the people, they had heard him use enigmatic statements and illustrations which were calculated to provoke thought. But never before had one of his addresses been a succession of parables *and nothing more*. This was something altogether novel. And to make matters more perplexing, the very occasion when he chose to resort to this new teaching method was one when they would least have expected him to do so, even if they had known in advance that a change of method was impending. It was a day when "great multitudes were gathered together unto him, so that he went into a ship and sat: and the whole multitude stood on the shore" (Matthew 13:2).

The presence of the multitudes is in fact the key to the understanding of Jesus' adoption of the parabolic method of instruction to the exclusion for the first time of the plain and direct preaching of the gospel of the kingdom in which he had also hitherto engaged (e.g. Matthew 4:23; 9:35). His popularity was at its height. His fame had spread afar, fanning the glowing embers of Jewish patriotism into flame, and raising in the breasts of all the hope that he would assert himself as a secular king and lead them to victory against the Roman tyrant. For himself, therefore, no less than for the enthusiastic crowds who thronged to hear him in feverish expectation that he would declare a holy war against the infidel, the situation was charged with direst danger. For him it revived the struggle of the wilderness Temptation. So for them it was, and had to be, a turning point lest disaster should befall both them and him. How then was he to act? To have told them bluntly that he had no intention of asserting himself as King would have had two immediate tragic consequences, one issuing from the other. It would have obviously turned all men from him at once in disgust and disappointment; but it would also (a far more serious matter) have exposed his Messianic claim to downright denial and contempt.

It was here that the parabolic method came so wonderfully to the rescue. It enabled him to state the true facts concerning the Kingdom in a way that would excite interest rather than disgust, and most effectively discourage the misguided longing of the worldly-minded that he should there and then assert himself as their deliverer by resorting to the use of force. That is, it made an appeal to the spiritually-minded which, without enraging the materially-minded, left the latter so unsatisfied, that they of their own accord drifted away from him without disturbance of any kind. As for the spiritually-minded, the parables—accompanied as they were by repeated appeals to search out their hidden meaning—came as a challenge both to their faith and to their powers of discernment. From every point of view, then, the adoption of nothing but parables as the means of instructing the over-enthusiastic crowds, was both inevitable and desirable.

It is essential to bear in mind that it was not Jesus, but they, who made it so. His change of method was an act of judgement on them, but one which they, with their wholly mundane and unspiritual interests, fully deserved. What would have been the use of his shocking the feelings of bloodthirsty zealots in his audience, bent as they were on military revolt, by stating that their true duty was not to wrest power from the hands of the Roman procurator but to submit to wrong and injustice? He would by that means have accomplished nothing. He might even have been made by them to put his own preaching to the test upon the spot and have died the victim of their revengeful violence! But the very fact that they would have been impervious to any appeals which he might have made (to meekness, to gentleness, and to readiness to resist not evil but instead to love their enemies) was proof conclusive that they had no genuine interest in that Kingdom which was truly God's. Better was it, therefore, that the Kingdom should be preached in an enigmatic way that would make no appeal to them, than in a direct way that would only earn their ungodly contempt for it. He, too, would not cast pearls before swine.

In a sense, their own self-chosen indifference to spiritual things pronounced judgement upon itself—a truth of which the parables were but a concrete illustration, as Jesus himself made clear to his disciples.

They came to him and asked, "Why speakest thou to them in parables?" This request followed hard upon the parable of the Sower (the first of the series spoken on that memorable day) and hard upon the significant intimation of its revolutionary meaning with which Jesus brought it to a close—"Who hath ears to hear, let him hear" (Matthew 13:9,10). Jesus, in reply to their enquiry, gave as his reason, "Because it is given unto you to know the mysteries of the kingdom of heaven, but to them it is not given" (verse 11). We need to grasp the meaning of this statement properly for not otherwise shall we understand the words that followed it. Something was "given" to the disciples which was denied to the misguided crowds around them; and it enabled them "to know the mysteries of the kingdom of heaven". That this "something" did not make the parable at once plain to them is only too painfully obvious: they had themselves to ask him to interpret it to them!—and others besides (Luke 8:9; Matthew 13:36; cf. Luke 12:41). He was not telling them, then, that they already had a full understanding of what the Kingdom was—their understanding was, alas, all too deficient. But what they did have (and it was this which so sharply marked them off from the worldly-minded crowds about them) was the willingness to learn what was the *real* character of the Kingdom. They evinced an interest in its spiritual nature which was altogether lacking in the mass of the nation at that time. They, therefore, would come to understand it better as time went on, but not so the people at large— they would become steadily *less* capable of appreciating the Gospel of the Kingdom. As Jesus at once proceeded to put it, "Whosoever hath, to him shall be given, and he shall have more abundance: but whosoever hath not, from him shall be taken away even that he hath" (Matthew 13:12). Never were the value of spirituality and the futility of material-mindedness set in starker contrast. "Therefore", said Jesus, "speak I to them in parables: because they seeing see not; and hearing they hear not, neither do they understand" (verse 13).

This solemn verdict had already been justified by the reception which had been accorded to Jesus' teaching. The

Pharisees' preoccupation with present reward and earthly treasure had darkened their spiritual vision exactly as Jesus had warned them it would (Matthew 6:21-23, cf. Luke 11:34-36). They had attributed his miracles to satanic agencies and thus shown their contempt for the Kingdom of God as thus revealed to their gaze (Matthew 12:28). On every hand deaf ears had been turned to both John's and his own call to repentance, and with self-satisfied hearts the religious leaders had spurned his testimony. So with ample reason Jesus added, "And in them is fulfilled the prophecy of Esaias". It was fulfilled in two senses: first it predicted, "By hearing ye shall hear, and shall not understand, and seeing ye shall see, and shall not perceive"—so Jesus expressly adopted the parabolic method in conformity with it. But he did so only because that state of affairs had been reached which Isaiah had again foretold and which alone warranted such an action on his part: "For this people's heart is waxed gross, and their ears are dull of hearing, and their eyes have they closed; lest at any time they should see with their eyes, and hear with their ears, and should understand with their heart, and should be converted, and I should heal them" (Matthew 13:14,15).

Yet amid the people, as in Isaiah's day, was "a very small remnant". And to these (his own disciples) Jesus then proceeded to address himself, saying, "But blessed are your eyes"—placing all the emphasis upon the word "your". "But blessed are *your* eyes, for they see: and *your* ears, for they hear" (verse 16). That is, his disciples were receptive whereas the crowds were obdurate. They had that childlikeness of disposition which was (and is) the prerequisite of a proper understanding of the Kingdom. For this quality of mind Jesus had already publicly thanked God. He had been denouncing the unresponsive cities of Galilee, and uttering solemn threats of judgement; but in wrath he remembered mercy, as Matthew indicates by saying, "*At that time* Jesus answered and said, I thank thee, O Father, Lord of heaven and earth, because thou hast *hid* these things from the wise and prudent, and hast revealed them unto babes". And that in this God was true to His own essential spirituality Jesus acknowledged by adding, "Even so, Father: for so it seemed good in thy sight" (Matthew 11:25,26).

This earlier acclamation of the disciples' humbleness of mind, which was such congenial soil for the sowing of the Word, had had a most significant sequel. "Thou hast revealed these things unto babes", Jesus had said. But how had God revealed them? Through Jesus, and no other. "No man knoweth the Son, but the Father; neither knoweth any man the Father, save the Son, and he to whomsoever *the Son* will *reveal* him" (Matthew 11:27). It was this same profound truth which Jesus once more took care to impress upon these "babes" when they asked him why he taught in parables. Not only were they blessed because they had eyes with powers of perception, and ears sensitive to hear; there was also something unique for them to see, and to hear—himself and his teaching! "For verily I say unto you, That many prophets and righteous men have desired to see these things which ye see, and have not seen them; and to hear those things which ye hear, and have not heard them" (Matthew 13:16,17; cf. Luke 10:21,22; 23,24). He was the Messiah, the King! and they his associates. So his parables, then, like all else he said and did, were penetrated• with Christology. He was their pivotal point and the ultimate secret of their meaning. And this he at once went on to show by adding, "Hear ye therefore the parable of the sower" (Matthew 13:18), and then proceeding to interpret it.

The King and the Kingdom

Matthew in his thirteenth chapter records seven parables, and Mark, in his fourth, records three. Matthew's fall naturally into two groups—four addressed to the crowd (the Sower, the Wheat and Tares, the Mustard Seed and the Leaven), and three addressed to the disciples in "the house" (Treasure in a Field, the Pearl of great price, and the Net). The three selected by Mark have a topical connection: they are all parables of harvest (the Sower, the Seed growing secretly, and the Mustard Seed). From this it is obvious that each inspired writer arranged his material

according to a plan of his own. This, in turn, makes the
fact that the parable of the Sower heads *both* series of
parables, Matthew's and Mark's alike, a matter of some
significance. It is not sufficient to explain the coincidence
by saying that the Evangelists automatically placed the
parable first in their respective series because they knew
that it happened to head the succession which Jesus himself recounted on that famous day. This explanation is true
so far as it goes, but it begs a pressing question. Why did
Jesus give pride of place to that particular parable? What
motive had he for so doing?

Reading carefully we soon stumble upon a vital clue. In
both Matthew's list and Mark's, every parable, save one,
begins with the formula (or some slight variation of it),
"The kingdom of heaven is like ...". The exception in each
case is *the parable of the Sower*. Turning to Luke's Gospel
we find the same to be true there too. Actually he quotes
the parable in isolation and several chapters separate it
from the twin parables of the Mustard Seed and the
Leaven. But whereas the first of these is introduced by the
double question, "Unto what is the kingdom of God like?
and whereunto shall I resemble it?" and the other by the
single question "Whereunto shall I liken the kingdom of
God?" We find that it is quite different with the parable of
the Sower. Luke simply states, "He spake by a parable",
and at once proceeds to narrate it, "A sower went out to
sow his seed", etc. (Luke 13:18-21; 8:4,5). And the same is
the case with other parables such as the Rich Fool, the
Good Samaritan, the Barren Fig Tree, etc. In their case
also no comparison is suggested with the Kingdom of God.

This fact must be significant. It can only mean that
when Jesus deliberately prefaced a parable with the statement, "The kingdom of heaven is like ..." he meant it to be
understood that he was revealing a certain aspect of the
Kingdom, or some special truth connected with it, through
the medium of the particular similitude which he was
about to employ. Since therefore only one parable in a
whole succession of parables was given without that form
of introduction on the occasion in question, Jesus clearly
intended it to stand apart from the rest because of some

topical uniqueness which distinguished it from them.

What distinctive truth, then, had the parable of the Sower to reveal? A twofold truth, at once general and specific. It is the general truth which interests Luke, for he quotes Jesus as saying, "The seed is the word of God" (Luke 8:11). That is, the parable is true of preachers of God's Truth in every age, and therefore comprehends the activities of them all. In keeping with this, Luke not only records the parable in isolation from the others spoken on the same occasion, but also makes it a kind of preface to his account of the preaching first of the Twelve (9:1) and then of the Seventy (10:1). In his scheme, as it were, the parable is at once an introduction to the preaching work of the earliest believers (and so, also, of all their successors), and a prophecy of the mixed reception which would be accorded to their witness.

But, then, who sent forth these "sowers" of the Word? None but the One who was the greatest sower of all time—*the* Sower, in fact. Enfolded within the general truth was thus another, a more precise and specific truth, namely, that Jesus himself was "the Sower" *in the first instance.* Consistently with this, Mark actually quotes him as saying in his interpretation of the parable, *"The* sower soweth the word" (Mark 4:14). Matthew is even more explicit: he makes Jesus' interpretation begin with the following significant sentence, "When anyone heareth the word *of the kingdom* ..." (Matthew 13:19). So Luke's "word of God", has in Matthew resolved itself into "the word of the kingdom": that is, for the wider definition of Luke, Matthew has substituted a particular illustration of it. This can only mean that Jesus himself attached a dual significance to the parable, so that Matthew, with his special interest in Jesus as King, very naturally seized on the phrase, "the word of the kingdom". But, having done so, Matthew, in pursuit of the same special interest also noted, and carefully set down, the recurrent preface to each of the subsequent parables, "The kingdom of heaven is like ...". That is, for him the Sower was also the King, and all the subsequent parables were but so many

147

different pronouncements about the Kingdom *by the King himself.*

In the light of that fact we need to classify his series of parables afresh. We have already divided them into two groups, those spoken out of doors to the multitude, and those spoken later "in the house" to the disciples. That division still holds good, but we must now detach the parable of the Sower from the other three spoken in the open, and make it an introduction to two balancing groups of three parables: (a) the Tares, the Mustard Seed, the Leaven; (b) the Treasure in the Field, the Pearl, the Net. Finally, to balance that introduction, we note that Matthew has also recorded an eighth parable, an appendix, as it were, to the whole series. And, as by now we would expect, this too is related to the central theme, the Kingdom. "Jesus saith unto them, Have ye understood all these things? They say unto him, Yea, Lord. Then said he unto them, Therefore every scribe which is instructed *unto the kingdom of heaven* is like unto a man that is an householder, which bringeth forth out of his treasure things new and old" (Matthew 13:51,52).

Now, as we know, Mark's series of parables is much shorter than Matthew's, but it is nevertheless arranged on the same plan. With him, too, the parable of the Sower is introductory, and the two parables which follow it are prefaced respectively by, "So is the kingdom of God as if ..." and, "Whereunto shall we liken the kingdom of God?" (Mark 4:26,30). Nor is this all. Looking closer we discover first that the similitude of the Candle is inserted by Mark between these parables and that of the Sower; and secondly, that like Matthew's parable of the Instructed Scribe it contains vital lessons for the disciples *as custodians of the Gospel of the Kingdom*. We thus deduce that in Mark's arrangement it serves the same purpose as the eighth and culminating parable in Matthew's scheme.

The Sower

We are now in a position to examine the first parable in each series in detail. It is the King who is speaking, speaking primarily of himself (and so, by implication, of his associates also). But his self-revelation is enigmatic only. What is the effect on his audience? To appreciate it, let us remind ourselves of the nature of that audience. It is a huge crowd agog with excitement and expectancy, drawn, says Luke, "out of every city" (Luke 8:4). It is wondering whether the One who forms the centre of its interest is the long-awaited King, and hoping that he will declare himself at last to be so, and sound the call to arms. Breathlessly the people wait for his manifesto—and what do they hear? First a peremptory summons, which is a becoming assertion of sovereignty, indeed! (Mark 4:3). "Hearken!" So the hush deepens, and ears are strained to hear. Then follows the strangest and most unexpected of pronouncements: "Behold a sower went forth to sow; and when he sowed, some seeds fell by the wayside ... some fell among stony places ... some fell among thorns ... but other fell into good ground, and brought forth fruit, some an hundredfold, some sixtyfold, some thirtyfold". Then came another peremptory call, "Who hath ears to hear, let him hear". After that, just silence, while he allowed them time to reflect! Never was an anti-climax more disconcerting. Even the disciples shared the general consternation. Bewildered and abashed they "came and said unto him, Why speakest thou unto them in parables?" (Matthew 13:10). This was no time for riddles, but for action! If the situation struck even them that way, what must have been its effect on the multitude? The whole incident would strike them as being senseless. To be fobbed off with an invitation to sit down and think when they expected a call to rise and act—why, the whole situation was farcical! "This man the King? Ludicrous! Whatever is he supposed to be talking about?" Such would be the sentiments which their disappointment would provoke.

Yet therein lay the irony. Jesus was, though appearances so perplexingly belied fact, the King indeed! And he stressed the fact in his reply to his disciples' enquiry. "He answered and said unto them, Because it is given unto you to know the mysteries *of the kingdom of heaven*, but to them it is not given" (Matthew 13:11). He would have them remember that he assuredly was the King, and that the

149

fault lay not with him, but with the crowd which entertained so erroneous a notion both of the King and of his Kingdom. It was written of him, "The Spirit of the Lord GOD is upon me; because the LORD hath *anointed* me to *preach* good tidings unto the meek" (Isaiah 61:1). Only in so far, then, as he fulfilled that mission—that is, only in as far as he was a Sower of the Word —could he truly manifest himself as the King. The parable was therefore a challenge to the people to recognize him as King despite the fact that he in no way conformed to their false conception of the Lord's Anointed. It was, in effect, Jesus' answer to their silent questioning, Is this man the Christ? And it was more besides, for it simultaneously informed the crowds that their reaction to it and to him would reveal what manner of persons *they* really were.

Some would immediately drift away from him never to return to listen to him again: they were the soil by the way side—the Word meant nothing to them. Others would accept him, though only for a while, lacking the courage to be steadfastly loyal to him—they were the stony soil. Yet others would accept him with greater determination than these, only, alas, to allow mundane interests eventually to choke the Word—they were the soil thick with thorns. Finally some would accept him, and faithfully serve him to the limit of their powers—they being the good soil. So whereas the crowds cherished definite illusions about Jesus, he himself had no illusions about them. He *knew* what they would do, and in his riddle said so. The parable, then, was a piece of prophetic autobiography (based of course on his experiences as a preacher up to this point), but its character escaped even the disciples. When they begged him tell them what it meant, he complied, but the crowds outside were deliberately left to work matters out for themselves. Such was his procedure in every instance. "With many such parables spake he the word unto them, as they were able to hear it. But without a parable spake he not unto them: and when they were alone, he expounded all things to his disciples" (Mark 4:33,34). The Kingdom was for none but the spiritually minded. Such were the only persons fit to enter it. For those engrossed with material interests it could have no appeal—a fact which explains why Matthew, Mark, and Luke all take care to point out the close connection of the parable of the Sower with the saying, "Whosoever shall do the will of my Father which is in heaven, the same is my brother, and sister, and mother" (Matthew 12:50; 13:1; Mark 3:35; 4:1; Luke 8:1-18,19-21).

The Kingdom revealed

We can now appreciate to the full both why the parable of the Sower came to be delivered, and why it assumed the particular form which it did. But we can also see that it would have been ineffective unless other parables had followed it to lay stress on those aspects of the mystery of the Kingdom which the worldly-minded crowds were unprepared to accept. The succeeding parables were therefore its natural and indispensable complement. To those then we must now turn. As we might expect, they were all designed to correct the commonly held notions of the Kingdom and the manner of its foundation which were so much at variance with the Scriptures. And in serving this purpose they also formed a fitting basis for the further enlightenment of the disciples whose sympathies, all too often, lay strongly with the excited crowds around them.

Taking Mark's brief series first, we at once find the position of the similitude of the Candle to be significant. Having answered the disciples' query as to why he preached exclusively in parable on this outstanding occasion, Jesus proceeded to chide them for their own lack of perception. "He said unto them, Know ye not this parable? and how then will ye know all parables?" (Mark 4:13). His interpretation of the first parable then followed (verses 14-20). Having received it from his own lips, and so been let into a great secret, they were then reminded of the responsibilities attaching to their newly gained knowledge. "He said unto them, Is a candle brought to be put under a bushel, or under a bed? and not to be set on a candlestick?" To reinforce that truism Jesus made appeal to one of his favourite axioms, "For there is nothing hid, which shall not be manifested". But not content with that, he then proceeded to state another axiom, "Neither was anything kept secret, but that it should come abroad". This second axiom hinted at a deliberate concealment of some kind, which was to lead on to an eventual exposure of the matter concealed. Jesus, therefore, invited them to search out what that matter was, declaring once again, "If any man have ears to hear, let him hear" (Mark 4:21-23). Now, as we have had occasion to note earlier, Jesus had declared his disciples' ears to be blessed because they did in fact hear what he had to say (Matthew 13:16), and had also on the same occasion drawn their attention to the greatness of their privilege in so knowing the mysteries of the Kingdom, contrasting them in this respect with the unenlightened, self-seeking multitudes around from whom was to be taken even what they had (Matthew 13:12). But it is clear from Mark that Jesus then proceeded to offset any tendency to complacency which this might awaken in them, by reminding them that the very same principle would hold good in their case too. Not only did he say, "If any man have ears to hear let him hear"; he also at once added the caution, "Take heed what ye hear (Luke—"how ye hear"); with what measure ye mete, it shall be measured to you: and unto you that hear shall more be given. For he that hath, to him shall be given: and he that hath not, from him shall be taken even that which he hath" (Mark 4:23-25).

The similitude of the Candle, then, must have had a significance other than the obvious. Its obvious meaning was that now that they had become custodians of the truth concerning the King and the Kingdom, they were to spread that knowledge abroad as a candle sheds light all around it. Neither worldly interests ("a bushel"), nor sloth ("a bed") were to be allowed to hinder their work of witness. But for this an added reason was given—enigmatically. What was the disciples' *duty*, it was also God's *intention*, to do. That is, eventually, God would reveal Jesus to the world as King, "For there is nothing hid, which shall not be manifested" (verse 22). What is "hid" by man is his secret sin and shame, but that, said Jesus on another occasion, will one day be exposed before all, "for there is nothing covered that shall not be revealed; neither hid, that shall not be known". Hypocrisy is futile in view of the immutability of this divine law (Luke 12:1,2). But on that memorable "day of parables" Jesus was not concerned with the bearing of this law on human hypocrisy (though the notion of Judgement was nevertheless implicit in his words as we shall see in a moment, for the disciples would eventually have to give an account to God of their steward-ship as candles). Primarily he was concerned with its bear-ing on himself, the Sower, the unrecognized King. God had concealed from Israel's gaze the true vision of Messiah—but only in order to reveal it decisively in due course, for "neither was any thing kept secret, but that it should come abroad". That "time to reveal", said Jesus in effect, had come! *He* was the candle in the full sense, and nothing was to hinder its shining. For those with ears to hear, the riddle he had just propounded to the people would not remain a mystery. Nay, more; even though he would con-tinue to remain unrecognized as the King by the mass of the nation, the time would nevertheless certainly come when he would be openly recognized by all as the promised Messiah. This meant that there was to be a second "com-ing" as well as the first, though it was to be long future from that day of shame and rejection, for (to quote his axiom once more) "neither was anything kept secret, but that it should come abroad". The future Day, then, would reveal all things.

It was this thought that led Jesus to remind the disci-ples of the solemn obligation placed upon them to use their spiritual hearing aright, and to increase their fund of knowledge, so that they should prove unashamed in that Day of final reckoning. And this concern with the ultimate Day, the Day of his own showing forth and of their judge-ment, led him naturally to reveal, in a further parable, that long delay would have to ensue before the Kingdom of which he was King would actually be set up in visible form on earth. "He said, So is the kingdom of God, as if a man should cast seed into the ground; and should sleep, and rise night and day, and the seed should spring and grow up, he knoweth not how. For the earth bringeth forth fruit of herself; first the blade, then the ear, after that the full corn in the ear. But when the fruit is brought forth, immediately he putteth in the sickle, because the harvest is come" (Mark 4:26-29).

This parable has unquestionably a bearing on the slow spiritual development of the believer, but that significance is secondary. Its primary significance has to do with the slow development of God's purpose to set up the Kingdom. The crowds wished it to be set up hastily; the disciples shared their longing, and likewise wished it to be set up hastily. Jesus said, in effect, the Kingdom will most certainly be set up hastily, *but the time for that is still far away in the future*. Harvest is the sudden termination of a slow process of development; so the setting up of the Kingdom will rapidly consummate a slow but sure—a barely perceptible but none the less *living*—process of divine working in the affairs of men ("the ground"). Jesus has Judgement Day in mind throughout this parable: that Day will constitute the time of divine Harvest. When world affairs have reached their appointed stage of readiness ("when the fruit is brought forth"), swift action by God will supersede human rule ("immediately he putteth in the sickle") and the Kingdom *of God* will at last be set up *on earth* ("because the harvest is come").

Thus the parable of the Sower, and the parable (for it is a parable) of the Candle, both took Jesus' first coming as their starting point, but envisaged also his second coming; the one by talking of the seed sown in the good ground bringing forth fruit, and the other by talking of the open manifestation of the hidden secret. The parable of the Seed growing secretly bridged the historical gulf between the first advent, in shame, and the second, in glory. That there would be *two* advents of Messiah was the one thing which the nation at large failed utterly to realize; it was the mystery into which it was the privilege of Christ's personal associates to be initiated first. Even John, the greatest of the prophets, failed to grasp fully the relationship between the two—to disentangle "the acceptable year of the Lord" and "the day of vengeance of our God". As for the worldly-minded throng to which Jesus spoke in this enigmatic way, it had no predisposition even to entertain the notion of such a distinction. It reasoned blindly; Jesus did not conform to the popular notion of the King, therefore Jesus was not the King.

This false deduction was cruelly ironical. As a result of it the people in the end unwittingly fulfilled the very Scriptures which they so wantonly refused to understand! for not only did they turn away from Jesus—at last they slew him. In their eyes his beginning of the Kingdom was no beginning at all. But to that misguided conclusion Jesus gave an enigmatic answer in the parable of the Mustard Seed. "He said, Whereunto shall we liken the Kingdom of God? or with what comparison shall we compare it? It is like a grain of mustard seed, which, when it is sown in the earth, is less than all the seeds that be in the earth; but when it is sown, it groweth up, and becometh greater than all herbs, and shooteth out great branches; so that the fowls of the air may lodge under the shadow of it" (Mark 4:30-32).

"A grain of mustard seed" was in those days a proverbial term to describe something microscopically small. But a seed has the germ of life within it, and if planted it grows. The mustard seed, in particular, grows into a bush as tall as a tree, whose branches can support the weight of many birds. The Kingdom, said Jesus, is something similar. In his person, despite all that the people thought, the Kingdom was present in the earth—in miniature only, but nevertheless potentially in its eventual universal form. As the seed becomes a tree, so was the small beginning to the Kingdom made in him certain to result in its eventual world-wide establishment on earth. The parallel between the full-grown mustard tree and the tree of Nebuchadnezzar's dream (Daniel 4:11,12) would not escape the notice of Jesus' audience. He was predicting once again the fulfilment of all the Scriptures bearing on the visible and real character of the Kingdom, but also hinting at a long interval of time yet to elapse before that fulfilment was complete. That is, he invited men to see in him the grain of mustard seed, and the embryonic mustard tree. The parable, then, like so many others, was a revelation of himself; a discourse on the Kingdom *by none other than the King himself*, as all with eyes to see would not fail to perceive.

To those without

The plan of Mark's fourth chapter is by now transparent, and the reason for his choice of parables obvious. His is a survey study of the working of God's purpose in human history. In part, Matthew's treatment of the parables is this also. Only in part, though. Actually, as we have noted, the six parables which he quotes after the introductory parable of the Sower fall into two groups of three. After the first group Matthew states, "All these things spake Jesus *unto the multitude* in parables" (Matthew 13:34). Before the second he comments, "Then Jesus sent the multitude away, and went into the house, and *his disciples came to him.*" (Matthew 13:36). As we might expect, the character of Jesus' audience determined the nature and theme of the group of parables which he recounted in each case. The first three were intended primarily for outsiders; the last three were meant exclusively for those who believed in him. Let us consider each sequence in turn.

It goes without saying that each group has a topical unity. In the case of the first group this lies in the fact that *a suggestion of delay is common to all three parables.* In the parable of the Tares the delay extends from sowing-time to harvest; with the Mustard Seed we have a mention only of the beginning and the end of its growth; as for the Leaven, it takes time to permeate the meal in which it is placed. Now when we note that these parables were spoken directly to an unbelieving (or, at best, half-believing) audience, the reason for importing into them the element of delay is obvious. The crowds were expecting Jesus to found the Kingdom soon: not otherwise would he have so deliberately spoken so many parables to them on that very theme. The parables were, therefore, designed to show that though the Kingdom would indeed be founded, it would not be founded there and then, but only after a long lapse of time.

Interpreting the parable of the Tares Jesus said, "He that soweth the good seed is the Son of man; the field is the world; the good seed are the children of the Kingdom; but the tares are the children of the wicked one. The enemy that sowed them is the devil; the harvest is the end of the world; and the reapers are the angels" (Matthew 13:37,38). From this it is obvious that Jesus intended the parable to bear its share of witness to the universality of the Kingdom, and so also of the Gospel. But, rivalling his own work of sowing "good seed" throughout the world, would be the activity of the devil in sowing "tares", evil plants bearing a close resemblance, particularly *in the early stages of growth*, to good grain, and thus serving as a symbol of a counterfeit system of faith which would be mistaken by some to be genuine. Thus, far from asserting himself at once by coercive means the King (and, with him, all the children of the Kingdom) intimated that he would have to contend against a false and rival order until the time came (the time of divine Harvest, once again) for him to send forth his reapers and burn up the tares (that is, destroy the rival order). Until that time came, however, the true church would have to endure many vicissitudes and much opposition, sustained only by the quiet confidence that a day of Judgement would assuredly set wrong things right. *"Then"* said Jesus, with that Day in mind, "shall the righteous shine forth as the sun in the kingdom of their Father" (verse 43).

This explanation helps us to determine Jesus' purpose in addressing the parable to the multitude. He was reminding them that admission to the Kingdom is not automatic but to be decided by a piercing scrutiny of each candidate's worthiness. And he did so in terms which John the Baptist had made familiar, and with the same intention, namely, to persuade the people that a wicked life would offset their descent from Abraham, and that only those who were sincerely children of the Kingdom could qualify to enter it. This notion that the Kingdom was not for all was as unpalatable for the Jews when it came from the lips of Jesus as when it came from those of John the Baptist, but Jesus, like John, presented it to them as a challenge—a challenge to decide to accept the Kingdom as primarily a *spiritual* institution, universal in its scope, and not founded for the exclusive blessing of the Jews. Ultimately the preaching of the Gospel divides men into two categories—"the wicked" and "the just"; those who serve Mammon and those who serve God. No man, said Jesus with the aid of the parable, can be a member of both categories; the Judgement at the end of the world will decide for each man whether or not he is to be for the Kingdom and the Kingdom to be for him. That is, Judgement must precede the setting up of the Kingdom— which is only another way of saying that the Kingdom pertains for "the children of the kingdom" (yes, and for the King himself also!) to the life which lies beyond this mortal life. And it was to this momentous fact that the nation was altogether blind at that critical time when the King appeared in their midst.

A long time, then, had to elapse before the King came into his own. So spoke the parable of the Tares. The parable of the Mustard Seed followed, making it plain that not all the discouragement and opposition in the world could frustrate God's purpose or prevent the King from finally coming into his own (Matthew 13:31,32). And to this was added the parable of the Leaven. It ran, "The kingdom of heaven is like unto leaven, which a woman took, and hid in three measures of meal, till the whole was leavened" (Matthew 13:33).

The resemblance between this and the preceding parable is obvious. In both cases a process begins and comes to completion. Is the parable of the Leaven, then, merely a restatement of the other? No; it is more than that. Its distinctive feature is that the active agent, the leaven, is this time "hid". It does its work *unseen*. So, though this parable, like the one that precedes it, bears witness to the certainty of the consummation of God's purpose in the earth, it also specially stresses that the outworking of that purpose is unseen and unheeded by the world at large. God's work in Jesus was at that time unrecognized, and seemed small and ineffectual by human standards even to those who recognized it. But as the leaven eventually affects the whole of the dough, and its work proceeds relentlessly until that stage is reached, so, too, is the case with the out-working of God's purpose. Nothing can stay its progress, and eventually the whole world will be affected by it. So the lesson of the Candle is also taught by the Leaven. What is hidden in one generation will assuredly come to light in another. "There is nothing hid, which shall not be manifested; neither was anything kept secret, but that it should come abroad". (How shot through with this notion is every one of the parables!)

To those within

As we have stated, the three parables examined above were addressed to, and their lessons primarily concerned, the multitude. But, as the parable of the Candle shows, the principles which they expressed apply to all manner of situations. In the case of the parable of the Mustard Seed, for example, the notion would not be absent from Jesus' thoughts, as he recounted it, of the expansion of the Gospel throughout the world, an expansion beginning from that day and initiated by his own Ministry. Similarly the Word of God works in the life of the faithful believer like leaven in meal, slowly permeating and transforming it, thus fitting him for the Kingdom of heaven which is properly the theme of the parable.

Be that, however, as it may, the fact remains that Matthew's first group of parables was of direct concern to the outsiders rather than to "the children of the kingdom" who then companied with Jesus. So for the benefit of the latter, special additional parables were recounted. These men were being increasingly initiated into the mystery of the Kingdom. Some things were startlingly novel to them, fresh discoveries as unexpected as the treasure upon which the man stumbled as he dug in the field. Others were the object of their longings, and the long-awaited satisfaction of their most spiritual desires, as the pearl of great price was to the merchant man who went "seeking goodly pearls". What response were they prepared to offer to their inestimable privileges? For the joy of his discovery, the man digging in the field was prepared to sell all that he had to buy that field (Matthew 13:44). The pearl merchant, likewise, sold all that he had to buy that one pearl which outvalued all his others (Matthew 13:45,46). The moral was obvious. The disciples, too, had come into possession of something unique. There was therefore one way only of showing their appreciation of it—to give up everything else in its favour, to accord the quest of the Kingdom priority over every other pursuit, however laudable and worthwhile it might chance to be. Were they equal to the demands of their discipleship? The parables presented them with the question, but left them to supply the answer.

What if some of them felt tempted to say, No, and to renounce their discipleship now that they appreciated the exacting nature of its demands? To deal with that contingency there followed the parable of the Net. Prove unequal to the demands of discipleship some of them certainly might, but none could escape from the Gospel Net, having once been taken by it. There was no question of their being able to contract out of the responsibilities which they had assumed by undertaking to become followers of Jesus, nor of their gaining exemption from a final divine scrutiny of their stewardship. "Again", said Jesus, "the kingdom of heaven is like unto a net, that was cast into the sea, and gathered of every kind: which, when it was full, they drew to shore, and sat down, and gathered the good into vessels, but cast the bad away" (Matthew 13:47,48).

"Cast the bad away ..." The fishermen among Jesus' company would appreciate the grimness of the words. They would know how quickly waste and inedible fish decomposed in the hot climate of Galilee, and how fire had to be used to dispose of them and their stench. "So shall it be at the end of the world," said Jesus, by way of explanation, and in order to lead them forward in thought, as he had repeatedly done in previous parables, to the eventual Day of the Kingdom's establishment on earth. "The angels shall come forth, and sever the wicked from among the just, and shall cast them into the furnace of fire: there shall be wailing and gnashing of teeth" (verses 49,50). Wailing—at the folly of wasted opportunity, and gnashing of teeth at the terrors of the ordeal which will succeed Judgement for "the wicked".

"Have ye understood all these things?" Jesus then asked. "They say unto him, Yea, Lord" (verse 51). They knew now the course which events would follow in the case both of the Kingdom and of themselves as "children of the Kingdom". If they were wise they would adjust their outlook and conduct accordingly, and review the ancient Scriptures afresh in the light of their new knowledge. As Jesus put it, contrasting them with the learned but misguided legalists of their day who failed so lamentably to grasp the import of the Scriptures, "Therefore every scribe which is instructed unto the kingdom of heaven is like unto a man that is an householder, which bringeth forth out of his treasure things new and old" (verse 52).

Let us never forget that the privilege which is ours today, after so long a lapse of time, of being able to read and understand the words of Jesus for ourselves, is one which we owe to some of these faithful "scribes". May it be our wisdom to emulate their steadfastness, and our joy to share their assured reward, when at last the Son of man comes in his Kingdom.

JESUS—HEALER & TEACHER

8
AND HE ORDAINED TWELVE

Christ's training of his disciples

THE famous "day of parables" was a veritable turning-point in the Ministry of Jesus, and its location toward the beginning of Mark's Gospel strongly suggests that it occurred at an early, rather than at an advanced, stage of that Ministry. Its position in Matthew's Gospel is consistent with this view, for though his account of it appears almost mid-way through his record, it occupies roughly the same situation in his chronological scheme as in Mark's. Outstanding events in the Ministry hitherto had been the cure of the Capernaum demoniac, the cleansing of the leper, the healing of the palsied man, the incident of the eating of corn on the Sabbath day, and arising out of it, a series of clashes with the Pharisees which culminated in the great Beelzebub controversy. Throughout this (in many ways) tense period, during which his popularity with the masses steadily rose and the disdain of the religious leaders hardened into violent, even murderous, hostility, Jesus had been the centre and focus of attention of vast crowds. And this was not due solely to his powers as a healer, for as with his acts of healing not one of his answers to his critics, of his public discourses, or even of his isolated sayings, failed to signify unmistakably that he claimed to be the Christ. Feeling was thus everywhere at fever pitch, and the wild unspiritual enthusiasm of the crowds who flocked to see and hear him was becoming a decided embarrassment and danger. The day of parables had thus inevitably to come sooner or later, and better soon than late. And come it did. Great events were still to follow: the stilling of the storm, the related healing of the Gadarene demoniac, the healing of Jairus' daughter and of the woman with the issue of blood, the two miraculous feedings—these, and sundry other wonderful events still lay in the future, and were to serve as further revelations of himself to the world. But the time to disabuse the misguided masses with their ill-conceived notions of the Kingdom had already arrived. So the process of sorting the wheat from the chaff began in earnest.

On a smaller scale it had begun already with the appointment of the Twelve to be apostles. We cannot with any confidence state when that was. Mark and Luke make it subsequent to the incident of the eating of corn on the Sabbath day and the healing of the man with the withered hand which followed it, but they each hint that some time separated the choice of the Twelve from these events (Mark 3:1-6,7-12; Luke 6:1-11,12). Matthew, on the other hand, records that choice some two chapters earlier than the healing of the man with the withered hand (Matthew 10:1-4). Of this we can be certain, however, that it took place a good while *prior* to the day of parables, for over that matter the three Evangelists concur. That is, Jesus had begun to discriminate between his professed followers well before the critical day of parables, and his actions that day and onward were but the logical outcome of the process which had begun much earlier.

The little flock

It can be taken for granted that many of those who sought the company of Jesus—who "followed him", as Mark 2:15 has it—were worthless adherents of his cause. Others were more genuinely attached to him, though not all accompanied him on his travels. Some did, like the "certain women ... which ministered unto him of their substance", of whom Luke speaks (8:1-3); but others, like Martha and Mary, remained at home, and there entertained him from time to time (Luke 10:38-42). The number of such disciples would naturally vary from place to place. In the neighbourhood of Nain, at least, they were fairly numerous (Luke 7:11), but in other places (Chorazin, Bethsaida, etc., Matthew 11:20,21) they would be very few indeed. Yet, whether they were many or few, their needs were the same, and for their benefit Jesus would constantly repeat his teaching, and even vary it as special circumstances demanded. Nothing would in fact be more natural for him to do than this, especially when we reflect that he more than once made a circuit of "all the cities and villages" of Galilee (Matthew 4:23; 9:35; 13:54). Yet how perversely do so many modern scholars ignore this obvious fact, and cavalierly impugn the reliability of the gospels as records of Christ's words, on the ground that there are "discrepancies" between them. (It is not difficult to guess what these men would in turn have said had the gospels been found instead to be in perfect verbal agreement when setting down the sayings of Jesus!) The plain fact is that time and again Jesus would express the same sentiments in slightly different form, whether for the guidance, the warning, or the enlightenment of his dispersed body of disciples. They were his "little flock," and like a faithful shepherd he would carefully attend to their every want. Even in the case of those who were his constant companions he found it necessary to restate certain truths repeatedly, as we have already had some occasion to see (e.g. Matthew 5:29,30; 18:8,9; and Matthew 10:26; Mark 4:22; Luke 8:17; 12:2), and this factor alone is sufficient to dispose of many alleged discrepancies.

As to the actual number of those who closely followed Jesus on his travels we can only guess, though they are in one place stated to be "many" (Luke 8:3). It is only of the number of the Apostles that we can be certain. Theirs was to be a special mission. As Mark has it, "He goeth up into a mountain, and calleth unto him whom he would: and they came unto him. And he ordained twelve, that they *should be with him*, and that he might send them forth to preach, and to *have power to heal sicknesses* and to *cast out devils* (Mark 3:13-15). Yet their special duties did not make the services of the rest of the disciples superfluous. Far otherwise, as Matthew shows, for immediately before relating the choice of the Twelve, he records significantly, "And Jesus went about all the cities and villages, teaching ... and preaching ... But when he saw the multitudes, he was moved with compassion on them, because they fainted, and were scattered abroad, as sheep having no shepherd.

165

Then saith he unto his disciples, The harvest truly is plenteous, but the labourers are few; pray ye therefore the Lord of the harvest, that he will send forth labourers into his harvest" (Matthew 9:35-38). Whether the "disciples" here mentioned were a whole band of disciples then accompanying Jesus, or only the Twelve who were being initiated into duties which later they would have to fulfil, either singly or in pairs, the facts were the same—the choice of the Twelve was no rebuff to the general body of believers but a practical, statesmanlike step toward the organization of urgent work of witness in which all were alike engaging. What was sound counsel for the Twelve was thus no less valid for the rest of the disciples also, as the correspondence between the instructions given to the Twelve (Matthew 10:1-42) and the Seventy (Luke 10:1-16) amply proves. Nor is that counsel anything but valid for Christians today when due allowance has been made for special factors which in the first instance sometimes (but only sometimes) conditioned what Jesus had to say. And if further proof of that were needed we have it in Luke's sequel to Jesus' choice of the Twelve, for, Luke continues, "And he came down with them, and stood in the plain, *and the company of his disciples*, and a great multitude ... And he lifted up his eyes *on his disciples*, and said, Blessed be ye poor ... " etc. (Luke 6:17-20). Thus Jesus' special counsel to the Twelve and his more general discourses to his followers can for our purpose in this study well be merged and considered together, especially as it is impossible for us to decide whether any of those who heard Jesus' periodic comments were always the same people. Though the original companions of Jesus enjoyed a unique privilege in coming under his direct personal influence yet we too, thanks to their faithful preservation of his sayings, can in measure partake of that privilege; and, doing so, we can like them come little by little to acquire his standards and his outlook. His training of them can be (and in fact should be) a training of us also.

Worthy of me

Jesus dealt with all would-be disciples on their merits. The cured Gadarene demoniac was not a fit person to be a member of his retinue. But though Jesus spared him experiences which he could not endure, yet he knew what was the best service which the man was capable of rendering to the Gospel. So whereas he besought Jesus "that he might be with him", Jesus deliberately, but with kindly motive, sent him away, saying, "Return to thine house, and shew how great things God hath done unto thee". The eagerness with which this former sufferer discharged his duty was proof of the sincerity of his joy, even though it had only this one means of outlet. "He went his way, and published throughout the whole city how great things Jesus had done unto him" (Luke 8:37-39).

Sad by contrast was the spirit in which others either offered, or withheld, their service as disciples. One rather incautious scribe once said, "I will follow thee whithersoever thou goest" (Matthew 8:19). He little realized what his brave promise entailed. Jesus quickly made him aware, though with what result we are left to guess. "Jesus said unto him, Foxes have holes, and birds of the air have nests; but the Son of man hath not where to lay his head" (Luke 9:57,58). The way was truly hard if the scribe really wished to traverse it. His secure and settled life would have to be abandoned, and as an itinerant preacher he would have to depend upon others' hospitality for his food and clothing, like the Twelve and Seventy who had been bidden to go forth on their errand of mercy without money or baggage (Matthew 10:9-11).

There was another man whom Jesus adjudged fully capable of undertaking such a commission, and therefore wished to enrol among his retinue. "Follow me", was his simple request on this occasion. But the prospect appalled the man. He pleaded family responsibilities—dear to the Oriental—as a pretext of non-compliance, saying, "Lord, suffer me first to go and bury my father". Years might well elapse before his father died and he became free, having buried his father and wound up his affairs, to join the company of Jesus. But those, alas, would be wasted years, and

167

the crisis which led to his call was too urgent to allow of such delay. So, peremptorily, "Jesus said unto him, Let the dead bury their dead: but go thou and preach the Kingdom of God" (Luke 9:59,60). Jesus' language was significant for two reasons. It implied firstly that the man was not himself one of "the dead": that is, he was already a disciple, and the call was to full-time service in future, in contrast to less regular service hitherto. But, secondly, it revealed that Jesus was calmly setting himself on a par with the High Priest—nay, more, it meant that he was demanding that even this half-hearted disciple should regard his discipleship as no less than a form of High Priestly service which excused him from those responsibilities that seemed to him so pressing! The Law, while strictly forbidding any of the general body of priests to "be defiled for the dead among his people", nevertheless made this concession, "But for his kin, that is near unto him, that is, for his mother, and for his father, and for his son, and for his daughter, and for his brother ... may he be defiled" (Leviticus 21:1-3). In the case of the High Priest, however, even this compassionate concession was withheld: "He that is the high priest among his brethren ... shall not uncover his head, nor rend his clothes; neither shall he go in to any dead body, nor defile himself for his father, or his mother" (Leviticus 21:10,11). This was the stringent law, with its urgent emphasis upon the sanctity of the priestly office, which Jesus invoked for the guidance of his wavering disciple. And there was a profound reason why it was apt for him to do so, for apart from its immediate practical purpose, this law had also a wonderful prophetic import. It intimated that the ultimate High Priest who would one day assume office as the one Mediator between God and man, would possess a *deathless* nature. Jesus, knowing himself to be the One destined to fulfil this (like every other) type, thus saw in it an anticipation of his own eventual assumption of the divine nature, and, with it, of his work as intercessor for his sinning brethren. So though he was not as yet the High Priest, he was none the less the High Priest *elect*. This meant that his disciples were potential kings and priests, too, as they would later come to realize clearly (cf. Revelation 1:6, etc.). Jesus was thus only bidding this waverer to act in a manner consistent with his status when giving him the curt command, so pregnant with meaning, "Let the dead bury their dead". And the further instruction added to this, "but go thou and preach the kingdom of God", bade the man give his service to God, full time, as the priest did his.

In so doing Jesus certainly did not mean that the man's consecration as a disciple would exempt him in future from the obligation to do good to all men, father and mother included. On the contrary, so insistent was Jesus that no ceremonial law, however stringent, must ever take precedence over *love to the living*, that he actually invoked this same law as witness in his exposure of the perverted religiosity of the priest and Levite in the parable of the Good Samaritan. All that he did on this other occasion was put a spiritual interpretation upon that law, and pronounce his disciple exempt from all family obligations based purely on *physical* relationship. He was thus being true to his own dictum uttered on that famous occasion when "he stretched forth his hand toward his disciples, and said, Behold my mother and my brethren! For whosoever shall do the will of my Father which is in heaven, the same is my brother, and sister, and mother" (Matthew 12:49,50). He was calling upon this other disciple to conceive of his discipleship as a new existence, with new loyalties and new standards of right and wrong—in brief, as life on a new plane, with the Kingdom as its goal.

In the circumstances, the commission which Jesus placed upon the man was too urgent to admit of delay. To another (and more genuinely enthusiastic) disciple the same task of appreciating just how urgent it was, came in a different but no less abrupt way. This man, like the incautious scribe, said, "Lord, I will follow thee". He doubtless did so, knowing full well what that decision spelt for him in terms of privation and the severance of old ties. But though he knew this, he betrayed a distinct reluctance to accept it, for he qualified his expression of readiness to follow Jesus by adding, "but let me first go bid them farewell which are at home at my house". Such a leave-taking was

at that time an affair of many days. But the urgency of
Christ's call just did not allow of such an extravagant
waste of time, nor of respect for a rival loyalty, any more
than did the call made by Abraham's servant to Rebekah
to become Isaac's wife. "Her brother and her mother said,
Let the damsel abide with us a few days, at least ten; after
that she shall go". "Hinder me not", pleaded the servant in
reply. "And they said, We will call the damsel, and enquire
at her mouth. And they called Rebekah, and said unto her,
Wilt thou go with this man?" Without hesitation the
answer came, "I will go", and with no qualification as in
the disciple's case. Jesus made it clear to that disciple that
he expected no less ready a response on his part, by saying, "No man, having put his hand to the plough, and looking back, is fit for the kingdom of God" (Luke 9:61,62).

With Jesus it was a fixed rule, "He that loveth father or
mother more than me is not worthy of me: and he that
loveth son or daughter more than me is not worthy of me.
And he that taketh not his cross, and followeth after me is
not worthy of me", adding, as so often, "He that findeth his
life shall lose it: and he that loseth his life for my sake
shall find it" (Matthew 10:37-39). These particular words
were addressed to the Twelve as they set off on their first
preaching tour, but the sentiments expressed by them
were often repeated, we can be sure. Once when "there
went great multitudes with him", Jesus "turned, and said
unto them, If any man come to me, and hate not his father,
and mother, and wife, and children, and brethren, and sis-
ters, *yea, and his own life also*, he cannot be my disciple"
(Luke 14:25,26).

Jesus was not advocating detestation of one's nearest
and dearest in this case any more than in the case of the
hesitant disciple, though to modern ears it may sound as
though he was. He was merely employing a familiar
Hebraic idiom for purposes of emphasis, as when God said
through Hosea, "I will have mercy and not sacrifice"
(Hosea 6:6), or through Malachi, "I loved Jacob and I hated
Esau" (Malachi 1:2,3). The people would not misunder-
stand the situation. Love for those nearest and dearest to
them was still expected by Jesus, but it was to be no longer

a purely reflex, possessive, love—a doing of kindness only to those from whom kindness is received—but a love richer and wider in its sympathies, springing from a transcending loyalty to himself.

Jesus pressed the lesson home with the help of two illustrations. The first was simple enough and its moral obvious. "For which of you, intending to build a tower, sitteth not down first, and counteth the cost, whether he have sufficient to finish it? Lest haply, after he hath laid the foundation, and is not able to finish it, all that behold it begin to mock him, saying, This man began to build, and was not able to finish" (Luke 14:28-30).

The second illustration which Jesus used was no mere reiteration of the first: it bit deeper. And necessarily so, for uncompleted discipleship exposes a man to much more than the ridicule of his fellows. The story this time ran, "Or what king, going to make war against another king, sitteth not down first, and consulteth whether he be able with ten thousand to meet him that cometh against him with twenty thousand? Or else, while the other is yet a great way off, he sendeth an ambassage, and desireth conditions of peace" (Luke 14:31,32). Placed in such a dilemma the weaker king can either accept his stronger opponent's demands for total surrender *and escape with his life,* or cling to his army and his rights, only to lose them both *and his life with them.* "So likewise," commented Jesus, "whosoever he be of you that forsaketh not all that he hath, he cannot be my disciple" (Luke 14:33).

Seeking to save his life by his own means, a reluctant disciple succeeds only in losing it, as inevitably as does a weaker king who decides to join battle with a stronger. Discipleship, then, when once begun, must be pursued faithfully to the last, or it ends in ruin. Such was the burden, not only of this parable, but also of Jesus' conclusion to his address for he added, "Salt is good: but if the salt have lost his savour, wherewith shall it be seasoned? It is neither fit for the land, nor yet for the dunghill; but men cast it out". If *men* "cast out" insipid salt, what will not God do with a disciple who is no disciple? Such was the challenge implicit in this further comment. And, as his manner was, Jesus forced it home upon his listeners with the cryptic counsel, "He that hath ears to hear, let him hear" (Luke 14:34,35).

Think not ...

With how rude a shock must many have woken up to the fact that Jesus, as King, had no immediate rosy prospect to offer either his actual, or his would-be disciples. The popular illusion that the establishment of the Kingdom was imminent had time and again to be offset. For example, to the Twelve, as he sent them forth on their first errand, he saw fit to say, "Think not that I am come to send peace on earth: I came not to send peace, but a sword. For I am come to set a man at variance against his father, and the daughter against her mother, and the daughter in law against her mother in law. And a man's foes shall be they of his own household" (Matthew 10:34-36). These words would not have been spoken had it not been necessary to counter certain secret longings in the hearts of the Apostles, but how great an anticlimax they would have formed for those among the crowds who were excitedly expecting physical struggle against their hereditary foes the Romans. "A man's foes shall be ... they of his own household!" How flat and unheroic a manifesto this would have sounded for one who claimed to be the King! And the same would be true of several other statements in this address to the Twelve. "Behold, I send you forth as sheep in the midst of wolves: be ye therefore wise as serpents, and harmless as doves"(Matthew 10:16). "Harmless as doves ...!" How grotesque this would have sounded to the bloodthirsty assassins who were ever ready to join themselves to any self-appointed Christ who championed the cause of national independence.

This process of disillusionment, so essential if the people were to be taught aright, and if the King were to reveal himself for what he truly was, went on uninterruptedly throughout the Ministry. At every turn time-honoured fallacies had to be exploded. Reviewed in the context of the historical situation at that time, many of the sayings of

Jesus assume startlingly fresh point and meaning for us. Thus the view then generally held was that it would be ruthless military action, and the service of strong men with intrepid hearts, which would usher in the Kingdom; but Jesus said, "Except ye be converted, and become as little children, ye shall not (i.e. *never*) enter into the kingdom of heaven" (Matthew 18:3). Again, the current notion of the Kingdom was that it would be largely a matter of government by the Jews for the Jews, but with Jesus it was an axiom that "Many shall come from the east and west, and shall sit down with Abraham, and Isaac, and Jacob, in the kingdom of heaven. But the children of the kingdom shall be cast out into outer darkness: there shall be weeping and gnashing of teeth" (Matthew 8:11,12; cf. Luke 13:28-30). And to such sayings as this must be added one other matter, which to us seems trivial, but which served as a constant affront to the patriotism of the Jews at that time, groaning as they were under the burden of Roman taxation—Jesus was a friend of *publicans*, those hireling traitors to their own nation's cause and pawns of the uncircumcised infidel who gathered his taxes for him. Jesus' friendship with these men was for the mass of the people proof positive that he was not after all the Messiah for whom they were waiting. He was not indeed! but he *was* the Messiah none the less and to foster that conviction in the minds of his disciples was his constant preoccupation.

Greatest in the kingdom

The King was the Kingdom in miniature, as the miracles amply demonstrated. But so also were his companions, those who accepted him as Messiah when all others doubted or denied the fact. Jesus declared the lowliest of these to be greater than John because they were already "in the kingdom of heaven", in it there and then, whereas John's entry into it would not come till the day when men should "see Abraham, and Isaac, and Jacob, and *all the prophets*, in the kingdom of God" (Luke 13:28). It was these same companions whom Jesus had in mind again when he opened his Sermon on the Mount (as was fitting) with a regal pronouncement, "Blessed are the poor in spirit: for *theirs* is the kingdom of heaven". In fact Matthew points out that these particular words were addressed directly to "his disciples", though that does not mean that they were not intended also for the enlightenment of the multitudes (Matthew 5:1-3). Six more Beatitudes followed. They too exalted not the manliness (more properly, manlikeness) which is so congenial to human nature with all its pride and self-assertion, but the gentler spiritual virtues which are the tokens of a converted heart; but in contrast to the first Beatitude (and a further one which concluded the series of general pronouncements proper) these others were more in the nature of *promises* of blessing, which could only be realized when the Kingdom was eventually set up on earth, such as "Blessed are the meek: for they *shall* inherit the earth ... Blessed are they which do hunger and thirst after righteousness: for they *shall* be filled" (Matthew 5:4-9). But with a significant difference in the verbs Jesus also said, "Blessed are they which are persecuted for righteousness' sake: for theirs *is* the kingdom of heaven" (verse 10). The same distinction in tense recurred when Jesus on another occasion "lifted up his eyes on his disciples, and said, Blessed be ye poor: for yours *is* the kingdom of God. Blessed are ye that hunger now: for ye *shall* be filled. Blessed are ye that weep now: for ye *shall* laugh" (Luke 6:20,21).

Nothing doctrinal can be argued from the distinction (least of all the notion that the Kingdom is not to be a visible dominion on earth) for all the pronouncements in question were addressed to the same body of people. Yet insofar as Jesus made such a distinction it is safe to conclude that he meant something by it. He seems to have made it in order to lay the greatest stress on the disposition indispensable to membership of the Kingdom, whether now or in the future. Isaiah had predicted of him, "The LORD hath anointed me to preach good tidings unto the meek" (Isaiah 61:1). Jesus in turn declared the prophecy fulfilled when he sent back John's two disciples with the message, "the poor have the gospel preached to them" (Matthew 11:5), and said to his own faithful band, "Blessed be *ye* poor: for yours is the kingdom of God" (Luke 6:20). The words, "in spirit", which occur in the first Beatitude—"Blessed are the poor *in spirit*: for theirs is the kingdom of heaven"— are probably an explanatory comment interpolated by Matthew rather than by Jesus. But be that as it may, the words lay an essential emphasis on the attitude of mind which the true believer must possess: the genuine Christian must be lowly in mind and utterly self-effacing. Not without good reason did Jesus lay down, and lay down *first*, "If any man will come after me, let him *deny himself* ..." What followed—"and take up his cross", merely went the next logical step and revealed that self can only properly be so denied by being *put to death* (Matthew 16:24).

Jesus repeatedly brought this solemn fact home to his disciples, choosing as the most appropriate times to do so those occasions when that self-assertiveness which is native to our human nature had led them into error. Luke records two such occasions. On the first, "there arose a reasoning among them, which of them should be greatest". They were careful to conceal the dispute from Jesus. It had in fact taken place in the course of a journey (Mark 9:33,34) and they were now indoors, but Jesus with his amazing insight was aware that it had taken place, and took prompt action. "Perceiving the thought of their heart", says Luke, Jesus "took a child, *and set him by him*". The action was significant. The disciples had in effect wrangled as to who should occupy the seat of honour next to Jesus. So by way of answer Jesus accorded that place *to a child!* Word next followed action, and "he said unto them, Whosoever shall receive this child in my name receiveth me: and whosoever shall receive me receiveth him that sent me: for he that is least among you all, the same shall be great" (Luke 9:46-48).

Mark records an interesting sequel to this incident. He writes, "And John answered him, saying, Master, we saw one casting out devils in thy name, and he followeth not us: and we forbad him, because he followeth not us" (Mark 9:38). The action of the disciples is understandable for the power to cast out devils was vested in the Twelve (Matthew 10:1). Yet who were they to limit the possession of it? Their fussy insistence that this man, who so palpably possessed the same power as themselves, should either join their company or desist from using it, tragically matched the concern for technicalities shown later by the heartless synagogue ruler (Luke 13:11-16). They were concerned with their own prestige and privileges rather than overjoyed that Jesus' power was shared by yet another of those whom he went on to call "these little ones that believe in me" (Mark 9:42). So Jesus gently rebuked them, saying to John, "Forbid him not: for there is no man which shall do a miracle in my name, that can lightly speak evil of me. For he that is not against us is on our part" (Mark 9:39,40).

To the original incident there was not only this significant sequel. It had also an interesting prelude, which gave all the more point to what Jesus had to say. Matthew introduces his version of the incident thus, "*At the same time* came the disciples unto Jesus, saying, Who is the greatest in the kingdom of heaven?" The fact that the disciples themselves actually framed a question is illuminating. It strongly suggests that they feigned a purely academic interest in the problem when Jesus enquired, "What was it that ye disputed among yourselves by the way?" In reply to that request for information we know from Mark (9:33,34) that, "they held their peace", but Matthew makes it clear that they then tried to save their faces with a counter-question. Their guile, however, failed to deceive Jesus. But what interests Matthew is not their guile so much as *the time* at which the incident took place. His time note specifically connects it with an incident which took place just before. Of this Matthew says, "And when they were come to Capernaum, they that received tribute money came to Peter, and said, Doth not your master pay tribute? He saith, Yes". Whether that tribute was paid to the Romans or into the Temple funds does not affect the issue (though, probably, it was a levy for the upkeep of the Temple), for Jesus as Son of God was equally the predestined heir of the world and Lord of the Temple. A little later, when Peter "was come into the house, Jesus prevented (i.e. forestalled) him, saying. What thinkest thou,

Simon? of whom do the kings of the earth take custom or tribute? of their own children, or of strangers?" Peter could give but one answer, "Of strangers". This gave Jesus his cue, so he added, "Then are the children free". By this Jesus meant that Peter, in thus rashly committing his Master to pay tribute, had not paused to reflect who that Master was. Jesus was not a subject *but a King,* and so exempt from the obligation to pay custom or tribute. Yet, King though he was, it was fitting that he should by humble action demonstrate the essentially spiritual character of his Kingdom and of the conditions of entry thereinto. So, having thus reminded Peter of his regal status Jesus added, "Notwithstanding, lest we should offend them, go thou to the sea, and cast an hook, and take up the fish that first cometh up; and when thou hast opened his mouth, thou shalt find a piece of money: that take, and give unto them for me *and thee*" (Matthew 17:24-27). How sordid by contrast with such humility and such non-assertion of self were the pettiness and pride of the disciples as they vied for the highest place. Small wonder that Matthew is eager that we should not miss the connection between the two incidents.

The second manifestation of such pettiness and pride which Luke records took place (of all times!) during the Last Supper. How it must have grieved the heart of Jesus, not only because he had had occasion to rebuke such folly before, or even because it took place so late in the Ministry, but more especially because his own death—that death which was the supreme expression of self-denial in the cause of others—was imminent and filled his thoughts. His crucifixion was, as we shall see again later, the culmination of a whole life of self-sacrifice. So to silence his disciples' wranglings, and recall them to sanity, Jesus made a gentle appeal to his own manner of life in support of the criterion of true greatness which he wished them to adopt, one which is utterly alien to human nature. "He said unto them, The kings of the Gentiles exercise lordship upon them; and they that exercise authority over them are called benefactors". This would be common knowledge to the Apostles not only because all those in authority love to enforce their wills on others, but also because the Seleucids of Syria and the Ptolemies of Egypt had claimed virtue in so doing and actually assumed the title of "Benefactor". "But ye shall not be so", said Jesus; "but he that is greatest among you, let him be as the younger; and he that is chief, as he that doth serve. For whether is greater, he that sitteth at meat, or he that serveth? is not he that sitteth at meat? but I am among you as he that serveth". Who was the "I"? The same one who at once went on to say, "And I appoint unto you a kingdom, as my Father hath appointed unto me" (Luke 22:24-29). This was to be a real kingdom, but that only stressed how stringent were the spiritual conditions for enjoyment of it. Only the genuinely humble can qualify for such exaltation!—a law which is as binding today as then, for the Kingdom is one and the same for every generation of believers.

Mercy for the merciful

We are by now well aware of the fullness of meaning with which Jesus used the term "mercy". That meaning was fixed for him by the Old Testament, especially by Hosea's use of it in the famous dictum, "I will have mercy and not sacrifice". It connoted a yearning loving kindness which reflects God's compassion toward sinful man. In the Christian it is an indispensable attribute, for only to the merciful will mercy be shown in the final reckoning, as Jesus declared (Matthew 5:7). Yet that law holds good as much for the present as for the future. In fact at every stage of the Christian's experience the rule is, "With the same measure that ye mete withal it shall be measured to you again" (Luke 6:38).

No better illustration could be found of that rule in the Synoptic Gospels than the parable of the Two Debtors. The actual emphasis of the parable is on the final judgement for it is prefaced by the words, "Therefore is the kingdom of heaven likened unto a certain king, which would take account of his servants". The king forgave the immense debt owed him by one servant, yet the latter forthwith exacted full compensation from one of his own debtors who owed him a relatively trivial sum. News of the wicked servant's ingratitude and lack of mercy reached the King who declared to him, "O thou wicked servant, I forgave thee all that debt, because thou desiredst me: shouldest not thou also have *had compassion* on thy fellowservant, even as I had pity on thee?" As this foolish man dealt with others so God would deal with him, "And his lord was wroth, and delivered him to the tormentors, till he should pay all that was due unto him". Jesus then brought the lesson home to his disciples, "So likewise shall my heavenly Father do also unto you, if ye *from your hearts* forgive not every one his brother their trespasses" (Matthew 18:23-35).

That lesson is taught in so effective and self-contained a form by the parable that it can be considered in isolation from its context. Yet that context is most revealing. Jesus had not been content to check and correct his disciples' tendency to rivalry (Matthew 18:1-5). He had also joined considerateness and forgiveness to humility, issuing a stern warning (which we have considered earlier) against offending fellow-believers. He had then bidden his followers emulate God in His desire to save all sinners, and themselves act as shepherds seeking to save lost sheep (Matthew 18:6-14). He gave them a specific illustration of what he meant by this. Anticipating that state of affairs which would obtain later when his present company would have swollen in numbers, and the spirit of rivalry would hold even greater power for harm, he had gone on to give them instructions how to act when "offences" arose. "If thy brother shall trespass against thee, go and tell him his fault between thee and him alone: if he shall hear thee, thou hast gained thy brother" (Matthew 18:15). Jesus was concerned with the motive no less than with the act. The danger always is that Christians, putting sacrifice before mercy, might become engrossed with the act to the exclusion of that kindly and compassionate motive which alone can sanctify it. Jesus meant that the purpose with which one brother should thus point out to another "his fault" should be not *to censure* but *to save*. The next step—to take a further brother (or two) as witness—must also be performed with the same charitable end in view. Only if the wrong-doer is obdurate, and thus wantonly persists in offending his brother (thus incurring the terrible punishment which Jesus pronounces against such action—e.g. verse 6) should the matter be brought to the notice of the church for official disapproval to be expressed (Matthew 18:16,17).

This procedure, prompted by compassion at every turn, as Jesus insisted, struck Peter forcibly. It moved him to enquire of Jesus, "Lord, how oft shall my brother sin against me, and I forgive him? till seven times? Jesus saith unto him, I say not unto thee, Until seven times:but, Until seventy times seven" (Matthew 18:21,22). Peter might well have asked why the command to forgive was so stringent; but the parable of the Two Debtors followed swiftly to render such a question superfluous. It silenced all potential protest for it implied that all Christians who have occasion to forgive their brethren are themselves in much greater need of forgiveness by God than their brethren are in need of forgiveness by them. That is, Jesus took the repeated sinfulness of his disciples as his starting-point, and used God's compassionate forgiveness of it as a claim upon them to be forgiving in their turn. If they withstood that claim they would automatically forfeit the blessings of divine compassion. "After this manner therefore pray ye", said he, making one of the petitions, "And forgive us our debts, as we forgive our debtors"; and then commenting on it as follows, "For if ye forgive men their trespasses, your heavenly Father will also forgive you: but if ye forgive not men their trespasses, neither will your Father forgive your trespasses" (Matthew 6:9,12,14-15).

His own sin places the disciple permanently in God's debt—and so under the obligation to forgive his brother's sin. "If he trespass against thee seven times in a day, and seven times in a day turn again to thee, saying, I repent; *thou shalt forgive him*", said Jesus on another occasion to his followers (Luke 17:3,4). The rigour of the demand appalled the Apostles in particular, for they "said unto the Lord, Increase our faith". His retort was consummate. They wanted their faith *increased*—so that meant that they felt they had some faith, at least! Very well! then let them realize that however small it was, even if it was relatively as tiny as a mustard seed, if it was a *living* faith, as the seed was a *living* seed, then like the seed it would grow of its own accord and make the impossible possible (verses 5,6). Moreover he told them that this was no matter of choice but of *duty*. "Which of you, having a servant plowing or feeding cattle, will say unto him by and by, when he is come from the field, Go and sit down to meat? And will not rather say unto him, Make ready wherewith I may sup, and gird thyself, and serve me, till I have eaten and drunken; and afterward thou shalt eat and drink? Doth he thank that servant because he did the things that were commanded him? I trow not. So likewise ye, when ye have done all those things which are commanded you, say, We are unprofitable servants: we have done that which was our duty to do" (Luke 17:7-10). A sinner cannot lay down his own terms; he must accept God's, however distasteful they may be. Yet if he does so, and obediently forgives his brother, he can in faith rest assured that his own sins are forgiven also. Compassion towards others is in fact the ground of confidence in God's compassion towards oneself: "Judge not", said Jesus, "and ye shall not be judged: condemn not, and ye shall not be condemned: forgive, and ye shall be forgiven" (Luke 6:37).

Ask—Seek—Knock

Penitence is an act of faith, for, firstly, it regards a wrong-ful act as sin—that is, as an offence *against God*—and so presumes the existence of God; and, secondly, it presuppos-es that God is willing to grant pardon for that act if it is sincerely regretted, and so impels a man to seek His for-giveness. Thus, paradoxical though it sounds, the logical outcome of sorrow for sin against God is approach to Him in prayer. Prayer restores the communion with God which sin so tragically interrupts, and no man who is truly con-trite need—or should—feel disqualified from approach to God when the sin which he deplores happens to have been particularly heinous. What delights God is the sinner who *repents*: there is more joy in heaven over such an one "than over ninety and nine just persons, which need no repen-tance". The self-righteous Pharisee who stood praying in the Temple was conscious of his virtues to the total disregard of his sins. The publican, on the other hand, "standing afar off, would not lift up so much as his eyes unto heaven, but smote upon his breast, saying, God be merciful to me a sinner". "I tell you", said Jesus, "this man went down to his house justified rather than the other: for every one that exalteth himself shall be abased; and he that humbleth himself shall be exalted" (Luke 18:9-14).

The humility which Jesus here commended so warmly sprang, we note, from a consciousness of personal unworthiness. All the more significant therefore is the fact that the incident which Luke records immediately after this parable is that in which the disciples rebuked those mothers who had brought their babes for Jesus to bless, and were in turn rebuked by him for doing so. "Jesus called them unto him, and said, Suffer little children to come unto me, and forbid them not: for of such is the kingdom of God. Verily I say unto you, Whosoever shall not receive the kingdom of God as a little child shall in no wise enter therein" (Luke 18:15-17). As we have already seen, to do this—to receive the Kingdom as a child—entails beginning life afresh; that is being *converted* and making a new beginning, with all that that implies in terms of repentance and confession of personal unworthiness (Matthew 18:3). No Christian, then, can be truly humble who is not more conscious of his own faults than of others. It was for this reason that Jesus declared such a consciousness of personal unworthiness, and the cheerful forgiveness of others' faults which is its logical consequence, to be essential to effectual prayer. Though he laid down, "What things soever ye desire, when ye pray, believe that ye receive them, and ye shall have them", yet he had at once to qualify that statement by insisting that such faith would be nullified if a man so engaged in the act of prayer was at the same time unready to forgive the faults of others (Mark 11:24-26).

Thus, for Jesus, a man's acknowledgement of his own need to be forgiven by God and consequent readiness to be forgiving like God, were presupposed in all that he had to say about prayer. These things apart, however, his main insistence was on *confidence* as the mainspring of prayer. The parable of the Unjust Judge was spoken specifically to prove that "men ought always to pray, and not to faint" (Luke 18:1). The widow of the parable was a model of persistence and dauntlessness, and her ceaseless request, which no amount of delay could deter her from making, was, "Avenge me of mine adversary". In the end that request was granted. Arguing *a fortiori*, Jesus then commented, "And shall not God avenge his own elect, which cry day and night unto him, though he bear long with them? I tell you that he will avenge them speedily". Finally there followed the cryptic question, "Nevertheless when the Son of man cometh, shall he find faith on the earth?" (Luke 18:2-8).

That concluding question, seemingly so irrelevant, does more than urge the disciples to have a faith which matches the persistence of the widow: it also throws light upon the meaning of the parable. The widow pleaded to be avenged of her "adversary". As she was avenged, said Jesus, so also will the elect be. But when? As in her case, after long delay. And then how? Speedily. It is here that his mention of the coming of the Son of man becomes luminous. The parable covers *the whole sweep of Christian discipleship* with all its frustration and yearning for deliverance from the thraldom of sin. Long delay must inevitably intervene before that deliverance is finally realized; but when it comes—as come it will when God intervenes as Judge to save His elect, through Jesus—it will come swiftly and decisively. Therefore no discouragement must be allowed to daunt the Christian. His faith in God's goodness and power to save must never waver. To faint is to doubt—to doubt the indubitable, be it noted—and so to lose the vision of God which alone imparts to prayer its power and effectualness.

Jesus' own vision of God was ever bright, and this primarily because he had no need to be forgiven like other men, so that petitions for pardon had no place in his prayer. Yet he, like all others, needed the constant succour of God—and (*unlike* most others) had constant resort to it in prayer. He was in the act of prayer when he received his

Anointing of the Spirit (who can therefore doubt that what he then received he had been asking God to grant?) (Luke 3:21,22). His momentous choice of the Twelve was preceded by an entire night of prayer to God (Luke 6:12,13). When, on one occasion, the disciples failed to cast out a demon and asked pathetically, Why could not we cast him out? his answer indicated that they had overlooked both the need and the power of prayer (Mark 9:14-29). It was his own repeated recourse to prayer which emboldened them to ask him to teach them to pray (Luke 11:1).

He did as bidden, and gave them the model Prayer (Luke 11:2-4). But more important than any formula which men may use, is the spirit in which they use it. So a parable followed to teach the disciples that prayer is never out of season, and that discouragement must never be allowed to weaken the confidence in which acceptable prayer should be offered. Midnight was an unbecoming hour for one man to invoke the co-operation and help of another, but the urgency of his need emboldened him to persist despite every unfavourable circumstance, so that his request was in the end granted (Luke 11:5-8). Applying the lessons of the parable in detail, Jesus commented, "And I say unto you, Ask, and it shall be given you; seek, and ye shall find; knock, and it shall be opened unto you. For every one that asketh receiveth, and he that seeketh findeth; and to him that knocketh it shall be opened" (verses 9,10).

So much for the confidence which prayer demands. But for what should such importunate request be made? An illustration followed to answer that automatic question. Men know what is good for their children, "If a son shall ask bread of any of you that is a father, will he give him a stone? or if he ask a fish, will he for a fish give him a serpent? Or if he shall ask an egg, will he offer him a scorpion?" What children ask for is not the counterfeit which, though it so closely resembles the genuine, is avoided by them because it is either useless or harmful. And what they seek—the good—they have every reason to expect to receive, and do in fact receive. The moral was twofold. The disciple must want *only what is good for him*; and wanting it, he can be confident of receiving it, "Good for him ..." Yes, but in what sense? Jesus made it plain that it was to be what is good for him *in the ultimate sense*. "If ye then, being evil, know how to give good gifts unto your children: how much more shall your heavenly Father give the Holy Spirit to them that ask him?" (verse 13). This assertion by Jesus was exquisitely in character. He had said enough elsewhere to assure men that God will satisfy their essential physical needs. It is not with these, but with the disciple's *spiritual* needs, that he is now concerned. The parable itself is, of necessity, concerned with material matters—the physical relation of father to son, and the child's bodily wants—each of which (in keeping with the purpose of the parable) is *good*. But the counterpart of these is spiritual—the spiritual relation between God and His children, and His concern for their spiritual needs. If it is the satisfaction of these which they desire most, then they shall have it. As Matthew's variant puts it—"how much more shall your Father which is in heaven give *good things* to them that ask him?" (Matthew 7:11). All these "good things" are in Luke's version covered by the all-embracing term "Holy Spirit" (not *the* Holy Spirit, be it noted) in order to lay bare their essential character and purpose. As therefore men must "seek first the kingdom of God and His righteousness", so must they make the attainment of them the dominant topic of their prayer. Such is Jesus' meaning here, and it is in perfect accord with all his teaching elsewhere, and, in particular, with his education of his intimate circle in the essentially spiritual character of the Kingdom of which he was the undoubted King. Viewed in the light of this fact, the model Prayer, with its almost exclusive concern for spiritual matters, shines with a greater brilliance (Matthew 6:9-13; Luke 11:2-4). What a man most fervently and *sincerely* prays for is an index to what he himself is.

The true riches

We have just seen how Jesus, to drive home a lesson, had no hesitation in drawing a parallel between God and an unjust judge. In the same way also he once asked his disciples to emulate an unjust steward. This man, rightly charged with dishonesty and corruption, acted with a promptitude and shrewdness in his own interests which excited the admiration even of the master he had wronged. "The lord commended the unjust steward, because he had done wisely". It was "wisely", because he applied his own materialistic philosophy to the uttermost, and not because what he did was honest—far from it! What he did was to secure his future by astute action; astute because it was properly related to the demands of the situation in which he found himself (Luke 16:1-8). Those who, because they are related to a quite different kind of future, ought to act with even greater urgency and with a consuming concern for the demands of their peculiar situation, are, alas, far less to be commended than this unscrupulous man; for, as Jesus sadly stated, "the children of this world are in their generation wiser than the children of light". He therefore called upon his disciples to emulate this man and in turn to make *their* present opportunities also a means to future security. Those opportunities are unhappily set in a worldly context, but they must be directed to an other-worldly end. As Jesus put it, "And I say unto you, Make to yourselves friends of the mammon of unrighteousness; that, when ye fail, they may receive you into everlasting habitations" (verse 9). He explained what he meant, and in terms which were characteristic: "He that is faithful in that which is least is faithful also in much". In saying this he was setting down a special standard of values for the disciples. All that pertains to the present is "least": by contrast, that which is related to the ultimate future of the children of light is "much". What men are today, so they will be declared to be in the final assessment: "he that is unjust in the least, is unjust also in much". So the question was inevitable: "If therefore ye have not been faithful in the unrighteous mammon, who will commit to your trust the true riches? And if ye have not been faithful in that which is another man's, who shall give you that which is your own" (Luke 16:11,12).

"The true riches"—who will not make them the goal of all his longings? Alas, no one will unless he is first convinced that they are indeed the *true* riches. Nay, more; who does not grasp that because he is a disciple, the life to come *is already his own,* and on that account is so determined not to lose possession of it that he deems no present sacrifice too irksome; his discipleship, that is, is a challenge to him to decide where his loyalty really lies. Either way he is a slave, but no slave can serve more than one master, and the master whom he chooses today will be his for eternity. Of this profound truth the sad story of the Rich Young Man is proof conclusive. "Sell all that thou hast", said Jesus to him, "and distribute unto the poor, and thou shalt have treasure in heaven: and come, follow me" (Luke 18:22). The demand was too great, "for he was very rich" (verse 23).

To us the call "follow me" may not so starkly involve such a heroic sacrifice, yet in some way or other we each have great possessions which we are loath to sacrifice for any spiritual cause, discipleship to Christ included. They tend always to loom larger in our estimation than treasure in heaven, for mammon is, in the ordinary course, more powerful an influence in our lives than God. Yet the blunt fact is that we cannot be slaves to both, any more than could the first disciples, or this admirable and upright young man. Which then is to be our master? Let us be mindful with what eternal consequences our answer, either way, is fraught!

JESUS—HEALER & TEACHER

9
I HAVE A BAPTISM TO BE BAPTIZED WITH
Portents of Calvary

IT is the fashion among many scholars today to treat
Matthew's Gospel somewhat patronisingly, especially
where (as quite frequently happens) he declares certain
events to have been the fulfilment of Old Testament
prophecy—the birth of Jesus, for example (1:22,23), or the
flight of Joseph and Mary into Egypt (2:14,15), or the
slaughter of the babes of Bethlehem (2:16-18). When they
encounter such passages these scholars betray a distinct
disdain for the Evangelist's method, as though he has been
unduly naïve, or even stupid, in observing parallels
between the facts which he records and the messages of
the ancient prophets. Yet what such men fail to take into
account is that, if Matthew was at fault in this, so also was
Jesus, for in this respect, as in every other, the Evangelist
was merely following the example set by his Master. In the
same way as Matthew applied Old Testament prophecy to
the work and witness of John the Baptist (3:1-3), so too did
Jesus before him (11:9,10). And similar illustrations
abound.

Some, realizing this to be so, reply that in this matter
Jesus was simply accommodating his message to the opin-
ions and outlook of his age, but such a verdict conflicts
utterly with our findings thus far, and pays scant honour
to Jesus. The truth is that his every action was conditioned
by the teaching of Old Testament Scripture. Isaiah, long
before, had warned the people, "By hearing ye shall hear,
and shall not understand; and seeing ye shall see, and
shall not perceive". This gave Jesus all the warrant he
needed for changing his preaching style at a crucial stage
in the Ministry, and adopting the device of speaking to the
mass of the people in nothing but parables. Nay, more, it

told him exactly how he ought to act in circumstances of such great tension. On the strength of Isaiah's words, because the people had already proved themselves to be too spiritually deaf, blind and obtuse to want to heed his teaching, Jesus saw himself not only permitted, but even *obliged*, to present it to them in an enigmatic form, for this enabled him to expose their unspirituality in the very process of revealing truth. Hence his answer to his disciples—"Whosoever hath not, from him shall be taken away even that he hath. *Therefore* speak I to them in parables". Hence, too, his added comment, "And in them is fulfilled the prophecy of Esaias" (Matthew 13:12-14).

In the volume of the book

In this, as we by now well know, Jesus acted characteristically. He could say, with a fullness of meaning not possible in the case of any other man, "Thy word is a lamp unto my feet, and a light unto my path" (Psalm 119:105). And nowhere in the gospels does that emerge more clearly, perhaps, than in the brief but pregnant record of the Temptation. Each assault upon his integrity was repulsed with the steadfast answer, "It is written ..." (Matthew 4:4,7,10). His course of action was laid down for him in Scripture, and he was resolved to follow it faithfully to the end. None but he fully understood that course; and that means also that none but he fully understood the Scriptures. Their true meaning, where they bore specifically on his mission, was lost on all but himself. It was a long hidden secret, and part (nay, in a sense, the real purpose) of his mission was to make that secret known—hence his axiom, "Neither was any thing kept secret, but that it should come abroad" (Mark 4:22). The tragedy of the situation on the famous day of parables lay in the fact that Jesus was obliged to reveal that secret in covert form to the mass of his listeners. Yet the Scriptures had allowed in advance for just such a contingency, as Matthew so shrewdly observed: "All these things spake Jesus unto the multitude in parables; and without a parable spake he not unto them: that it might be fulfilled which was spoken by the prophet, saying, I will open my mouth in parables, I will utter things which have been kept secret from the foundation of the world" (Matthew 13:34,35).

Here was a paradox indeed! Parables used to reveal secrets! It sounds a contradiction in terms, yet it is true; for, as we have seen, the parables divulged a secret, even though they did so enigmatically, a mystery which even the last and greatest of the prophets had not been able fully to solve—namely, that the Messiah had a *dual* role to fulfil; that the King would have to appear *twice*; that long time would separate "the acceptable year of the Lord" from "the day of vengeance of our God". This was a revelation indeed, but to the populace at large it was never made openly: only the disciples had the facts revealed to them explicitly. But so novel was the revelation, even to them, and so much was it an affront to their dearest longings and convictions, that they, too, proved unable to receive it. To us, in retrospect, their stupidity seems almost criminal, yet there is much to be pleaded in extenuation of it when once we appraise aright their circumstances and the power of their inherited beliefs. Their failure, however, makes Jesus' grasp of his mission all the more amazing by contrast. Even when he told them of it, and told them repeatedly, they failed to comprehend it—yet he knew it through and through.

And Jesus knew it not only through and through, but also *from the outset*. Not otherwise can the record of the Temptation make sense. He who underwent that dread experience, underwent it because he knew what his true duty was and yet at the same time had both a will capable of revolt and the power available to him to make the revolt effectual. Such are the stark facts. But the glorious fact which allows us to face them with joy and exultation to temper our horror, is that he survived the ordeal, submitted his own will to the will of God, and throughout acted in the spirit of the Psalm, written long ago expressly of him, "Lo, I come: in the volume of the book it is written of me. I delight to do thy will, O my God" (Psalm 40:7,8).

To fulfil that prophecy Jesus had to have not only a fervent desire to perform God's will but also a proper knowledge of it. Now that such knowledge on his part was *complete* before he started out on his mission is a fact which cannot be disputed. He knew the end from the beginning and expressly confessed what the "end" would be—and *had* to be—by the very form of "beginning" which he chose to give it. For him, as for all others, baptism was a symbolic death—but in his case it was also a prophetic symbol, an anticipation of the Cross, a portent of Calvary.

Death, however, is but half of the process of baptism. The beauty of this simple rite lies in its duality: it is not complete, either in fact, or in symbolic meaning, till he who sinks beneath the water also emerges from it and reappears to view. So the Jesus who went down into the waters of Jordan "to fulfil all righteousness" also "went *up out of* the water" (Matthew 3:13-17). As his submersion portended his Crucifixion so did his reappearance anticipate his Resurrection. And we can be sure that as he understood the meaning of the one aspect of his baptism so did he understand the meaning of the other also. He was aware both that he would die and that he would rise again—*and this from the very outset of his Ministry*. He had himself solved "the mystery of the kingdom of heaven" before ever he set out to make it known to others. That mystery lay in the fact that the King would have to appear twice; and that the first "appearance" which he was then about to make would end in a rejection of his Kingship which would (paradoxically) be its most effectual vindication! He, therefore, as the sole master of that secret, saw a significance in many incidents which escaped the notice both of the ultimate perpetrators of that bloody deed and of the faithful band who followed him in the persuasion that he was indeed the King. As for the latter, not until the Resurrection had actually taken place did they become fully capable of seeing all things in a proper light, and even then it was necessary for him specially to point out the correspondence between events and Scripture before all became plain to them. "He said unto them, These are the words which I spake unto you, while I was yet with you, that all things must be fulfilled, which were written in the law of Moses, and in the prophets, and in the Psalms, concerning me. Then opened he their understanding, that they might understand the scriptures, and said unto them, Thus it is written, and thus it behoved Christ (i.e. *the King*) to suffer, and to rise from the dead the third day: and that repentance and remission of sins should be preached in his name among all nations, beginning at Jerusalem" (Luke 24:44-47). Where, therefore, Matthew's Gospel, or any other, points out the correspondence between history and prophecy, we have echoes of the Lord's (what is more, the *resurrected* Lord's) own words on this historic occasion. Who then are these "scholars" who beg so condescendingly to differ?

Veiled hints

Whatever, during the Ministry, had either escaped the notice of the disciples or baffled their understanding, became doubly precious afterwards when its meaning was made plain. It is this fact, as we have seen, which explains the careful arrangement by the Evangelists of their historical material. They seem almost to delight in savouring the terrific dramatic irony of so many of the incidents which they record (now that they are in a position to do so!), though their real concern, of course, is not to do this but only to throw the greatness of Jesus, or the tragedy of those incidents, into even sharper relief. As we might expect, they do this not only in those cases where the claims of Jesus were the vital issue, but also where his consciousness of his redemptive mission was uppermost in his mind. An obvious example is the occasion when John's disciples posed their question, "Why do we and the Pharisees fast oft, but thy disciples fast not?" Part of Jesus' answer—the only part which had any relevance at the time for either John's disciples or those of Jesus—we have already fully considered: "Can the children of the bridechamber mourn, as long as the bridegroom is with them?" "But", added Jesus ominously, "the days will come, when the bridegroom shall be taken from them, *and then shall they fast*" (Matthew 9:15).

Now all three Evangelists carefully preserve this precious saying. And we do well to realize why. It was not simply because in retrospect they saw in it a proof that

Jesus knew that he would have to die; least of all that they thought that he chose to say so *gratuitously*. Rather was it because they had come to see that the prediction bore an intimate relation to the question which prompted it. Jesus had come expressly to fulfil (and thus abolish) all ritual and ceremonial forms, as he had just told the Pharisees enigmatically, leaving them to solve the riddle. It was pre-occupation with such forms that moved John's disciples to choose this very same time to ask him why he permitted his disciples to disregard them. What the Evangelists came to see was that in the same way as Jesus had just hinted at the *need* for him to die (by telling the Pharisees that he was the Physician who would eventually heal all sickness), so in his reply to John's disciples he revealed what particular crisis would actually precipitate his death. It would be a stubborn and misguided attachment to ritual for its own sake, a concern for the type which blinded men's eyes to the archetype, which would eventually drive the Pharisees to arraign him on a charge of blasphemy and to bring about his death.

It was Matthew's recognition of this fact that Jesus had foreseen the exact course which events would follow which led him to construct his twelfth chapter so carefully. Here again the issue was the same—Which was sovereign, the Law or the authority of the Son of Man? And once again the prophetic dictum "I will have mercy and not sacrifice" was for Jesus the key to the problem. As he by his righteous life and by his saving mission fulfilled the sabbath, so he could lawfully heal on the sabbath; so, ignoring the punctilios of the Pharisees, he healed the man with the withered hand. "Then", says Matthew significantly, *"Then* the Pharisees went out, and held a council against him, *how they might destroy him"* (Matthew 12:14). Though Mark here, as previously, omits Jesus' quotation of Hosea's words, yet, to compensate for this, his conjunction of these two facts—the overriding of the Law by Jesus, and the plotting of his death by these zealots for the Law—is actually more effective than Matthew's, for he it is, and not Matthew, who records that Jesus before healing the man asked his audience, "Is it lawful to do good on the sabbath

days, or to do evil? to save life, *or to kill*?" The irony of his
record is therefore really more impressive than that of
Matthew's. They flatly refused to answer Jesus' question—
"they held their peace", as Mark soberly puts it. But no
sooner had Jesus performed his cure, outraging their misguided zeal for the sabbath, than they proceeded without
delay to show that, they had no compunction whatsoever
about plotting to "kill"! "And the Pharisees", adds Mark
dramatically, "went forth, and *straightway* took counsel
with the Herodians against him, how they might destroy
him" (Mark 3:4,6).

"The Pharisees", we note, "took counsel with the
Herodians". That is, the patriots took counsel with the pro-
Roman aristocracy! Such was the measure of their desperation; for, as Luke tells us, "they were filled with madness;
and communed one with another what they might do to
Jesus" (Luke 6:11). Nor was this the only occasion on
which such an evil coalition was made and irreconcilable
policies were shelved in favour of an alliance against one
who was adjudged to be a common foe, for later "the
Pharisees also *with the Sadducees* came, and tempting
desired him that he would show them a sign from heaven"
(Matthew 16:1). With what sinister intent they made that
request we have already had occasion to note. What is
important for us at this earlier stage is that the Pharisees,
in thus joining forces with their traditional political
opponents, were clearly endeavouring to make a charge of
blasphemy against Jesus more likely to issue in his death.

Once more the Scriptures of the prophets told Jesus how
to act. He had the power to paralyse all opposition, as he
had later to produce a sign, "but", says Matthew, "when
Jesus knew it, he withdrew himself from thence". We then
read that "great multitudes followed him". It is not hard to
imagine what their hopes and longings were, but Jesus
merely "healed them" and, to discourage further excited
throngs from gathering, and so to obviate the danger that
they might make a demonstration in his favour, "he
charged them that they should not make him known".
Matthew tells us why; it was in order that it might be fulfilled which was spoken by Esaias the prophet, saying,

"Behold my servant ... He shall not strive, nor cry; neither shall any man hear his voice in the streets. A bruised reed shall he not break, and smoking flax shall he not quench, till he send forth judgement unto victory. And in his name shall the Gentiles trust" (Matthew 12:15-21). That is, Jesus deliberately forbore not only to fill the role of a secular Messiah, but also to use force even in his own defence against the malice of his foes. He sought safety in flight, thus acting on his own counsel to the Twelve when sending them forth, for he had foreseen that not only himself, but they also, would be persecuted: "When they persecute you in this city, flee ye into another", he had told them, adding by way of encouragement, "The disciple is not above his master, nor the servant above his lord" (Matthew 10:23,24). Even he would have to suffer as they did, so to that suffering they ought to submit uncomplainingly, availing themselves only of such means of avoiding it as flight would afford.

But flight, allied as it was to non-resistance, could not give lasting security either to his disciples or to himself. It was only too obvious that implacable foes would exploit the situation to their own advantage, and to his and his disciples' ruin. The course he chose to follow could only end in his death at their hands, once circumstances proved propitious for them to apprehend and try him. Whenever, therefore, they asked for a sign (not to satisfy their curiosity, far less their doubts, be it noted, for they deemed him an impostor) he promised them but one sign—"the sign of the prophet Jonas". He told them why, but in a form calculated to baffle both them and his disciples until the sign had actually become fact, saying, "For as Jonas was three days and three nights in the whale's belly; so shall the Son of man be three days and three nights in the heart of the earth" (Matthew 12:38-42; cf. 16:1-4).

The correspondence between himself and Jonah did not end there, as his subsequent comments hinted. He pointed out that it was Ninevites (i.e. Gentiles) who had repented at the preaching of Jonah, and that it was also a Gentile queen who had come from the uttermost parts of the earth to hear the wisdom of Solomon. By this means, inasmuch as he declared himself to be greater than both Jonah and Solomon, he intimated that he was the One of whom it was written, "In his name shall the Gentiles trust". This was, moreover, no merely gratuitous statement of truth: it implied that privileges which the Jews regarded as exclusively theirs were to become just as much the possession of the Gentiles—that acceptability before God had to be reckoned in terms of spirituality and not of racial extraction. Implicit here, therefore, was the universality of the Gospel, with all that that spelt by way of the supersession of the Law and Temple. It was just a case of John's teaching— "Think not to say within yourselves, We have Abraham to our father" (Matthew 3:9)—being taken to its logical conclusion.

This had been done by Jesus long before in his home town of Nazareth. His discourse in the synagogue there commanded the attention and awe of all: "All bare him witness, and wondered at the gracious words which proceeded out of his mouth". But his small amount of healing work in the neighbourhood was an affront to their local pride, and their muttered protests were known to him. "And he said unto them, Ye will surely say unto me this proverb, Physician, heal thyself: whatsoever we have heard done in Capernaum, do also here in thy country". His next words indicated that he had no intention of obliging them, for their motive was wrong; it was not based on acceptance of him as a prophet. "And he said, Verily I say unto you, No prophet is accepted in his own country" (Luke 4:22-24).

There was a wider meaning to that word "country" than his hearers were aware of, as he at once proceeded to make plain. Their unwillingness to accept his prophetic authority was characteristic of the whole nation. The very city of Capernaum which they so envied was just as unbelieving as Nazareth (Luke 10:15), and likewise representative of the whole country, so Jesus reminded them of the significance of two Old Testament incidents. These showed that not only did the people tend in every age to reject the prophets of God, but that these prophets had sometimes shown favours to the alien which were withheld from the

Chosen! "I tell you of a truth, many widows were in Israel in the days of Elias, when the heaven was shut up three years and six months, when great famine was throughout all the land, but unto none of them was Elias sent, save unto Sarepta, a city of Sidon, unto a woman which was a widow. And many lepers were in Israel in the time of Eliseus the prophet: and none of them was cleansed, saving Naaman the Syrian" (Luke 4:25-27). The recital of these facts—incontrovertible facts of Scripture though they were—raised a howl of protest, for their implications were too obvious to miss. That the Holy People should be rejected in favour of the alien—it was utterly unthinkable! "And all they in the synagogue, when they heard these things, were filled with wrath, and rose up, and thrust him out of the city, and led him unto the brow of the hill whereon their city was built, that they might cast him down headlong". Something, doubtless the power of his personality which during his discourse had so overawed them (verse 20), stayed them in their mad intention, and "he passing through the midst of them went his way" (verses 28-30). Yet it was a near thing, and one charged with omen. It was but a foretaste of the ultimate rejection of him when once again he would be thrust out of the city (this time the Holy City) and be in fact done to death by an angry and outraged people.

It was for this reason, therefore, that later he wistfully told the disciples of John, "The days will come, when the bridegroom shall be taken from them, and then shall they fast" (Matthew 9:15). Those disciples were concerned with literal fasting: Jesus however attached a new meaning to that term. He used it to anticipate that desolation and affliction of soul, that numbed despair, which his own disciples would experience when they saw him crucified and slain. When those "days" eventually came, it is interesting to observe that Jesus' first words to the two disciples on the road to Emmaus were "What manner of communications are these that ye have one to another, as ye walk, *and are sad?*" (Luke 24:17). This was fasting indeed, and such as they had not reckoned with.

Plainness of speech

The choice and training of the Twelve had an ulterior purpose which escaped them at the time. Little did they appreciate as they first went forth that this and later excursions of the same kind were designed to give them an experience of working without the bodily presence of Jesus which would serve them in good stead when the time came for the Bridegroom to be taken away from them altogether. Yet if there was some excuse for them at this stage because Jesus had not made specific and explicit reference to the fact that he would have to die, there was certainly none by the end of his Ministry, for a critical stage was reached mid-way through it when he began to reveal to them in detail what would befall him. This stage coincided with the maturing of their conviction that he was the Christ. They had, of course, followed him in the first place because they believed him to be Messiah, but stage by stage a more robust and enlightened conviction must have developed to supersede their first intuitive judgement on him. His claims and his symbolic ways of making them, his calm assumption of ultimate authority, the new revelation made on the famous day of parables, a revelation made no less in the parables themselves than in his interpretation of them—all these things would consolidate, intensify and enrich their original faith in him. But as their confidence increased so did the disbelief of the masses and the rancour of his foes, making it all the more necessary that they, his disciples, should be sure of their ground. So, finally, near Cæsarea Philippi, he put them to the test.

First he plied them repeatedly with the question, "Whom do men say that I the Son of man am?" The answers varied. In one town he was reckoned to be John the Baptist returned to life, in another to be Elijah, in another Jeremiah or some other prophet. Then, to bring matters to a head, he one day asked them bluntly, "But whom say *ye* that I am?" Peter was first with the answer— an answer which was primarily a confession of his own faith, but which doubtless also voiced the feelings of most, if not all, the other disciples: "Thou art the Christ, the Son of the living God" (Matthew 16:13-16).

Peter's answer was bold and uncompromising. And it was matched by a warmth of approval on the part of Jesus which Peter could not have foreseen. Said Jesus, "Blessed art thou, Simon Bar-jona: for flesh and blood hath not revealed it unto thee, but my Father which is in heaven" (verse 17). It was not Peter's earthly father, Jona, nor his own unaided intellect, that had led him to see things this way, but that same God whom he had just avowed to be Father to Jesus. This was a staggering privilege, and, as Jesus proceeded to show, another no less staggering sprang from it. A church—*the* Church—would be founded on the momentous truth which Peter had uttered; an eternal Church, moreover, for "the gates of hell shall not prevail against it" ("Not prevail ...", the words were ominous; they meant that death would assail the Church, even though it would be in vain, and Jesus was shortly to show how it would do so). In the foundation of that Church (that new supra-national Israel) Peter would also have the privilege of playing a vital and authoritative role: "I will give unto thee", said Jesus, "the keys of the kingdom of heaven" (verses 18,19). He it was who would admit the first aspirants into that kingdom when the time came for such authority to be exercised.

But meanwhile much had still to happen which would seemingly make mockery of Peter's belief that Jesus was indeed the Christ. The task of preparing his disciples' minds to meet that shock now became Jesus' first concern. First he decreed that they should keep his Messiahship a secret (verse 20). This would both serve as a sobering restraint on their own enthusiasm, and also remove the danger of popular agitation in support of him. And necessarily so, for he had heavy and unexpected tidings for them. He himself had come to Jordan both convinced that he was Messiah and aware of what his Messiahship entailed for him in terms of suffering and death. As yet his disciples, however, had come to see that he was Messiah without realizing in the slightest that this necessitated his death. The need to make them aware of this was therefore imperative. Accordingly, "*from that time forth* began Jesus to show unto his disciples, how that he must go unto

Jerusalem, and suffer many things of the elders and chief priests and scribes, and be killed, and be raised again the third day" (verse 21).

The news left the disciples stunned and incredulous. He—he the Christ—would have to suffer and die? the very idea was monstrous! So once more Peter took the lead. Not under the promptings of the Father this time, however, but in obedience only to his human prejudices and the false notions of the time. Ostentatiously, almost patronisingly, "Peter took him, and began to rebuke him, saying, Be it far from thee, Lord: this shall not be unto thee. But he turned, and said unto Peter, Get thee behind me, Satan: thou art an offence unto me: for thou savourest not the things that be of God, but those that be of men" (verses 22,23). The fierceness of Christ's words betrayed the strength of his feeling, and his use of one phrase in particular—"Get thee behind me, Satan"—in turn betrayed why he felt so strongly. Here was one of his own company—the very one, moreover, who had been the first to acknowledge him boldly as Christ—seeking to deflect him from the path of duty, and thus renewing for him the anguish and the conflict of his wilderness ordeal.

It is tempting to speculate that this was the very occasion when Jesus first told his disciples of that ordeal. The sequel strongly confirms this guess, for none but Jesus himself has ever actually been in the position to gain the whole world and also to lose his own soul in the process (verse 26). How much greater both in poignancy and power, then, would his appeal sound to them, *if they were aware* that he was speaking straight out of his own bitter experience in the wilderness. There in a flash he saw "all the kingdoms of the world, and the glory of them" (Matthew 4:8); but there, too, he had to remain loyal to his duty which decreed that that glory could not pertain to him until first the path of shame had been faithfully trodden. He was thus doing no more than insist, once again, that "the disciple is not above his master, nor the servant above his lord"—hence his added appeal: "If any man will come after me, let him deny himself, and take up his cross, and follow me" (Matthew 16:24).

The Twelve had heard similar words before this—"He that taketh not his cross, and followeth after me, is not worthy of me" (Matthew 10:38). At that stage the words could have been no more than just picturesque to them. But now all was changed. Jesus had just revealed that he "must be *killed*". There was therefore no mistaking his meaning when he next bade them acquiesce in the Cross even for themselves. He was clearly divulging, so far as he himself was concerned at least, that the death which had to be undergone was death by crucifixion.

Mark, with the same definiteness as Matthew, states that this was the occasion when Jesus "*began* to teach them, that the Son of man must suffer many things, and be rejected of the elders, and of the chief priests, and scribes, and be killed, and after three days rise again". He omits, we note, the reference to Jerusalem, but as this is implicit in the mention of the Sanhedrin ("the elders, chief priests and scribes"; cf. Acts 4:5 etc.) which met only in Jerusalem, his report tallies with Matthew's. We can thus safely conclude that Jesus' teaching at this stage concerning his death was general rather than circumstantial (Mark 8:31). But thanks to both we know that, as time progressed, Jesus came to deal with that matter in greater detail, and presumably for the benefit of all his disciples scattered over Galilee as he moved south from Cæsarea Philippi which bordered on the northern confines of the land. "They departed thence, and passed through Galilee; and he would not that any man should know it". And for such secrecy Mark gives us the reason, "For he taught (i.e. taught *repeatedly*) his disciples, and said unto them, The Son of man is delivered into the hands of men, and they shall kill him; and after that he is killed, he shall rise the third day" (Mark 9:30,31).

This brief statement gives us once more only the gist of Jesus' teaching, but it is important because, though it is seemingly but a repetition of the first summary of Jesus' words at Cæsarea Philippi, it diverges in one detail, and so reveals that Jesus had introduced a new factor into that teaching. Before, it had been, "the Son of man must suffer" (Mark 8:31; cf. Matthew 16:21; Luke 9:22), and the newness of the teaching had lain in the facts, firstly that Messiah was to be a *suffering* Messiah, and secondly, that he *had* to be so—"the Son of man *must* suffer". Here, in this second summary we have it revealed why the need for Messiah to suffer was imperative. "The Son of man is *delivered* into the hands of men", said Jesus. But who could so "deliver him" into the hands of *men*? Clearly none but God! His Crucifixion would therefore be according to God's will. So that was why he had said, "the Son of man must suffer". Men would sooner or later wreak their vengeance on him and give vent to their bitter hatred of him, and in that sense his death was inevitable. But they would be powerless to destroy him *unless God also chose to deliver him up*. This, said Jesus now, was precisely what would happen. His listeners were stunned. As Mark has it, "They understood not that saying, and were afraid to ask him" (Mark 9:32).

How long this quiet, almost secret, tour of Galilee for the instruction of his scattered disciples lasted we are not told. Luke merely indicates that Jesus was observing a definite time-table at this stage, so that "it came to pass, when the time was come that he should be received up, he stedfastly set his face to go to Jerusalem". Luke then reveals that the first stage of the movement south took Jesus through part of Samaria, and that he sent messengers before his face to reserve lodging for him. Then it was that James and John revealed themselves as Sons of Thunder, for because the Samaritans "did not receive him, because his face was as though he would go to Jerusalem", in indignant protest they sought permission to call down fire from heaven to consume them (Luke 9:51-56).

There was, alas, a double irony in their wild—albeit understandable—request. Not until after the great confession of Cæsarea Philippi, and that solemn setting of the seal to their conviction that their Master was King which there took place, would they in any case have been so incensed and dared to seek such power. Yet that confession had been followed first by the repeated instruction of the Twelve in the need for the King to suffer and die, and then by that pastoral tour by Jesus to instruct the scattered sheep of his little flock; a tour on which they had just accompanied him, and during which he had divulged that God required him to die. And to make matters worse, James and John had actually had the priceless privilege of witnessing the Transfiguration which had followed so hard upon the confession and which, as we shall see in a moment, bore such a close relation to the tour. Just at the time, therefore, when their minds should have been exercised with the explanation of this mystery they forbore to enquire (Mark 9:32) and so failed to see how needful was his death if men's lives were to be *saved*. Small wonder they found time to think of *destroying* them!

This unhappy incident would leave a deep impression upon the apostolic band, and who can doubt that it was as a direct result of it that Jesus gave James and John the surname Boanerges (Mark 3:17)? It certainly appears that from now on Jesus laid special stress on the fact that he had come to *save* men's lives, and did so particularly for the benefit of James and John. His journey through Samaria soon brought him into Perea, the province east of Jordan (Matthew 19:1), and there another incident in which these same two disciples featured gave him an opportunity to lay such stress on the redemptive character of his death, and thereby to shatter yet further the illusions still being cherished by these two zealous men. All three Synoptists mention a particular occasion when, *en route*, Jesus took the Twelve aside, and gave the most circumstantial outline to date of what would befall him at the end of this momentous procession southwards: "He took again the twelve, and began to tell them what things should happen unto him, saying, Behold, we go up to Jerusalem; and the Son of man shall be delivered unto the chief priests, and unto the scribes; and they shall condemn him to death, and shall deliver him to the Gentiles: and they shall mock him, and shall scourge him, and shall spit upon him, and shall kill him: and the third day he shall rise again" (Mark 10:32-34). Luke, who uses all his dramatic skill to depict the Crucifixion as the tragic culmination of the Ministry, is content to add that "they understood none of these things", and even that "this saying *was hid* from them, neither knew they the things which were spoken" (Luke 18:31-34). But Mark and Matthew at once proceed to give a telling illustration of the fact, one which, as Matthew shows, happened almost immediately afterwards, for "*then* came to him the mother of Zebedee's children with her sons, worshipping him, and desiring a certain thing of him. And he said unto her, What wilt thou? She saith unto him, Grant that these my two sons may sit, the one on thy right hand, and the other on the left, in thy kingdom". As proof that much of what he had told them of his sufferings and of the spiritual nature of his kingdom had been lost on them, "Jesus answered and said, Ye know not what ye ask. Are ye able to drink of the cup that I shall drink of, and to be baptized with the baptism that I am baptized with? They say unto him, We are able. And he saith unto them, Ye shall drink indeed of my cup, and be baptized with the baptism that I am baptized with: but to sit on my right hand, and on my left, is not mine to give, but it shall be given to them for whom it is prepared of my Father" (Matthew 20:20-23; cf. Mark 10:35-40).

The ten were swift to protest, but only, it seems, as a result of that same pretentiousness which James and John had just betrayed. So when Jesus observed that they "began to be much displeased with James and John" he "called them to him, and saith unto them, Ye know that they which are accounted to rule over the Gentiles exercise lordship over them; and their great ones exercise authority upon them. But so shall it not be among you: but whosoever shall be great among you, shall be your minister: and whosoever of you will be the chiefest, shall be servant of all". Then, to clinch matters, and to teach them once again that the disciple is not above his master, he added, "For even the Son of man came not to be ministered unto, but to minister". Nor was this all, for he came to minister to the uttermost; in fact "*to give his life a ransom for many*" (Mark 10:41-45; cf. Matthew 20:24-28). Sad—nay tragic— was the disregard for these weighty words shown at the Last Supper, when the Twelve fell once more to disputing as to which of them had precedence over the others (Luke 22:24-27). But that disregard extended not only to the exhortation to be humble but also to the prediction of the self-denying death which he would suffer and to the altruism which inspired him to undergo it. Indeed, not until they had properly grasped the need for his death and come to understand its true character could they even begin to esteem humility as the greatest virtue. And the same is true of us. One of the most important lessons which we, too, have to learn is the fact that before honour is humility—that the cross must come before the crown.

Glory through shame

The great truth that it behoved Christ (and so, by extension, every Christian also) first to suffer, and only then to enter into glory, received its most powerful expression in the Transfiguration. This took place within a week of Peter's great confession of faith at Cæsarea Philippi; and the fact that, in addition to himself, James and John were the only other ones to witness so momentous an event rendered their subsequent blindness to the sufferings of Christ, and their resultant false conception of greatness in the Kingdom, all the more inexcusable. Yet the candour with which the gospels soberly set down the faults of these pillars of the early Church is a most effective guarantee of their general truthfulness and reliability. We have therefore immeasurably greater reason to be grateful that we can trust the gospels than to be critical of those of whom they so frankly speak.

All three Synoptists closely connect the Transfiguration with the significant events which took place near Cæsarea Philippi. And in this they were guided not only by the order of the historical events which they record, but more especially by the sequence of thought revealed in the words which Jesus uttered after rebuking Peter for seeking to dissuade him from submitting to a martyr's death. Mark adds one interesting detail to those set down by Matthew, namely, that it was "when he had *called the people unto him* with his disciples also", that Jesus proceeded to lay down the criterion of true discipleship—"Whosoever will come after me, let him deny himself, and take up his cross, and follow me"—and to present man with the chal-

lenge to renounce the world now as the condition of entering into life, or to reckon with losing both the world, and
life itself, in the day when he will execute judgement upon
all. To drive home that challenge Jesus added these sombre words, "Whosoever therefore shall be ashamed of me
and of my words in this adulterous and sinful generation;
of him also shall the Son of man be ashamed, when he
cometh in the glory of his Father with the holy angels"
(Mark 8:34-38).

"In this generation ...": the words implied that the coming in glory was to be in another, a later, generation. And
necessarily so, for he had not long before revealed that
death awaited him in Jerusalem at the end of the procession southwards which he was shortly to undertake. No
matter: he would nevertheless still come in glory, a fact
which in its turn clearly necessitated and foretold his resurrection from the dead. He was insisting by this means,
then, that belief in his Messiahship, so boldly avowed by
Peter, was in no way incompatible with his death at the
hands of the leaders of the people. Knowing that he would
rise again he was serenely confident that he would himself
vindicate and authenticate his own truism, so startlingly
paradoxical, that "whosoever shall lose his life for my sake
and the gospel's, the same shall *save* it" (Mark 8:35). And
he was confident of even more than that, for he at once
proceeded to add, "Verily I say unto you, That there be
some of them that stand here, which shall not taste of
death, till they have seen the kingdom of God come with
power" (Matthew—"till they see the Son of man coming in
his kingdom") (Mark 9:1).

Now it is manifest from the fact that all three
Synoptists at once relate the story of the Transfiguration
that they all three regarded that signal event to be the fulfilment of this remarkable prediction by Jesus.

Let us look first therefore at the prediction. Not all, we
note, but only "some" were to be privileged to witness this
epiphany. As for them, they would "in no wise taste of
death" *before* they had witnessed it. So they would taste of
death *after!*—that was the obvious implication. But what
was its relevance? Much every way; it signified that the

epiphany which they would behold would not be the ultimate coming in glory of which Jesus had just been speaking, but at best only a foretaste of it, and therefore that as
the ultimate coming presupposed the rising from the dead
of the suffering Messiah, so would this primary coming
speak to them also of resurrection, and thus, too, of *death*
as something to be undergone by them, no less than by
their Lord, before the earnest became the reality.

Let us then now look at the fulfilment of the Lord's prediction. It took place six days after the giving of the
promise (Matthew 17:1; Mark 9:2), eight days in all after
Peter's confession (which means that his rebuking of Jesus
must have taken place two days after that confession)
(Luke 9:28). With only Peter, John and James to accompa-
ny him, Jesus went up into a mountain to pray, "And *as he
prayed*", says Luke, "the fashion of his countenance was
altered, and his raiment white and glistering" (Luke 9:29),
and he was, as Mark and Matthew put it, *"transfigured*
before them" (Mark 9:2; Matthew 17:2).

The conclusion is irresistible. As Jesus at Jordan had
prayed for the Spirit and received it (Luke 3:21,22), so here
he prayed to be transfigured, and his prayer was
answered, and thereby his promise to his disciples fulfilled. The disciples in question were his most intimate
associates, the three who alone were earlier allowed to witness his raising of Jairus' daughter (Luke 8:51), and were
later to be privileged to witness his agony in Gethsemane
(Mark 14:33). To these then was accorded the inestimable
privilege of seeing the glorified Son of man, "coming in his
Kingdom", *while he was still in the flesh*; that is, of witnessing a physical manifestation of what was otherwise to
be observed in him only by the spiritual eye of the behold-
er. Isaiah had said of his coming, "And the glory of the
LORD shall be revealed, and all flesh shall see it together"
(Isaiah 40:5). That glory was indeed revealed throughout
his Ministry, nay, throughout his life, but being as yet
revealed only in his spiritual perfection, it passed unobserved by all but a few. But the Transfiguration served to
demonstrate to the disciples that that perfection guaranteed his eventual advent "in *his own glory,* and the glory of

the Father, and of the holy angels", and anticipated the day when all flesh would see it together (Luke 9:26). The three disciples witnessed this his glory, for themselves, as on this one brief unrepeatable occasion it shone forth unhindered before them. It was as though the veil of flesh which obscured the physical manifestation of that glory had been removed; and, impossible though it is for us fully to understand how it all happened, we can be sure that the whole experience was none the less *real* for being a vision. To adapt a modern expression, it was as though Jesus and his apostles had penetrated the "time barrier". By some process, incomprehensible to our time-bound, finite minds, he momentarily passed into the ultimate state of glory, which for him and them alike lay beyond death. In keeping with that fact the disciples became conscious of the effects of that process *only upon awaking from sleep*—a symbolic death—and then beheld not only him but two long-dead worthies also: "Peter and they that were with him were heavy with sleep: and *when they were awake* (RV fully awake), *they saw his glory*, and the two men that stood with him" (Luke 9:32). Luke, who is the only one of the Evangelists to supply us with this interesting item of information, is also careful to point out that the two men in question, Moses and Elijah, also "appeared in glory" (verses 30,31). Matthew and Mark are content to say that they talked with Jesus, but Luke goes further and tells us what was the topic of their conversation—"they spake *of his decease* which he should accomplish in Jerusalem". This meant that he would not attain to ultimate glory except through death—and on the basis of it. And the fact that it should be these two particular personages—the one the symbol of the Law, and the other at that time the very personification of prophecy—who should there discuss Jesus' impending death, was for this reason most significant. It indicated that the Law and the Prophets would find their culmination and fulfilment in that death. So, fittingly, when their conversation was over, the illustrious figures of the past at once began to fade from view. Peter, overwhelmed, hastened to ask Jesus for permission, ere it was too late, to erect three tabernacles, "one for thee, and one for Moses, and one for Elias" (verse 33). But this, as was quickly shown, could not be. A cloud at this stage enveloped both the disciples and their Master, filling their hearts with fear (verse 34). "And a voice came out of the cloud, saying, This is my Son (or, my beloved Son), my chosen, hear ye him. And when the voice came, Jesus was found alone" (Luke 9:35-36, RV).

The combination of voice and symbolism was terrific. It signified that the One about to die was essentially superior to all who had gone before, being a unique manifestation in flesh of the Father Himself—"This is my *Son*"; that he was the Anointed, the Chosen One, long foretold by Psalmist and Prophet alike, and destined to be heir of all the world (Psalm 2:7,8; Isaiah 42:1); that what he said was the final and authoritative revelation of God, superseding all that had preceded it, as God had said to Moses should come to pass (Deuteronomy 18:15). Those concluding words, "hear *him*", thus lent divine weight to the challenge so recently issued—"he that loseth his life for my sake shall find it"—and bade men believe and act upon it notwithstanding the shameful death which he would shortly suffer. Thus the Transfiguration, like the Temptation, was an experience which could have befallen one man only, and the record of it is charged with Christology in the same way as that of the Temptation, for each was complementary to the other.

So the vision ended, abruptly, dramatically; "Suddenly looking round about, they saw no one any more, save Jesus only with themselves" (Mark 9:8, RV). Amazed and bewildered, the three disciples then set off down the mountainside with Jesus. As they proceeded on their way, "he charged them that they should tell no man what things they had seen, till the Son of man were risen from the dead" (Mark 9:9). His mention of his resurrection seemed to them to accord ill with the glorious vision of the coming of the Kingdom which they had just witnessed, "and they kept that saying with themselves, questioning one with another what the rising from the dead should mean" (Mark 9:10). All they asked him to explain was how the predicted coming of Elijah fitted into the appointed train of events. He gave his answer by once more rehearsing the testimony of Scripture to his own sufferings and pointing to John the Baptist's tragic death as the initial fulfilment of Malachi's prophecy.

Soon they rejoined the rest of the disciples, but the privileged three kept their amazing secret to themselves until events had finally reconciled them to the shame and degradation of the Cross and had made it both impossible and unnecessary for them to keep it any longer. As for Jesus, "he steadfastly set his face to go to Jerusalem", knowing that though he would suffer and die, he would as assuredly return alive from the tomb as Jonah had returned from the belly of the whale, and would then at last enter into that glory which was rightfully his own.

He would not have been human had the prospect of that glory not loomed large in his thinking and become the object of his longing. He knew that he would at the last fulfil all that John had said of him to the uttermost, and naturally yearned for that time to come—"I came to cast fire upon the earth; and would that it were already kindled!" (Luke 12:49; RSV, Moffatt, etc.). But never could he contemplate that prospect without thinking also of the ordeal of suffering which he had first to endure—and to long too for that to be past—"I have a baptism to be baptized with: and how am I straitened till it be accomplished!" (verse 50).

10
WHY TEMPT YE ME?

Christ and his Gainsayers

JESUS' unique grasp of his mission put him in the position not only to correct the misconceptions of his followers but also to dispose of the fallacies of his foes. If it is right to say that he could declare, with a fullness of meaning not possible in the case of any other man, "Thy word is a lamp unto my feet, and a light unto my path", the same is no less true of the closely related saying, "Thou through thy commandments hast made me wiser than mine enemies: for they are ever with me" (Psalm 119:98).

Of quick understanding
Jesus was constantly beset by unscrupulous adversaries bent on discrediting him by fair means or foul. Yet despite the ingenuity with which these men devised their questions and problems, the facility and mastery with which he confuted them at every turn drove them to madness, until at last, in desperation, they determined to put him to death. They knew this to be the only method by which they could effectively silence him, for always the last word in each verbal battle lay with him, whether the encounter was with an overbearing synagogue ruler, Pharisees hot with zeal for the sanctity of the Sabbath, or a censorious host who was sceptical as to his prophetic powers.

The opposition which he encountered was no less than he could expect, and we can be sure that toward much of it he would be sympathetic. Though the enquiry of John's disciples, "Why do we and the Pharisees fast oft, but thy disciples fast not?" was tinged strongly with reproach, his answer was kind and gentle, for all that it was firm and authoritative. And the progressive, carefully graduated re-education by him of his disciples is further proof of his understanding of men's difficulty in accommodating their ideas and outlook to his teaching and to his demands upon them. For the duplicity and cunning of his sworn enemies, however, he held no brief at all, and he never hesitated to denounce them for their hypocrisy and criminal folly, as we have seen on several occasions already.

Once when scribes and Pharisees, who had come all the way from Jerusalem to observe and interrogate him, asked reproachfully, "Why do thy disciples transgress the tradition of the elders? for they wash not their hands when they eat bread", he abruptly presented them with a counter-question of far more serious import. "He answered and said unto them, Why do ye also transgress the commandment of God by your tradition?" The tradition was, at best, but the tradition *of men*; the commandments upon which it was overlaid were by contrast the commandments *of God*. Now, manifestly, where the lesser—the laws of men—stultify the greater—the laws of God—they must perforce be ignored. This was precisely the position on this occasion, and these critics of Jesus, by their very attachment to their revered tradition, themselves provided him with all the warrant he needed for ignoring it! They were, ironically, the best advocates in his defence! "For God commanded, saying, Honour thy father and mother: and, He that curseth father or mother, let him die the death. But ye say, Whosoever shall say to his father or his mother, It is a gift, by whatsoever thou mightest be profited by me; and honour not his father or his mother, he shall be free".

"God commanded ... but ye say ..." How witheringly effective was the contrast in Jesus' choice of words; and all the more so because what was comprehended by, "ye say", actually had greater weight for these men than what "God commanded"; for the contingency covered by this particular edict was regarded as conferring exemption upon a man from doing what God had expressly decreed—hence Jesus' denunciation of them: "Thus have ye made the commandment of God of none effect by your tradition" (Matthew 15:1-6).

Now what that contingency was is not easily decided. The text is allusive and this inevitably tends to make the sequence of thought obscure. Yet its allusiveness also

WHY TEMPT YE ME?

serves to make Jesus' reasoning plain (and so helps us to decide the precise nature of the tradition in question) if we treat it with the respect and care which it deserves.

One thing is already obvious: the tradition concerned a man who had by some sort of vow devoted his wealth to the Temple treasury. The next thing which emerges is that that man *informs* his parents of this, and thus signifies to them that he considers himself under no further obligation to apply the Fifth Commandment to the extent of giving them financial support. Now what completes the picture is the fact that Jesus quotes not only the Fifth Commandment, *but also, with it, another precept* taken from the Book of the Covenant—"He that curseth (AV and RV margin, "revileth") his father, or his mother, shall surely be put to death" (Exodus 21:17). Jesus would not have invoked this second precept without good reason—nothing is more sure. It therefore clearly bore upon the issue in question. Once this is conceded, we find this second Scripture providing the key to an otherwise insoluble difficulty. It denounced disrespectful or insolent speech by a man to his parents—so, clearly, the case envisaged by Jesus was one where the man's action in informing his parents that he had vowed his wealth to the Temple was a calculated rebuff to their legitimate demands upon him. That is, his vow had been made less out of respect for the needs of the Temple than out of contempt for those of his parents—not out of love for God but rather out of anger or resentment against his father and his mother. The moral issue was therefore whether the law declaring an oath to be binding took precedence over a son's solemn obligation to obey the explicit divine command, "Honour thy father and thy mother" (Exodus 20:12). Did his vow excuse him from blame for riposting impudently, "It is Corban!" when they pressed their claims upon him?

With typical perversity the Pharisees decreed "Yes". They gave honour to a rash or cynical vow rather than to a man's moral duty; to sacrifice rather than mercy; to technicalities rather than true love. That perversity was typical because their whole attitude to vows was fundamentally immoral. "Woe unto you, ye blind guides", said Jesus to them in fierce denunciation at the close of the ministry, for they affirmed, "Whosoever shall swear by the temple, it is nothing; but whosoever shall swear by the gold of the temple, he is a debtor!" "Ye fools and blind," said Jesus in blazing wrath, "for whether is greater, the gold, or the temple that sanctifieth the gold?" In the same way they said, "Whosoever shall swear by the altar, it is nothing; but whosoever sweareth by the gift that is upon it, he is guilty" (margin, "bound"). It was all of a piece with this law that they should have adjudged a son irrevocably committed by his vow to neglect his parents, rather than to succour them, regardless of the evil motive which led him to make it. But their seeming consistency sprang merely from a characteristic disregard of moral issues, and was at root illogical as Jesus proceeded to show, "Ye fools and blind; for whether is greater, the gift, or the altar that sanctifieth the gift? Whoso therefore shall swear by the altar, sweareth by it, and by all things thereon. And whoso shall swear by the temple, sweareth by it, and by him that dwelleth therein" (Matthew 23:16-21). That is, God's requirements are sovereign, and no man has authority to tamper with them. Any form of tradition which has the effect of making them null and void thus stands self-condemned. As zealots for such a tradition the scribes who invoked it against Jesus thus succeeded only in exposing their own moral perversity. And this he made unmistakably plain to them by appealing once again to the verdict of inspired Scripture. "Ye hypocrites, well did Esaias prophesy of you, saying, This people draweth nigh unto me with their mouth, and honoureth me with their lips; but their heart is far from me. But in vain they do worship me, teaching for doctrines the commandments of men" (Matthew 15:7-9).

Then it was that, calling the crowds together, Jesus chose to point out the intrinsic limitations of all purely ceremonial regulations, and exposed the fundamental misconceptions of the Pharisees. Then to conclude his clash with them, and also by way of answer to their original inquiry, he declared, "To eat with unwashen hands defileth not a man" (verses 10-20).

Always, for Jesus, it was a man's motives and moral state which mattered supremely, whereas for his critics these seemed always to matter least, or not at all. So for this reason he denounced them to their faces, and laid bare their hypocrisy: "Woe unto you, scribes and Pharisees, hypocrites! for ye are as graves which appear not, and the men that walk over them are not aware of them". Here was a stinging rebuke indeed, for, knowing the Law as they did, these men would perceive the point of the allusion. To walk over a grave was to be defiled. Likewise, said Jesus, in effect, to come into contact with them was to become morally corrupted (Numbers 19:16; Luke 11:44). Hearing this, a rash lawyer protested, "Master, thus saying thou reproachest us also" (verse 45). His was the voice of injured innocence, but he was quickly told that it was really the voice of calculated guilt: "Woe unto you also, ye lawyers! for ye lade men with burdens grievous to be borne, and ye yourselves touch not the burdens with one of your fingers". The responsibility of these men was tragically criminal for devising such futile and perverse burdens. "Woe unto you, lawyers! for ye have taken away the key of knowledge: ye entered not in yourselves, and them that were entering in ye hindered" (Luke 11:46,52).

Their mortification vented itself in spiteful retaliation: "As he said these things unto them, the scribes and the Pharisees began to urge him vehemently, and to provoke him to speak of many things: laying wait for him, and seeking to catch something out of his mouth, that they might accuse him" (Luke 11:53,54). Always therefore Jesus had to be on his guard, and alert to some sinister ulterior motive behind every apparently harmless question.

Now and hereafter

On one occasion Jesus "was demanded of the Pharisees, when the kingdom of God should come" (Luke 17:20). The question was in itself a harmless one; but it had been prompted by great cunning. These men knew that he presented himself as King, but denied his right to do so. Their question was thus on the one hand a mock challenge to him to assert himself as King, one which, like the demand for a sign, was designed to make him look a fool; and on the other a device whereby it was hoped that he would be goaded into making some assertion which might embroil him with the political authorities. Either way, then, it bristled with dangers.

Jesus was equal to the emergency, and his answer was disconcertingly enigmatic while being also perfectly true. It is best read in a modern version or with the assistance of the Revised Version margin. Moffatt renders it, "The Reign of God is not coming as you hope to catch sight of it; no one will say, 'Here it is' or 'There it is', for the Reign of God is now in your midst"; and the Revised Standard Version is equally helpful: "The kingdom of God is not coming with signs to be observed; nor will they say, 'Lo, here it is!' or 'There!' for behold, the kingdom of God is in the midst of you" (verse 21). The reply foiled them beautifully, and in turn issued a moral challenge to them to appreciate that the Kingdom had already been inaugurated. For so indeed it had. The coming of the King was itself an advent of the Kingdom: it already existed in miniature both in himself and in his company of disciples. This Jesus left for these men to sort out for themselves by saying, "The kingdom of God is in the midst of you", for unless they first grasped the significance of the immediate "coming of the kingdom", they could in no way become related to its eventual coming as a visible and tangible institution upon earth.

But to foil the cunning of these men was not enough. So as soon as opportunity permitted Jesus (doubtless in private) "said *unto his disciples*, The days will come, when ye shall desire to see one of the days of the Son of man, and ye shall not see it". That is, they too would duly begin to enquire like the Pharisees, "When is the kingdom going to be set up?" Not however in the same captious spirit, but in hope of their own deliverance and with anxious longing. He warned them that when that time came they were not to allow themselves to be misled by wishful thinking: "And they shall say to you, See here; or, see there: go not after them, nor follow them". When the day came there would be no mistaking it: "For as the lightning, that lighteneth out of the one part under heaven, shineth unto the other part unto heaven; so shall also the Son of man be in his day" (verses 22-24).

This was information which Jesus denied to his questioners. Only to those who believed in him did he ever reveal that there were two comings of the Son of man—the first quiet and unobtrusive, the second overt and spectacular. But he could not reveal this without also reminding them why, So he added, "But first must he suffer many things, and be rejected of this generation". Here was a further portent of Calvary, but contenting himself with a passing reference to it he travelled forward in thought to the ultimate coming, and proceeded to stress how sudden and calamitous a coming it would be for the world at large. It would both bring ruin to the ungodly, as had the Flood and the rain of fire and brimstone on Sodom, and also serve as a testing period for all disciples alive at the time. The danger for those disciples would be that, having an excessive interest in the things of this life, they would be loath to give the spiritual treasure of the life to come its proper priority, and seeking to save their material possessions would perish with them. So, said Jesus sombrely, "Remember Lot's wife. Whosoever shall seek to save his life shall lose it; and whosoever shall lose his life shall preserve it" (verses 26-33). The sudden call to Judgement would come to all at once, however employed or whatever the situation in which they found themselves (verses 34-36).

Perplexed, his hearers asked, "Where, Lord?" as just before the Pharisees had arrogantly asked him "When?" His reply was enigmatic—"Wheresoever the body is, thither will the eagles be gathered together" (verse 37). Perhaps it was some common proverb which Jesus here used, but in any case its import was plain. By it he assured them that all would duly happen with a fitness which the crisis demanded and that they need not stumble over details. Their concern should rather be with their own preparedness. So he at once went on to urge them to seek strength through earnest and unceasing prayer to endure the disappointment of not being allowed actually to witness one of the days of the Son of man. Never, despite all adverse circumstance, was their faith in his eventual coming once to waver, but all should instead match the tenacity and dauntlessness of the importunate widow (Luke 18:1-8).

No more twain

As Jesus passed through Perea on his fateful procession from Cæsarea Philippi to Jerusalem, a company of Pharisees came to him with a question. They asked, "Is it lawful for a man to put away his wife for every cause?" (Matthew 19:3). At that time the Pharisees themselves were divided on this issue. Some, adherents of the school of Shammai, declared that the law of Deuteronomy 24:1-4 signified that divorce was permissible, but permissible only for adultery; others, who agreed with Hillel, realizing that Deuteronomy 24:1-4 did not embrace cases of sexual sin (for these were actually punishable *by death* under the Law—Leviticus 20:10; Deuteronomy 22:22), then reasoned falsely that there did exist all manner of other grounds, some of them quite trivial, for divorce, The one party was rigid, the other lax—but each invoked the same passage of Scripture in its support! Thus the question posed to Jesus was ostensibly one which asked him which interpretation he supported, and so to state to which party he adhered. But both Matthew and Mark (10:2) indicate that it was actually a trick question. The truth is that the Pharisees were hoping to inveigle him into saying something which would either embroil him, like John the Baptist, with the divorced Herod and Herodias, in whose territory he was at the time, or which could be construed as heresy against the Law, for the sequel shows that the Law's provision for divorce was in the forefront of their thoughts. There was thus real cunning behind their query. But they underestimated the resourcefulness of their victim!

Jesus at once put the onus on them: "He answered and said unto them, Have ye not read, that he which made them at the beginning made them male and female, and said, For this cause shall a man leave father and mother, and shall cleave to his wife: and they twain shall be one flesh?" Lest they should miss the point of this original marriage law he then commented, "Wherefore they are no more twain, but one flesh". And having thus cited Scripture to support his verdict, and foiled their cynical intent without even alluding to it, he added, "What therefore *God* hath joined together, let not *man* put asunder" (Matthew 19:4-6). In saying this he was consistent to the testimony not only of the first words of Old Testament revelation but also to the last, for Malachi, the last of the ancient prophets, had declared "For the LORD, the God of Israel, saith that he hateth putting away". Malachi, like Jesus, had said this on the strength of Genesis 2:24, for he too had asked his contemporaries, "Did not he (i.e. God) make *one*?" (Malachi 2:14-16).

Though balked in their purpose, the Pharisees were not to be outdone. "They say unto him, Why did Moses then command to give a writing of divorcement, and to put her away?" To their chagrin, once again, they received an answer disrespectful not to Moses, but to themselves as men who failed to make the Edenic marriage law their guide. The fact was that Moses had "commanded" no such thing. "He saith unto them, Moses because of the hardness of your hearts *suffered* you to put away your wives". The change of emphasis was crucial: it left the primitive ideal of marriage all the brighter, so Jesus added, "but from the beginning it was not so" (Matthew 19:7,8). Then, and then only did he proceed to lay down his own law, saying, "And I say unto you, Whosoever shall put away his wife, except it be for fornication, and shall marry another, committeth adultery: and whoso marrieth her which is put away doth commit adultery" (verse 9).

His denunciation of the laxity of the disciples of Hillel could not have been made clearer. The law of Deuteronomy 24, while permitting divorce, was specially designed to discourage hasty resort to it: it both declared the act of divorce irrevocable and stipulated that it should always assume proper legal form. But the school of Hillel had stultified the deterrent purpose of this law by cynically using it as an excuse for easy divorce. And they had also for that reason done something else which was far more criminal: they had made it possible for a man to lust after another woman and to give his lust a cloak of legality and respectability by making it easy for him both to discard his wife and also to take the other woman. As for the discarded wife, like some chattel she too very quickly became another man's in most cases, if only out of sheer economic necessity, and the original evil was proportionately aggravated, marriage in both instances—the husband's and the wife's—losing all its Edenic meaning and sanctity.

For such deceit and legalised indecency Jesus had nothing but contempt. On two other occasions he denounced it (Matthew 5:31,32; Luke 16:17,18), and on both he did so to stress that the prevailing Pharisaic zeal for the Law was a hollow mockery, for the majority of them, it seems, were of Hillel's persuasion. He did so here again. And once again there was no mistaking his meaning—he declared Deuteronomy 24:1-4 to be henceforward *null and void!* One ground only would he in future allow for divorce, that very sin which the lax Hillelites encouraged—adultery.* In this sense he came down on the side of the Shammaites, but this did not mean that he endorsed their particular interpretation of the term "uncleanness" in Deuteronomy 24:1. He went much further than they, for he acted in keeping with the Law's stern condemnation of adultery. The Law punished it with death in order to uphold the sanctity of marriage. Jesus, with the same intention, declared it to be now the *sole* ground for the dissolution of marriage. This particular means of recognizing the enormity of adultery had the added virtue that it suited perfectly the anomalous situation of the pilgrim society for which Jesus was legislating—a society which had no legal status or right to deal with adultery in the summary fashion enjoined by the Law.

Now the marriage law of Genesis 2:24 was familiar to all, his disciples included. But never before had they heard it so uncompromisingly construed, or its implications so

---

*Fornication (Gk. *porneia*) has undoubtedly a restricted meaning (e.g. 1 Corinthians 6:9), but Revelation 2:14,20 are additional examples of its use by Jesus in a wider sense which embraces adultery (cf. 1 Corinthians 5:1; 6:18; 10:8).

ruthlessly laid bare. Mark tells us that indoors they "asked him again of the same matter". The exceptive clause— "except it be for fornication"—does not appear in his record: they presumably saw sense in it and it was not that which worried them. They received the same authoritative reply as before—marriage is sacred, binding, life-long (Mark 10:10-12). Its obligations cannot be circumvented by some legal trick.

Matthew resumes the record, from that point. Better, said the disciples in dismay, not to marry at all then! That, said Jesus, in reply, is for each to decide for himself, though not all are capable of foregoing marriage—"All men cannot receive this saying, save they to whom it is given". Yet some are indeed able to do so, and thus to make themselves eunuchs for the kingdom of God's sake. To these Jesus gave the counsel, "He that is able to receive it, let him receive it" (Matthew 19:10-12).

For all others, for those who choose to marry rather than to remain eunuchs for the Kingdom's sake, his previous counsel must be law: "They twain shall be one flesh". There at once is the first word on marriage in the Scriptures, and also the last. To that obligation no disciple can be disloyal and yet still call himself a disciple. And where this, with all its implications—spiritual, moral and practical—is in fact the law which men and women revere, they have no time for the prevarication of the Pharisees nor the inclination to allow any marriage to come to ruin, least of all their own.

The head of the corner

For the Jewish leaders Jesus' eventual arrival at Jerusalem was a disastrous event. From the very first moment he acted with an imperiousness which they dared not ignore. Either they had to bow before it, or to resist it to the death. By careful prior arrangement, it would seem, Jesus made his entry into Jerusalem a triumphal kingly procession. And in the process he revealed what manner of King he was. It was written in the book of the prophet Zechariah, "Rejoice greatly, O daughter of Zion; shout, O daughter of Jerusalem: behold, thy King cometh unto thee:

223

he is just, and having salvation; lowly, and riding upon an ass, and upon a colt the foal of an ass" (Zechariah 9:9). Of set purpose Jesus fulfilled this prophecy. Two disciples were sent on ahead to procure the foal which was tethered with its mother in a prominent position in a village near Jerusalem. The password, "The Lord hath need of them", satisfied the owners as to the credentials of the disciples (Matthew 21:1-3). Meanwhile a throng of other disciples, doubtless up from Galilee for the feast of Passover, was mustering on the road (Luke 19:37). Upon the arrival of the animals they enthusiastically threw their outer clothing over the bare backs of both creatures, not knowing which to choose. But Jesus knew, as did the two messengers who had led them to him, for the prophecy specified that it should be a colt. Matthew knew, too, and it is a mistaken sense of cleverness which makes so many modern critics think that he naïvely believed Jesus to have ridden both mounts, or, worse still, that to make the fulfilment of prophecy sound more convincing he deliberately invented those details of the story which speak of both the colt and its mother. Matthew was more at home with the parallelism of Hebrew poetry than are his critics: when he stated, "they set him thereon (i.e. on them)" he meant "on the clothes", not "on the animals" (Matthew 21:7), and it is sheer perversity which leads his critics to suggest otherwise.

So Jesus set off for the city, a self-confessed King. The enthusiasm of his disciples knew no bounds: "Many spread their garments in the way: and others cut down branches off the trees, and strawed them in the way. And they that went before, and they that followed, cried, saying, Hosanna; Blessed is he that cometh in the name of the Lord: blessed be the kingdom of our father David, that cometh in the name of the Lord: Hosanna in the highest" (Mark 11:8-10). By this time the throng had swollen: "And some of the Pharisees from among the multitude said unto him, Master, rebuke thy disciples" (Luke 19:39). He replied that the situation demanded just such a demonstration: "I tell you that, if these should hold their peace, the stones would immediately cry out" (verse 40).

The following day (Mark 11:12) he threw the city into yet another commotion by purging the great Court of the Gentiles, which traffickers were desecrating for their own material gain. He cleared it of their tables and booths, crying, "It is written, My house shall be called the house of prayer; but ye have made it a den of thieves" (Matthew 21:13). This done, he then began to preach in its porticoes, and to heal the blind and lame who came to him (verse 14). A tremendous stir was caused. "And when the chief priests and scribes saw the wonderful things that he did, and the children crying in the temple, and saying, Hosanna to the son of David; they were sore displeased". Once again they asked him to restrain this unseemly zeal. And once again he disconcerted them by his answer. "They said unto him, Hearest thou what these say? And Jesus saith unto them, Yea; have ye never read, Out of the mouth of babes and sucklings thou hast perfected praise?" (verses 15,16). He left them to complete the quotation "... that thou mightest still the *enemy* and the *avenger*" (Psalm 8:2), as earlier he had left it to the guilty conscience of those traffickers who profaned the sanctuary of the Gentiles to complete his quotation from Isaiah, "My house shall be called an house of prayer ... for *all* people" (Isaiah 56:7).

His preaching activity continued daily, from early morning (Luke 21:38), attracting the usual large crowds whose presence thwarted the murderous intentions of the authorities (Luke 19:47,48). But clearly the situation was for them intolerable and fraught with peril. They saw that in one way only could they hope to break his hold over the people—they would have to discredit him by some means or other. So like wolves, in full view of all, they descended upon him. "Tell us", said they, "by what authority doest thou these things? and who gave thee this authority? (Matthew 21:23). Their cunning however merely rebounded on themselves. They had chosen their time and place: the presence of the crowds suited them ideally because to discredit him in private would be purposeless. But the presence of those same crowds suited *him* ideally also! especially as they had reached a conclusion which the leaders themselves had been too cowardly and spiritually neglectful to reach. So he answered, "I also will ask you one thing, which if ye tell me, I in like wise will tell you by what authority I do these things. The baptism of John, whence was it? from heaven, or of men?" (verses 24,25).

The question caught them in their own trap. Say "No" they dared not. The vast throng all around them would have stoned them to death on the spot! But to say "Yes" was to answer their own question, for the acclamation made during the triumphal entry had been "Hosanna to *the son of David*: Blessed is *he that cometh* in the name of the Lord" (Matthew 21:9), and they knew that he regarded John as the forerunner and considered himself to be the Coming One. So to concede that John was a prophet was also to concede that Jesus was the Christ. A hush fell over the crowd as it waited for their answer. The hush deepened as they were seen to enter into muttered conclave. Exasperated by this turning of the tables, they reasoned with themselves saying, "If we shall say, From heaven, he will say unto us, Why did ye not then believe him? But if we shall say, Of men ..." And there the myriads of staring eyes filled them with alarm—"we fear the people; for all hold John as a prophet". At last, shamefaced and crestfallen they were obliged to answer, "We cannot tell. And he said unto them, Neither tell I you by what authority I do these things? (Matthew 21:25-27).

The humiliation and mortification which this incident brought to them needs no effort to imagine. Amid the derisive glances of the crowds they would try to make their way back whence they came, the cocksureness with which they had borne down on him having now all gone. But before they could move he had recited the Parable of the Two Sons and plied them with yet another devastating question—"Whether of them twain did the will of his father?" They had no excuse for not answering this time, and there was but one answer which they could offer— "The first". So forthwith Jesus interpreted the parable for them, and in the process answered the previous question concerning John to which they had declined to reply. "John came unto you *in the way of righteousness*", said he, "and ye believed him not". And he made explicitly clear what that meant for them—exclusion from the Kingdom of God (verses 28-32).

But John was not the first prophet—the first servant of the Householder—to be rejected, as Jesus went on at once to show in yet another parable, that of the Wicked Husbandmen (verses 33-39). He used the parable to reveal that he was perfectly aware what would be the tragic outcome for himself of this public humiliation which he had just inflicted on them. Servant after servant, said Jesus, came to the keepers of the Vineyard to gather the Householder's dues, but all were maltreated, and some slain. Then, in words rich in Old Testament allusion, he added solemnly, "Having yet therefore one son (i.e. one further Servant, a Son), his well-beloved, he sent him also last unto them saying, They will reverence my son" (Mark 12:6; cf. Isaiah 5:1-7; 42:1, etc.). His enemies would not miss the point of this: they knew his claims and here was a reflection of them in his parable too plain to miss, and a palpable answer to their own query, "By what authority doest thou these things?" With withering irony he then made the Wicked Husbandmen personate these same ruthless enemies, and so in effect made them confess, "This is the heir!" These, as he knew, were words which they would never be persuaded to use. Yet how exquisite a device this was for bringing solemnly home to them the dastardly nature of the words (words which were already framing themselves on their lips) and of the monstrous crime in which they would issue—"Come, let us kill him". Then to lay bare the jealous self-interest and pre-occupation with their own authority and power which drove them to such madness, he even made them add, "... and let us seize on his inheritance" (Matthew 21:38).

Here was a portent of Calvary indeed—a last minute portent almost. And he would have them appreciate in advance the dire consequences of their folly. So, as his custom was, he then asked them a question based on the parable: "When the Lord therefore of the vineyard cometh, what will he do unto those husbandmen?" Once again their answer was a foregone conclusion: "They say unto him, He will miserably destroy those wicked men, and will let out his vineyard unto other husbandmen, which shall render him the fruits in their seasons" (verses 40,41). Mark's Gospel reads as though Jesus at this point solemnly recited their own words back to them (Mark 12:9), before proceeding to ask, "Did ye never read in the scriptures, The stone which the builders rejected, the same is become the head of the corner: this is the Lord's doing, and it is marvellous in our eyes?" (Matthew 21:42).

The words of Psalm 118 had not long before rung out in their ears, "Blessed be he that cometh in the name of the LORD" (Psalm 118:26). The same words were soon to be addressed to them again by Jesus himself as he took leave of the Temple for the last time (Matthew 23:39). And already they had heard the Temple choirs rehearse the singing of the Hallel Psalms (Psalms 113-118) in preparation for the services of Passover Week. They too doubtless had been turning the words over in their own minds, as is natural at such times. Did the words then mean nothing to them? Had they not paused at all to wonder what was meant by the last Psalm in the series where it was written, "The stone which the builders rejected, the same is become the head of the corner?" (Psalm 118:22).

The words should have had a special interest for the Temple rulers for they were themselves the supervisors of the Levitical masons whose exclusive privilege it was to be still constructing the as yet unfinished Temple. But the words, alas, meant nothing to them. From now on, however, they had no excuse. Here was the Stone addressing them, and here were they, the builders, rejecting him. Could they expect to prosper when the time came for it to be made the head of the corner? Certainly not, as he went on at once to show in words of their own using: "Therefore say I unto you, The kingdom of God shall be taken from you, and given to a nation bringing forth the fruits thereof" (Matthew 21:43). They had rejected the Stone—therefore they too would be rejected in their turn. This was in harmony with all else that was written of the Stone—the *same* Stone—for it was according to Isaiah, to be "a stone of stumbling, and for a rock of offence to both the houses of Israel ... and many among them shall stumble, and fall, and be broken, and be snared, and be taken" (Isaiah 8:14,15). And more; Daniel, too had told of a Stone, one that would grind all kingdoms to powder and come itself to fill the whole earth (Daniel 2:34,35). This was clearly the same as the other. How awful then did Jesus make the responsibility of these men to be for their mad plot to kill him, and how paltry beside his own greatness and destiny did their concern for their little "brief authority" appear when he said to them, "And whosoever shall fall on this stone shall be broken: but on whomsoever it shall fall, it will grind him to powder" (Matthew 21:44). Yet they forthwith, none the less, "sought to lay hands on him!" (verse 46).

Cæsar and God

The chief priests were impotent in the presence of so large and enthusiastic a crowd to arrest Jesus there and then. The next step thus lay with their temporary allies the Pharisees (Matthew 21:45). These now "went and took counsel how they might entangle him in his talk" (Matthew 22:15). Having witnessed the discomfiture of the chief priests they might well have thought the better of joining issue with him and resigned themselves to the situation, but in their folly they thought they saw a ray of hope! True, he did not conform to their conception of Messiah, but nevertheless he professed to be King; so he could probably be induced to do himself mortal harm on that very account, if they were sufficiently astute! The high priests had failed because they had acted in flat defiance of his claim. They, the Pharisees, would be wiser, and play on it instead. But to succeed in their fell purpose they would need the pro-Roman Herodians as witnesses of his words. So accompanied by a contingent of these they confronted him with the craftiest of questions, one which was calculated to rouse the most passionate feelings of everyone within earshot. "Master", said they, with smooth-tongued hypocrisy, trying to make it impossible for him to prevaricate in the slightest degree, "we know that thou art true, and teachest the way of God in truth, neither carest thou for any man: for thou regardest not the person of men. Tell us, therefore, What thinkest thou? Is it lawful to give tribute unto Cæsar, or not?"

"Tribute to Cæsar"—no words could sound more hateful to the Jew of those days, with his independence gone, and his country garrisoned by foreign troops. We can therefore imagine the glint of triumph in the eyes of Jesus' questioners. They had made it impossible for him to refuse to answer, yet were he to say bluntly, "Yes", the crowd which had of late been hanging so attentively on his every word would at once turn on him and rend him. Yet were he to pacify them by a bold "No", straightway the Herodians would denounce him to the Roman procurator and secure his arrest as a dangerous agitator on a charge of sedition. His foes could thus barely restrain their pride in their own cunning, or conceal their sense of victory. Here, at last, they had him—him, the invincible—at their mercy!

Like a bombshell came his response to their assault, "Jesus perceived their wickedness, and said, Why tempt ye me, ye hypocrites? Shew me the tribute money". Someone from the crowd sped outside the sacred Court and returned hotfoot with a Roman denarius. With this coin they also transacted their daily business! More, they accepted all too readily the benefits of the settled government which Cæsar imposed upon them, and thus confessed an obligation to contribute to its upkeep, even though at such heavy cost. "Whose", asked Jesus, "is this image and superscription?" The question answered itself—"They say unto him, Cæsar's". Their coins, then, their precious wealth to which they were so jealously attached, they owed to Cæsar! So if they availed themselves of his coinage they could not consistently object to his demand to be paid in it for the service which he rendered them. More important therefore than the question whether they ought to give Cæsar his dues, was the question whether they were in fact honouring their obligations toward God. They had both an earthly *and* a heavenly ruler. And the demands of each had to be met. "Render (i.e. pay *as due*) therefore", said he, "unto Cæsar the things which are Cæsar's; and unto God the things that are God's" (Matthew 22:16-21).

The things that are God's

Nonplussed, and compelled against their wills to admire his dialectical skill, the Pharisees and Herodians slunk away after their encounter with Jesus (Matthew 22:22). In their turn the Sadducees took up the cudgels, only, however, to be routed and discredited like all before them (verses 23-32). Never before had proof been forthcoming to these men that the doctrine of the Resurrection was taught *in the Torah* on which they took their stand. No Pharisee had ever been able to cite such proof from Moses' writings. Small wonder therefore that the Sadducees utilized the law of levirate marriage to discredit the very notion of resurrection. But their confidence, as Jesus showed, was wholly misplaced, for they were, in effect, vainly endeavouring to set Moses against Moses. They came saying, "Master, *Moses* wrote unto us ..." He rejoined by saying, "Now that the dead are raised, *even Moses showed* at the bush, when he calleth the Lord the God of Abraham, and the God of Isaac, and the God of Jacob. For he is not a God of the dead, but of the living: for all live unto him" (Luke 20:28,37,38).

The Sadducees were stunned. It goes without saying that the crowds were, too. "When the multitude heard this, they were astonished at his doctrine" (Matthew 22:33). Even some of the scribes were constrained to pay ungrudging tribute to his wisdom—"Master thou hast well said" (Luke 20:39). Off they went to report to their discomfited Pharisaic allies, and these, when they had heard "that he had put the Sadducees to silence" came together again (Matthew 22:34).

One of the scribes returned with them and, having been impressed by his treatment of the Sadducees, appealed to him to settle another and equally vexing problem: "Which is the first commandment of all?" The enquiry was doubtless genuine, for it was to this same scribe that Jesus was to say a moment later, "Thou art not far from the kingdom of God" (Mark 12:28-34). Why then does Matthew say that the man submitted his question *"tempting* him" (Matthew 22:35). There is an obvious and fully satisfying solution to this problem. Let it be understood that the Pharisees were using this man as a tool to reopen the controversy in which they had been so sadly worsted earlier in the day and all is plain. Jesus had challenged them—"Render unto God the things that are God's". But what were those "things that are God's"? The Rabbis isolated over six hundred different precepts in all in the Law. Some they classified as 'weighty', some as 'light', and much argument raged as to which were which. The scribe's question therefore invited Jesus to pass a verdict on this thorny issue. He did, and in no uncertain terms: "Thou shalt love the Lord thy God with all thy heart, and with all thy soul, and with all thy mind. This is the first and great commandment. And the second is like unto it, Thou shalt love thy neighbour as thyself".

The question had concerned precepts in *the Law*. Jesus went further in his reply. "On these two commandments hang all the law *and the prophets*", said he, leaving them in no doubt as to how they ought to discharge their duty Godward (Matthew 22:37-40).

They will reverence My Son

It was by now time for Jesus to call a halt to this succession of inquisitions. The Pharisees had compelled him to prove his mettle; he would now put theirs also to the test. So, before they dispersed, "Jesus asked them, saying, What think ye of Christ? whose son is he?" There were in fact two answers to this question; the traditional one—"The Son of David"—which they gave him; and another which he himself had earlier given in the parable of the Wicked Husbandmen—"The son of God". Receiving the first, Jesus invited them indirectly to go on to add the second, by plying them with a problem: "He saith unto them, How then doth David in spirit call him Lord, saying, The LORD said unto my Lord, Sit thou on my right hand, till I make thine enemies thy footstool? If David then call him *Lord,* how is he his *son?*" (Matthew 22:41-45).

How the Evangelists—and Jesus himself—must have savoured the irony of the situation here! He was the "Lord" in question—"Lord", because, though sprung from David he was also sprung direct from God to whom David owed his very existence. He was at once "a rod out of the *stem* of Jesse", and, "a Branch out of his *roots*" (Isaiah 11:1); at once "the root" as well as "the offspring" of David (Revelation 22:16). And here was he in the midst of the very enemies who were destined to become his footstool— and they were sublimely unaware of the fact, as was proved by their inability to answer his question. "No man was able to answer him a word". Small wonder then, that "neither durst any man from that day forth ask him any more questions" (Matthew 22:46). Impotent to silence him any other way, they had but one means left of doing so—to kill him—or so they thought! For little did they appreciate that even death could not dispose of him, for it was written expressly of him, as David's Lord, "Thy people shall be willing in the day *of thy power*" (Psalm 110:3). Had they been wise therefore they would have kissed the Son (Psalm 2:12). Instead, they chose to slay him—and so to slay themselves!

JESUS—HEALER & TEACHER

11
OBEDIENT UNTO DEATH

The Saviour slain

BEING in a literary category of their own the gospels have of necessity to be judged by special standards, yet even when tested by the accepted canons of literary and dramatic criticism they are found to be artistic productions of the highest order. The action in each moves steadily toward a tremendous climax, with Jesus, the ultimate victim of his enemies' demented hatred, proving himself master of the situation at every turn, even, as we shall see, when actually about to breathe his last. With steadfast courage and serene resignation he proceeds toward what he knows to be certain doom, his every action deliberate and calmly premeditated. "It came to pass, when the time was come that he should be received up, he steadfastly set his face to go to Jerusalem" (Luke 9:51).

Journeying toward Jerusalem
The signal for the commencement of this momentous journey southwards to the Holy City was undoubtedly the Transfiguration. Luke certainly seems to make it the starting point, and from this stage onwards he punctuates his record with references to the steady progress of this journey by Jesus. The meeting with "a certain man" who said, "Lord, I will follow thee whithersoever thou goest", took place "as they went in the way", and the realization that the sands of time were now running out quickly for Jesus, helps to explain why his demands upon would-be disciples, and his handling of the faint and half-hearted, were so imperative (Luke 9:57-62). This was no time for prevarication or delay: the need was desperately urgent.

The nature of that need is exemplified in the commissioning of the Seventy. A period of intense activity lay immediately ahead for Jesus before those "days" came when the Bridegroom should be taken away. He sent the Seventy "two and two before his face into every city and place, whither he himself would come" (Luke 10:1). A good while before he had sent out the Twelve with a more independent mission, but one no less urgent even though they had more time available for the execution of it. Persecution was in fact to hasten them, to some extent conveniently, from city to city, ensuring that no one place would detain them too long from fulfilling their appointed task of witness and of calling men to repentance. "When they persecute you in this city", said Jesus, "flee ye into another: for verily I say unto you, Ye shall not have gone over the cities of Israel, till the Son of man be come" (Matthew 10:23). Here he had clearly in mind some solemn "coming"—some final visitation in person—to these same cities. It would seem that what Luke has to say as to the purpose of the work deputed to the Seventy helps us to identify this visitation.

The time assigned to each pair of workers could not have been long, and it would appear that they reassembled at one point on a given date to give Jesus a report of their work and the reception accorded to them (Luke 10:17). He in the meantime was probably travelling (virtually incognito) to visit and instruct his scattered sheep in Galilee, but his ultimate destination was still Jerusalem, and within a brief period he was consolidating the work of the Twelve and Seventy, going "through the cities and villages, teaching, and journeying toward Jerusalem" (Luke 13:22). We can almost sense an even greater stress than usual being laid by him at this time on the need for repentance. It was during this stage of the ministry that he warned the people at large, "Ye hypocrites, ye can discern the face of the sky and of the earth; but how is it that ye do not discern *this time?*" (Luke 12:56). This, we can be sure, was a sentiment which he would often express at this particular "time", and the report brought to him of the slaughter by Pilate of certain devout Galilæans, and of the casualties caused by the collapse of the tower of Siloam in Jerusalem, served his purpose well as striking object lessons in the need for spiritual preparedness (Luke 13:1-5).

That very theme—the need for spiritual preparedness—
is in fact the dominant topic of the middle chapters of
Luke's Gospel. The long discourse which goes to make up
the bulk of his twelfth chapter (doubtless a sample of
Jesus' instruction of his "little flock" at this critical time)
culminates in the call "Sell that ye have, and give alms;
provide yourselves bags which wax not old, *a treasure in
the heavens* that faileth not, where no thief approacheth,
neither moth corrupteth. For where your treasure is, there
will your heart be also" (Luke 12:33,34).

This call, we note, was meant to drive home a significant
promise—"Fear not, little flock; for it is your Father's good
pleasure to give you *the kingdom*" (verse 32). Fear implied
danger, and cause for dismay—and indeed there was more
than enough of these at the time! But to offset all discour-
agements, for him no less than for his sheep, was the
prospect of the Kingdom. That was (and still is) the
unchanging factor in an insecure and changing world; it
was a joy set before him and them to sustain and fortify
them in whatever ordeal and hardship loyalty to God
might bring to them. So, not unnaturally, Jesus moved forward in thought to the day of the eventual coming of the
Kingdom—and with the same consistent emphasis on the
need for preparedness. "Let your loins be girded about,"
said he, stressing the need for wakeful preparedness for
the great event to come. "And ye yourselves like unto men
that wait for their lord, when he will return from the wedding; that when he cometh and knocketh, they may open
unto him immediately" (Luke 12:35,36).

In those days wedding festivities were protracted. No
one was to know exactly on which day the absent bridegroom would return. But come he would, and faithful servants would not be taken unawares, even if his advent
were to take place far into the night. When he knocked
they would be ready to answer. "Blessed are those servants", then, said Jesus, "whom the lord when he cometh
shall find watching: verily I say unto you, that he shall
gird himself, and make them to sit down to meat, and will
come forth and serve them" (verse 37). Here was a gracious promise indeed, and one which Jesus could well

make, for in the case of the faithful his second advent would confirm the benefits of the first. He came then "to minister"—to die, that they might be forgiven; but he will also come again, to minister life more abundantly to them, so that he will, in that sense, once more "serve" them even though he is their Lord. Thus, "if he shall come in the second watch, or come in the third watch, and find them so, blessed are those servants" (verse 38).

But some had already failed to be watching when they should have been! Already he had "come" once—come to a people unprepared, for only a minority had heeded John's preaching and constituted themselves there and then "a people *prepared* for the Lord" (Luke 1:17). It was for that very reason that it was necessary for him to rebuke the majority of the Jews for their blindness to the signs of those very times. So, in parable, he went on to point out their failure to his disciples and make an object lesson of it. "And this know, that if the goodman of the house had known what hour the thief would come, he would have watched, and not have suffered his house to be broken through". The thief here, then, was himself: the goodman of the house symbolized those spiritual leaders against whose hypocrisy he had begun by warning his followers (Luke 12:1); the breaking through of the house spelt the dissolution of the old order, and the destruction of the Jewish state. Such were the sad consequences of his first, and generally unrecognized, advent. Would his second coming correspondingly catch his own elect unprepared? Let the past failure of others be a warning to them—"Be ye therefore ready also: for the Son of man cometh at an hour when ye think not" (verse 40).

Peter sensed that the expressive figure used by Jesus—based perhaps on a recent well-known burglary—was a parable of wider bearing than usual. So he put to Jesus the question, "Lord, speakest thou this parable unto us, or even to all?" Jesus' detailed but enigmatic reply seems to signify that it actually embraced both "us" and "all", for his coming was to have a significance for the world as well as for the saints!

First Jesus dealt with the "us". "The Lord said, Who then is that faithful and wise steward, whom his lord shall make ruler over his household, to give them their portion of meat in due season?" The figure was different—and deliberately different. Jesus has moved forward in thought to the time when he as "lord" would apportion the administration of his "household" (that is, the Kingdom) to those who were in the meantime his stewards. "Blessed", said he again, "is that servant, whom his lord when he cometh shall find so doing. Of a truth I say unto you, that he will make him ruler over all that he hath". This was characteristic teaching on the part of Jesus. Men will be what they are: those only will minister salvation to the world in the age to come ("meat in due season") who minister it now by faithfully girding up their loins and seeing that their lights are burning. As for those who fail in their duty, even they themselves will be denied a share in that "meat"; there will be no salvation for them, "But and if that servant say in his heart, My lord delayeth his coming; and shall begin to beat the menservants and maidens, and to eat and drink, and to be drunken; the lord of that servant will come in a day when he looketh not for him, and at an hour when he is not aware, and will cut him in sunder, and will appoint him his portion with the unbelievers" (verses 42-46).

So much for believers—good and bad. Jesus next went on to deal with the "all", for his coming will be of vital moment to all others who are alive when he returns. When he comes again millions will have heard of him and acquired fair knowledge of his teaching, while others will be ignorant of him. But both divisions of mankind are nonetheless accountable to him as Lord, and upon both, reformative chastisement will be visited: "That servant, which knew his lord's will, and prepared not himself, neither did according to his will, shall be beaten with many stripes. But he that knew not, and did commit things worthy of stripes, shall be beaten with few stripes." To this ominous statement Jesus appended a moral explanation, "For unto whomsoever much is given, of him shall much be required: and to whom men have committed much, of him they will ask the more" (verses 47,48). The explanation is enlightening. As with men, so with God: where He has "given" He expects a due return. He gave open-handedly to Israel, but because they proved to be only a disobedient and gainsaying people, their society came to ruin, in early vindication of Jesus' warning. The same will happen yet again (and, in a sense, is happening constantly). The civilized races bear a heavy responsibility to God for their culture is permeated with Christian teaching and traditions, yet for the most part they turn a blind eye to their moral accountability, vainly thinking that they escape from it just by ignoring it. Upon them will undoubtedly fall the heaviest cataclysms of the coming era of judgement; whereas the backward countries, who in a sense know not their lord's will, will (though seemingly only as an accident of history and of geography) suffer far less in the coming global conflict. Yet they too will suffer reformative judgement, for being men they are under the common obligation to do their lord's will even though they are in detail ignorant of it, for, as Paul showed, they too are "without excuse" (Romans 1:18-20).

Such a worldwide visitation of judgement and deserved punishment is an essential prelude to the establishment of the Kingdom upon earth, and will both herald and attend the advent of the King. So, if our understanding of the parable be correct, we find Jesus merely pursuing his thought to its logical end, when he goes on to add, "I am come to send fire on the earth; and what will I, if it be already kindled?" (Luke 12:49).

He beheld the city

Not long afterwards Jesus spoke another parable, this time to press home his stern warning to those alive at that time who would die before his second advent—"Except ye repent, ye shall all likewise perish". "A certain man", said he, "had a fig tree planted in his vineyard". The allegory was transparent. Was it not written of the vineyard—"It is the house of Israel"? and of the fig tree—"and the men of Judah (are) his (God's) pleasant plant"? In Isaiah's day God "looked for judgement, but behold oppression; for

240

righteousness, but behold a cry"(Isaiah 5:7). The state of affairs was no different in the days of Jesus. In his person and John's, God "came and sought fruit" on His fig tree, "and found none". Only one sequel then could there be: "Then said he unto the dresser of his vineyard, Behold, these three years I come seeking fruit on this fig tree, and find none: cut it down; why cumbereth it the ground?" The people would find in these words an echo of John's stern warning, "Now also the axe is laid unto the root of the trees: every tree therefore which bringeth not forth good fruit is hewn down, and cast into the fire" (Luke 3:9). Three years had passed since that warning had been given: and still it was being ignored by the nation at large. Jesus, in his parable, indicated that judgement ought to begin forthwith. What then was there to spare the city, at once holy and profane, whither he was bound? The parable once again gave the clue: his present period of intense activity gave Jerusalem—and with it, of course, the entire nation—a final chance. Like the dresser of the vineyard who pleaded with the owner, he in turn was pleading with God, "Lord, let it alone this year also, till I shall dig about it, and dung it: and if it bear fruit, well: and if not, then after that thou shalt cut it down" (Luke 13:6-9).

It is one of the sublimest samples of irony in the whole of the gospels that the fig tree was during this very year to prove itself fruitless, and thereby to seal its own doom, by sending Jesus himself to his death! A double drama slowly unfolded itself as he drew near to Jerusalem. What the city would do to him he would in due course have to do to the city. None but Jesus realized this at the time and there was a tragic pathos in the situation, when, toward the close of his procession southwards, "because he was nigh to Jerusalem ... they thought that the kingdom of God should immediately appear". This enthusiasm no doubt originated among his disciples, but a multitude was accompanying them and probably to some extent shared it. So another parable followed for the guidance of both sections of his retinue (Luke 19:11-27). His last words in their hearing, as he entered the house of Zacchaeus, had been, "The Son of man is come to seek and to save that which was lost" (verse 10). This momentous fact, though they little realized it, signified several things at once: Jesus would have to die; he would die simultaneously a rejected King and a life-giving Saviour; yet he would still one day come into his own as King and Judge, but not until some long future time; and meanwhile his disciples, possessing the salvation which he had died to procure for them, would be left to add a spiritual increase to it. All this Jesus contrived to compress into the compass of his parable, which began, "A certain nobleman went into a far country to receive for himself a kingdom, and to return. And he called his ten servants, and delivered them ten pounds, and said unto them, Occupy till I come. But his citizens hated him, and sent a message after him, saying, We will not have this man to reign over us".

The pounds, one to each servant, clearly symbolized the salvation which was the common gift made to all his disciples. While the servants awaited the nobleman's return, their duty was "to gain by trading". The nobleman's calling of them to him on his return was therefore a figure of Jesus' judgement of his disciples (to see if they had grown in grace and to reward them accordingly) and of his punishment of the spiritually barren among them—"For I say unto you, That unto every one which hath shall be given; and from him that hath not, even that he hath shall be taken away from him". Here were ominous words indeed: the spiritually undeveloped disciple (he "that hath not") would lose the life won for him by his Saviour's death ("that (which) he hath").

Now in his possession of this "pound" the "servant" stood apart from others—the "citizens"—for they were not disciples. That is, the present gift of life is not for all, but only for the man who *believes*, though the fact that it is his present possession is no guarantee that it will not be "taken from him" in the Day of Judgement! Only by adding a faithful life to it can he retain it. What then of those who deliberately reject the King's authority over them—the rebellious citizens? The disciples' Day of Judgement will be theirs also—"Those mine enemies, which would not that I should reign over them, bring hither, and slay them before me". These were ominous words, too—at once an urgent reminder to the undecided of the need to recognize and serve Jesus as King, and also a prophecy of the punishment which would assuredly be visited on the city, which would shortly reject and crucify him.

"And when he had thus spoken, he went before, ascending up to Jerusalem" (Luke 19:28). The Triumphal Entry into Jerusalem followed, with all that that signified. The Cleansing of the Temple took place not the same day, however, but the next; Mark making it clear that this was not an impetuous but a carefully premeditated action (Mark 11:11,15-17). And to that next day belonged one other momentous act. The year of intense activity was now, alas, over—and the needed repentance had not been forthcoming. The "citizens" had in effect said, "We will not have this man to reign over us". So the Fig Tree was doomed. What is more, a fig tree stood conveniently to hand to serve as a visible parable of the fact! As Jesus walked in from Bethany on this fateful morrow he espied in the distance a fig tree laden with leaves. Since fruit precedes leaves on the fig, Jesus had every right to find fruit on it. But the tree aptly symbolized the nation, for despite such promise of fruit by the tree, he found it was barren: profession was belied by practice. So the curse was inevitable and well justified, even though "the time of figs was not yet"—"No man eat fruit of thee hereafter for ever" (verses 12-14).

Luke omits this incident, but he conveniently recounts the sequel to it which so beautifully complements the parable of the Fig Tree in the Vineyard which he alone provides. He says, "When Jesus was come near, he beheld the city, and wept over it, saying, If thou hadst known, even thou, at least in this thy day, the things which belong unto thy peace! but now they are hid from thine eyes". The city's blindness to its peace explained why he had shortly before cursed the barren fig tree. And as the tree was even then withering, so now he went on to predict the city's certain doom, "For the days shall come upon thee, that thine enemies shall cast a trench about thee, and compass thee round, and keep thee in on every side, and shall lay thee even with the ground, and thy children within thee;

and they shall not leave in thee one stone upon another; because thou knewest not the time of thy visitation" (Luke 19:41-44). He had indeed come upon the Goodman unawares, and his house was unhappily to be broken through.

Jesus drove this home upon the Pharisees and rulers as they hotly engaged him in controversy and he turned their craftiness back upon themselves. He first confuted and confounded them with the parable of the Wicked Husbandmen to show them, as we have seen, how they had failed to recognize the time of their visitation. But he did not stop short there. A further parable followed—full of omen. It was once again the Son who spoke: "The kingdom of heaven," said he, "is like unto a certain king, which made a marriage for his son, and sent forth his servants to call them that were bidden to the wedding". According to Oriental practice, to accept an initial invitation to a feast was to commit oneself to respond to the final notice of it. Israel had consented to be "bidden". But when, as had happened, servants had been sent to them with the confirmation of the original invitation, "they would not come". This, for the Oriental, was an insult to the host, yet their divine Lord had overlooked this and at once sent forth other servants. But again they "made light of it, and went their ways, one to his farm, another to his merchandise", with typical perversity putting the things of this life before those of the next. "And the remnant took his servants, and entreated them spitefully, and slew them". Once again there was no mistaking Jesus' meaning, and once again he gave heavy tidings of certain Judgement—"When the king heard thereof, he was wroth: and he sent forth his armies, and destroyed those murderers, and burned up their city" (Matthew 22:1-7).

This prediction was much more circumstantial than that at the close of the parable of the Wicked Husbandmen. It portended the ruin of Jerusalem amid fire and sword. And that put beyond a shadow of doubt the dissolution of the Jewish State, and the cessation of Israel's special privileges, of which he had just been warning the leaders. So once again he parabolically predicted the call of the

Gentiles. The King's servants went out once more at his bidding, this time into the highways, and gathered together all as many as they found, both bad and good": and thus "the wedding was furnished with guests" (verses 8-10).

From one point of view the parable was complete at this juncture. But from another it lacked artistic unity, for the rejection of the first guests was because they were "not worthy", and it needed stressing that the second invitation also came from the King, whose will was sovereign and could not be flouted. So Jesus next portrayed the treatment of one among the second company of guests who, accepting the invitation (and so also the obligations which went with it) had the effrontery to present himself at the wedding without a wedding garment. This man, no less than the others whom he had helped to replace, was "not worthy". He, therefore, also received the punishment which he deserved. To his underservants the King said, "Bind him hand and foot, and take him away, and cast him into outer darkness". "There shall be weeping and gnashing of teeth", added Jesus, by way of explanation, "for many are called, but few are chosen" (verses 11-14). That is, grace brings responsibilities in its train, and "few", alas, will in the end be found to have honoured those responsibilities. For the "many", here represented by this one man, there will be nothing left but the outer darkness of eternal death. The judgement which eventually fell on wicked Jerusalem should thus be a warning to us all of the yet more dreadful fate which *could* befall us.

O Jerusalem, Jerusalem

How disconcerting must these sombre parables of Jesus have been to the enthusiastic multitude, who had thought the appearing of the Kingdom to be so near. And his actions were no less perplexing, for here indeed, in the events of one crowded week, was the grand climax of the Ministry, and of its last strenuous year in particular. Small wonder therefore that to that one week all the Evangelists assigned so much space in their respective gospels. Their problem was so to arrange its many dramatic incidents that the essential tragedy of them all was thrown into the clearest relief. Each, as we can now see, in his own inimitable way succeeded under Spirit guidance in solving this problem to perfection. And with Matthew's help in particular (for he more than the others has recorded what Jesus had to say during these momentous days) we can now round off our study of that double drama which we have seen steadily unfolding itself throughout the Ministry.

Having foretold in such transparent allegory the ruin of the city, and reduced his cleverest foes to silence, Jesus resolved that he would make his famous day of questions the last on which he would appear in the Temple. But he would not leave it without first denouncing his enemies to their face. "Then spake Jesus to the multitude, and to his disciples, saying, The scribes and the Pharisees sit in Moses' seat: all therefore whatsoever they bid you observe, that observe and do; but do not ye after their works: for they say, and do not" (Matthew 23:1-3). There followed a discourse full of withering satire (verses 4-33), inspired doubtless by Isaiah's precedent, for Isaiah's parable of the Vineyard (Isaiah 5:1-7) had likewise been followed by a succession of woes upon the ungodly (verses 8-25), ending in a sombre warning of certain disaster (verses 26-30). Jesus' discourse culminated in a detailed prediction of the savage treatment which would be meted out against his own emissaries. But, he being who he was, such savagery would not—could not—go unpunished, so he warned the offenders that upon them would "come all the righteous blood shed upon the earth" from the first martyrdom of the Old Testament historical Scriptures to the last, "Verily I say unto you, All these things shall come upon this generation" (Matthew 23:34-36). Yet he could not help but be filled with tender remorse at the thought of the horror which the beloved Holy City would have in consequence to witness and endure. Once more he wistfully lamented, "O Jerusalem, Jerusalem, thou that killest the prophets, and stonest them which are sent unto thee, how often would I have gathered thy children together, even as a hen gathereth her chickens under her wings, and ye would not!"

"Ye would not! ..." Such was the sorry verdict which he had to pronounce on his Ministry. So, dramatically, he brought it to a close forthwith, sounding the city's doom, and with it the doom of the Temple, in a few curt words. "Behold, your house is left unto you desolate". But did that spell the falsification of all the nation's longings, and the repudiation of those acclamations which he had inspired but shortly before? By no means. His first coming was about to end—in death, and so in the ruin of the city; but the second would inevitably follow. So he added—grimly, yet none the less buoyantly—"For I say unto you, Ye shall not see me henceforth, till ye shall say, Blessed is he that cometh in the name of the Lord" (Matthew 23:37-39).

"And Jesus went out, and departed from the temple", adds Matthew dramatically. No more would he appear in its courts. The remaining days before the fateful Passover, when he would be done to death, were to be spent in seclusion, in calm preparation for the coming ordeal, and in loving instruction and preparation of his intimate disciples. It was necessary that they should be made to grasp the nature of the dangers—physical and spiritual—which would assail them in the interval between those days and the time of his eventual coming. And it was essential too that he should gird himself for the long agony of his arrest, trial and martyrdom.

The bridge of history

With Jesus at long last disengaged from the crowds, "his disciples came to him for to show him the buildings of the temple". There were, alas, more serious things to think of, and all they received by way of reply was, "See ye not all these things? verily I say unto you, There shall not be left here one stone upon another, that shall not be thrown down". He then doubtless left them, dumbfounded, to ruminate over that tragic prophecy, while he himself sought privacy on the Mount of Olives. There Peter, James, John and Andrew sought him out. Away across the Kidron the massive bulk of the Temple stood out against the rest of the Holy City. That this should all come to ruin—the prospect filled them with perplexity! So, anxiously, they turned to him, saying "Tell us, when shall these things be? and what shall be the sign of thy coming, and of the end of the world?"

They received their answer. In graphic terms Jesus bridged the gulf of time between those days and the time of his second coming. His was no system of faith detached from the processes of human history, nor can any "brand" of Christianity begin to be true which has no room in it for the slow development of a divine purpose which conditions and overrides the affairs of men and culminates in the establishment of the Kingdom of God as a visible and tangible institution upon earth.

First he impressed upon them that a prolonged period of international disturbance would ensue, and though many of the terrible events to come would actually happen in their lifetime and fill them with alarm, the end would still lie in the future, even though imposters tried to affirm otherwise (Matthew 24:1-8). Of more immediate concern to them was the impact of these events upon themselves and their fellow believers. Persecution and martyrdom awaited them, which would induce some to renounce the faith, and with it their salvation; but patient endurance "to the end" would ensure the salvation of all the faithful. Not until the Gospel had been preached through every land, "for a witness unto all nations" would the final "end" come (verses 9-14). To the destruction of the Temple and Jewish State they had therefore to resign themselves, determining not to be misled either into becoming embroiled in the conflict of those times, or into being persuaded that he had at last returned (verses 15-26; cf. Luke 21:20-24). When the time arrived for him to come there would be no mistaking the fact (Matthew 24:27-28). He then proceeded to restate what they had heard him say before about the ultimate time of calamity (Luke 17:26-37), and to remind them how cataclysmic that would be: "Immediately after the tribulation of those (i.e. the last) days shall the sun be darkened, and the moon shall not give her light, and the stars shall fall from heaven, and the powers of the heavens shall be shaken: and then shall appear the sign of the Son of man in heaven: and then shall all the tribes of the earth mourn, and they shall see the Son of man coming in the clouds of heaven with power and great glory. And he shall send his angels with a great sound of a trumpet, and they shall gather together his elect from the four winds, from one end of heaven to the other" (Matthew 24:29-31).

Here at once was his answer to the questions, "What shall be the sign of thy coming? and of the end of the world?" In language which was intelligible to this small company of unlettered men, reclining in the calm of a spring day on a quiet hillside tucked away in a remote corner of the great Roman Empire, he divulged great and mysterious secrets, assuring them that when the earth was ripe for divine intervention, God would immediately put in the sickle, "because the harvest is come" (Mark 4:29). Jerusalem would once again be the cockpit of world politics (Luke 21:24)—as was natural, for he was the King, and Jerusalem his city (Matthew 5:35). The Fig Tree would once more bud in anticipation of the coming summer, and at long last the Kingdom would be "even at the doors" (Matthew 24:32,33).

Watch therefore!

When Jesus had ended this private discourse on the long vista of future history, it was still necessary for him to add, "But of that day and hour knoweth no man, no, not the angels of heaven, but my Father only". His caution had thus still to be, "Watch therefore: for ye know not what hour your Lord doth come" (Matthew 24:36,42). That he should speak of himself in this detached way must have produced a strange effect on his four disciples. It must have sounded as though this "Lord" whom they were expectantly to await would be some other person. And in a sense he would be, even though he would in actual fact be the same individual, for he who then spoke to them was shortly to enter on a new plane of existence—to be "as a man *taking a far journey*, who left his house, and gave authority to his servants, and to every man his work, and commanded the porter to watch" (Mark 13:34). And when he came it would inevitably be to test and judge his servants on the basis of their conduct in his absence. So too great an emphasis could not be laid by Jesus upon the need for wakefulness, watchfulness, preparedness. The true servant would be one who was both "faithful and wise", and so qualify to become a ruler with the King (Matthew 24:45-47). Conversely, the neglectful and drunken servant would be caught unawares and be cut asunder when his Judge came (verses 48-51).

Jesus, we note, did not now, as earlier, proceed to talk also of those two other classes of servant—the one who "knew his lord's will, and prepared not himself", and the one who "knew not, and did commit things worthy of stripes" (Luke 12:47-48). They, presumably, were not relevant object lessons to believers—for it was to, and of, believers only that Jesus spoke in his parables on the Mount of Olives. Instead, therefore, he gave two further allegories to stress the need for watchfulness. The first, that of the Ten Virgins, showed how disciples could either be wise or unwise; the second told them the eternal consequences of being either faithful or unfaithful, so that both together illustrated and drove home what Jesus had just had to say about the servant who was both "wise" and "faithful" (Matthew 25:1-30; 24:45). He only is wise who has acquired spiritual resources in preparation for the day of the Son of man's coming, like the Virgins who had oil in their lamps; and he only is faithful who has put his spiritual endowments to practical use, like those who traded with their talents.

Then, last of all, Jesus gave his disciples a glimpse of the ultimate Judgement, portraying himself as King of all the earth, granting the Kingdom and life eternal to those who were worthy of them, and assigning the unrighteous to "everlasting punishment" (Matthew 25:31-46). What a glorious challenging climax was this to all his parables! Not only was it a final epiphany of himself as the ultimate Judge; it also stood in majestic contrast to all the shame, spitting and cruel maltreatment to which he was shortly to be subjected by judges who were not worthy of the name. He, the King of the world, was to be done to death by the world! Never was there starker irony than this. And he alone knew it—then. It was, in fact, to cushion his disciples against the shock of what was soon to happen that he had recounted so many parables anticipating both his departure and subsequent advent in glory. As the shadow of the Cross crept over the Ministry, so, too, thanks to these parables, did the sunshine of the coming Day. But that made the prospect of the Cross no less a horror, or the suffering of it no less a certainty.

The King betrayed

Ever since the sojourn near Cæsarea Philippi Jesus had been progressively revealing to his disciples what would befall him at Jerusalem. Now, in this brief lull, his active Ministry at last concluded, he released the last item of information—the actual date of his crucifixion. Both in plain word and in parable he had foretold his departure, hinted that they would be left to labour without his bodily presence with them, and impressed upon them the significance for themselves of his ultimate advent in power and great glory. Henceforth, in the remaining hours of his earthly life, its tragic end was perforce to fill his thoughts —and ought to fill theirs also. As Matthew has it, "It came to pass, when Jesus had finished all these sayings, he said unto his disciples, Ye know that *after two days* is the feast of the passover, and the Son of man is betrayed to be crucified" (Matthew 26:1,2). This precise prediction revealed that he was aware of something which was proceeding unknown to every one else. He knew that his foes were in solemn conclave, scheming how "they might take him by subtilty, and kill him". He had temporarily (as they thought) withdrawn from the Temple porticoes. Should he reappear there, they knew they would be powerless as hitherto to arrest him amid the multitudes of those who so revered him for his grace and wisdom. So it had to be "by subtilty", and certainly "not on the feast day, lest there be an uproar among the people" (verses 3-5). But Jesus knew too that there was one who had sold himself to serve their fiendish ends, to divulge where and when he could be arrested far from the multitudes, and hastily condemned and despatched before ever the matter came to the ears of all but a small section of the populace. That certain one knew that Jesus was now spending his time in the quiet

retreat of a garden on the side of the Mount of Olives, that
no longer was he travelling in each morning from Bethany
and returning thence in the evening, as earlier in the
week, accompanied by excited crowds: he could now be
apprehended with convenient ease if only his enemies
knew.

Judas had already purposed that they should know—
and it was of this that Jesus was aware. The resolve had
entered Judas' heart at Bethany. There he had seen Jesus
anointed by a woman with precious ointment. In the eyes
of the disciples this had been a senseless and wasteful act,
and they had protested, "This ointment might have been
sold for much, and given to the poor". But Jesus had
rebuked them, saying, "Why trouble ye the woman? for she
hath wrought a good work upon me. For ye have the poor
always with you ..." Then came those chilling words—"but
me ye have not always. For in that she hath poured this
ointment on my body, she did it for my burial". They were
grieved at the loss of mere money, but she at the prospect
of losing her dear Lord! So Jesus added weightily, "Verily I
say unto you, Wheresoever this gospel shall be preached in
the whole world, there shall also this, that this woman
hath done, be told for a memorial of her" (Matthew 26:6-
13).

"Then", says Matthew dramatically (and one can almost
catch him emitting a gasp of astonishment as he says it),
"Then one of the twelve, called Judas Iscariot, went unto
the chief priests, and said unto them, What will ye give
me, and I will deliver him unto you? And they covenanted
with him for thirty pieces of silver" (verses 14,15). Luke
passes his sentence on this heinous act, not like Matthew
and Mark (14:3-11) by juxtaposing it with the gracious
deed of mercy by the woman, but by declaring instead that
"Satan entered into Judas" (Luke 22:3,4)! The jubilation of
the Jewish leaders can easily be imagined. To receive an
ally from so unexpected a quarter, both willing and able to
furnish them with just the information which they most
desperately needed! Nothing could delight them more.
"They were glad", as Luke laconically puts it, "and
covenanted to give him money. And he promised, and

sought opportunity to betray him unto them *in the absence of the multitude*" (verses 5,6).

The farewell feast

Thus it came about that while Judas schemed, Jesus prepared the rest of his disciples for the shock to come. The last day duly arrived, as was by now inevitable. As the hours spent themselves his enemies laid their careful plans. Finally the last fateful hour approached, and with majestic calm Jesus assembled his disciples to take his leave of them—Judas included, ironically, for he could not honour his foul and dishonourable contract except by spying on Jesus' movements to the last. As Luke so simply yet so effectively puts it, "*When the hour was come*, he sat down, and the twelve apostles with him. And he said unto them, With desire I have desired to eat this passover with you before I suffer: for I say unto you, I will not any more eat thereof, until it be fulfilled in the kingdom of God" (Luke 22:14-16).

Never was an occasion more solemn. The shame and the glory were once more in the forefront of Jesus' thoughts. But between the two lay for him an interlude of absence and for them long weary years of waiting. He would therefore give them—and all others after them—an unforgettable memento of the shame while they awaited the coming of the Day of glory. "As they were eating, Jesus took bread, and blessed it, and brake it, and gave it to the disciples, and said, Take, eat; this is my body. And he took the cup, and gave thanks, and gave it to them, saying, Drink ye all of it; for this is my blood of the new testament (covenant), which is shed for many for the remission of sins" (Matthew 26:26-28).

The words which Jesus here used were rich in Old Testament allusion. Indeed it is clear from his every phrase that all that was testified of him in Scripture now crowded in upon his thoughts. He saw Judas as that perfidious one—"even he that eateth with me"—whose evil deed was published in advance by the inspired Psalmist (Psalm 41:9; Mark 14:18 RV). He was led thereby to warn the betrayer of the dread consequences of his crime, even while stressing, "The Son of man indeed goeth, as it is written of him" (Mark 14:21)—"as it was determined" (Luke 22:22). He foresaw the defection of even these, his intimate associates. As he shortly afterwards walked with them to his quiet retreat on the Mount of Olives (Mark 14:26), he told them, "All ye shall be offended because of me this night: for it is written, I will smite the shepherd, and the sheep shall be scattered" (verse 27). It was also on the strength of this prophecy that Jesus, while still in the Upper Room, had told the self-confident Peter, "I have prayed for thee, that thy faith fail not: and when thou art converted, strengthen thy brethren" (Luke 22:32), and even now again in the Garden he had to tell him, "Verily I say unto thee, That this day, even in this night, before the cock crow twice, thou shalt deny me thrice" (Mark 14:30; cf. Luke 22:33,34). Small wonder that he had in the first place sent his disciples into Jerusalem to reserve the Upper Room, instructing them to tell the owner of the house, "The Master saith, *My time* is at hand" (Matthew 26:18). It was indeed "at hand", and in the Garden of Gethsemane was to be even nearer,"For I say unto you," said he, as they had started off for the Garden, "that this that is written must yet be accomplished in me, And he was reckoned among the transgressors". "For", he added, "the things concerning me have an end" (i.e. are being fulfilled) (Luke 22:37).

Gethsemane

Thus, with the composure that his penetrating insight into the meaning both of Scripture and of his own mission gave him, he went, as by now "he was wont", to the Mount of Olives. "And his disciples also followed him" (verse 39). All but one! for Judas had gone his way. Soon he would be back, and the harrowing ordeal, toward which Jesus' whole life—and with it, his entire Ministry—had been inexorably tending, would have begun. Then darkness such as he had never known before would come upon him, for he who had never sinned would come to be "reckoned with transgressors"— "reckoned" with them, not merely by chancing to experience death in their company (or even in the form normally reserved for the worst of them), but in some deeper sense which would bring him into direct contact with their sin, as before he had so often come into direct contact with their sickness. Long had he known that this *had* to be, but to shrink from it—not from the torture of the stake but from the experience in his own person of a desolation from which he had hitherto been totally exempt—was natural in one so holy. As the minutes of waiting slowly passed, and his predetermined bearing of those iniquities drew nearer, his spirit groaned under the suspense of the wait. He sought strength in prayer and in the company and fellowship of those three whose unique privilege it was to witness his Transfiguration in glory— Peter, James and John (Matthew 26:36,37). Yet, though he told them, "My soul is exceeding sorrowful, even unto death; tarry ye here, and watch with me", they failed him in his need. With fervent prayer he besought his Father, "O my Father, if it be possible, let this cup pass from me". No protests or complainings were there here, but only a respectful and submissive expression of his feelings and preferences as a man—hence his pledge of utter willingness to obey, "Nevertheless not as I will, but as thou wilt" (verses 38,39). Coming back to his disciples he was dismayed to find them sleeping. They, the King's attendants, asleep on duty! "Watch! said he, "and pray". Why? His own ordeal gave the reason—"that ye enter not into temptation". Nor was this all; speaking directly out of his own experience at that very time he added, pathetically— "the spirit indeed is willing, but the flesh is weak" (verses 40,41).

He could, indeed, never have qualified to bear men's sins had this—"the flesh is weak"—not been true of him so much as of them. He, no less than they, had to contend with its native unreadiness to do the will of God. But in that contention he always gained the mastery. And he did so here, for "He went away again the second time, and prayed, saying, O my Father, if this cup may not pass away from me, except I drink it, thy will be done". The change of emphasis was significant. Mild though the plea, "If it be possible" had been, it fell far short of the gentle

resignation of, "If this cup may not pass away from me ..."
And with the same resignation he reavowed his ready
acceptance of the bitter cup which he had perforce to
drink, by praying a third time, "saying the same words"
(verses 42-44). What these words cost him, however, can be
gauged by the fact that he sweat as it were great drops of
blood even though an angel had been sent to succour him
(Luke 22:43,44). Thus Jesus endured the remaining suspense calmly bidding his disciples to rest now, while they
had opportunity, for soon their slumber would be rudely
disturbed—and with perfect composure (now that he was
utterly resigned to the unique ordeal before him) he told
them why—"Behold, the hour is at hand, and the Son of
man is betrayed *into the hands of sinners*" (Matthew
26:45).

Soon the gleam of torches lit up the darkness in the distance, and the sound of tramping feet broke the calm of the
Garden. Jesus responded at once; "Rise, let us be going",
said he; "behold, he is at hand that doth betray me". And
before Judas could reach his Master's retreat Jesus himself had rejoined his disciples and was ready to greet his
betrayer upon his arrival (verse 46). There a rash disciple,
albeit unwittingly, translated Jesus' earlier human longing—"If it be possible"—into wrongful action, by drawing a
sword in his defence, but with the strength which his vigil
of prayer had brought to him. Jesus rebuked him. Angelic
aid in abundance was his for the asking, "But how then
shall the scriptures be fulfilled, that thus it *must* be?"
(verses 51-54). Knowing this, Jesus then faced the cowardly multitudes with regal calm, master of the situation to
the last. But "all the disciples forsook him, and fled"!

The guiltless condemned

For Jesus' foes, time was too pressing for legal niceties to
be observed. The appropriate members of the Sanhedrin
were all ready to respond at a moment's notice to the summons to meet, and were all mustered and waiting, though
it was far into the night, when Jesus was led in before
Caiaphas the High Priest. Far from there being witnesses
prepared to lay their charges against the prisoner as both

law and custom demanded, such witnesses had instead to be sought! But in no two cases, even so, was their testimony found to correspond. So Jesus met the flagrant illegality of the whole proceedings with silence, not deigning to sanction it even by rebutting the falsest of charges (Matthew 26:57-61; Mark 14:53-59). But his composure exasperated his foes and at last, in desperation, Caiaphas, contrary to every principle of Jewish justice, placed the onus of witness on the accused! "Answerest thou nothing? what is it which these witness against thee?" Once more, however, "Jesus held his peace", until this wicked judge could contain himself no longer, and called upon him to swear on oath, saying, "I adjure thee by the living God, that thou tell us whether thou be the Christ, the Son of God". The answer came, with meekness, yet with becoming dignity, "Thou hast said: nevertheless I say unto you, Hereafter shall ye see the Son of man sitting on the right hand of power, and coming in the clouds of heaven" (Matthew 26:62-64).

Here the irony of the gospels begins to build up to its most intense pitch. The answer was true—gloriously true. But all Caiaphas did was rend his clothes in horror, saying, "He hath spoken *blasphemy*; what further need have we of witnesses? behold, now ye have heard his blasphemy. What think ye?" All in concert answered, "He is guilty of death". Spitting and blows and taunts were aimed at the unresisting captive during the period of waiting for day to dawn, and even the defection of his own dear disciple Peter took place near enough for him to witness it (Matthew 26:65-75), and even to pass sentence on it with that one withering pathetic look which shamed Peter into shedding the bitterest tears of remorse (Luke 22:61,62).

At long last dawn came. The sentence already passed was quickly endorsed by the full Council and Jesus was hurried off to Pilate's court so that sentence of death might there be passed on him with the certainty that it could—and would—be carried into action. Now it was that the cunning of the night trial emerged undisguised, for Jesus had been made to confess that he was the Christ—the King of the Jews. For his malevolent and unprincipled foes this claim amounted to blasphemy deserving death; but even though they had not the authority to inflict that death, his claim still served their evil purpose excellently, since to Pilate it could be conveniently construed as an act of sedition against Cæsar.

Pilate, as it was Passover time, and so a time of danger to public security with so many zealous patriots all met together in one place, had, a few days before, left Cæsarea and taken up his quarters in Jerusalem. Herod Antipas, too, to maintain his pose of zeal for Judaism, and to curry favour with the people, had come to the Holy City to keep the feast. This was for Pilate a most convenient coincidence, for soon he found himself in dire straits. The prisoner assented to the charge of his foes that he had claimed to be the King of the Jews, but he silently ignored the false imputations which went with it, so much so that Pilate was moved to marvel (Matthew 27:11-14; Luke 23:1-3). He had seen political pretenders before, but never one like this man. They had been ferocious men of action, but here manifestly was no dangerous political extremist bent on destroying the Roman administration in those parts. So he frankly told Jesus' accusers, "I find no fault in this man". But they were certainly not going to let their prey slip out of their hands as a result of such a verdict, so, "They were the more fierce, saying, He stirreth up the people, teaching throughout all Jewry, beginning from Galilee to this place". Pilate was less inclined to check the truth of these outrageous lies when struck by that one word "Galilee". Here he saw hope of respite! "As soon as he knew that he belonged unto Herod's jurisdiction, he sent him to Herod" (Luke 23:4-7).

Herod was both flattered and delighted, but Jesus refused to recognize this wicked ruler's right to try him, and "answered him nothing", especially as thither, too, his implacable foes had pursued him. So Herod decided to recognize this man's claim to the Jewish throne in his own satirical way! He "with his men of war set him at nought, and mocked him, and arrayed him in a gorgeous robe". Here again, had the onlookers but realized the fact, the irony of the situation was terrific. Despite their raillery he was a King of the Jews indeed and ought to have been acclaimed not with ridicule but with sincerity and awe. So back he was sent to the luckless Pilate.

The procurator, finding himself once more on the horns of a dilemma, hit on a stratagem. He knew that it was merely petty jealousy for their own authority and vested interests which had inspired the clamour of his accusers. They refused to be fobbed off with a promise that Jesus should be whipped, so he decided instead to try to counter their malice by enlisting the sympathy of the inquisitive crowds outside. He offered these the opportunity of asking him to show clemency either to this inoffensive captive or to a dangerous terrorist Barabbas.

He had not reckoned, alas, with the ruthlessness of the chief priests. They soon mingled with the hesitant crowds and reminded them which of these prisoners had done most to further their national aspirations. So, to Pilate's dismay, the answer came, We want Barabbas! Nay more, so thoroughly had the priests done their insidious work, that when Pilate asked, "What shall I do then with Jesus which is called Christ? They all say unto him, Let him be crucified" (Matthew 27:15-22; Mark 15:6-14). It was useless for Pilate, who was by now filled with superstitious alarm by the news of his wife's dream about Jesus, to protest Jesus' innocence. Three times he tried to save his prisoner, but they (by now excited and insatiable) "were instant with loud voices, requiring that he might be crucified" (Luke 23:18-23).

The words which follow in Matthew's record are among the most awful to be found in Scripture. "When Pilate saw that he could prevail nothing, but that rather a tumult was made, he took water, and washed his hands before the multitude, saying, I am innocent of the blood of this just person: see ye to it". That was monstrous enough. But they in their frenzy shouted back, not knowing what a ghastly sentence they were pronouncing on themselves, "His blood be on us, and on our children". Finally, he "released Barabbas unto them: and when he had scourged Jesus, he delivered him to be crucified" (Matthew 27:24-26).

The crucified King

It was, we note, because Jesus claimed to be the King of
the Jews, that he was condemned by the Sanhedrin for
blasphemy; arraigned before Pilate and charged with
sedition; made the butt of Herod's and his soldiers' jests;
and finally sent off by Pilate to be crucified to satisfy a
menacing mob who had made themselves the tools of their
envious rulers and on their behalf had said, in effect, "We
will not have this man to reign over us". But, as though
that were not enough, before "the soldiers of the governor"
set off on their grizzly errand, they too "took Jesus into the
common hall, and gathered unto him the whole band of
soldiers. And they stripped him, and put on him a scarlet
robe. And when they had plaited a crown of thorns, they
put it upon his head, and a reed in his right hand: and
they bowed the knee before him, and mocked him, saying,
Hail, King of the Jews!" (Matthew 27:27-29). Finally as a
last cruel jest, having crucified him, they cast his claim to
kingship in his teeth, saying, "If thou be the king of the
Jews, save thyself"; and then to top it all, they placed a
superscription to his Cross, written moreover in three
languages altogether (Greek, Latin and Hebrew), "THIS IS
THE KING OF THE JEWS" (Luke 23:36-38). And to all this
abuse, Jesus' gracious answer was, "Father, forgive them;
for they know not what they do" (verse 34)!

Here was irony indeed—the most intense of all the irony
that is to be found in the gospels. If ever providence over-
ruled the whim and malice of men, surely it was here.
That Jesus should have endured such a death—such
shame, such degradation—for the Jews made utter nonsense of his claim; that fact alone settled for good and all
in their minds that he was not, could not be, the Christ.
Yet, irony of ironies, the superscription bore mute witness
to the fact that he was none other! It said, in effect (though
none intended that it should!), not that he could not be the
Christ because he so suffered, but that despite the fact
that he did so suffer—nay, in a sense *because* he did so suffer—he *was* the Christ indeed. No drama ever resolved
itself with such a disconcerting assertion of fact; fact to

which all gave their mock assent precisely because they thought it was not true!

Gloating over him, and jesting at the words inscribed above his head, the people and rulers, like the soldiers, "derided him, saying, He saved others; let him save himself, if he be Christ, the chosen of God". Even the thieves beside him cast the same in his teeth (Luke 23:35; Matthew 27:39-44). Little did any of them know that Jesus could, had he chosen, have thereupon done exactly what they thought he was incapable of doing. Little therefore did they realize that they were adding to the torture of the nails in his hands and feet the agony of the wilderness Temptation, and of the vigil in Gethsemane.

But one at last saw light—and he one of those same thieves who were crucified with him! The other thief in his torment had cried, "If thou be Christ, save thyself *and us*". "And us"—the man was concerned with his own ordeal to the exclusion of all else, and had made his agonized appeal not in hope but in contempt. At which the other rose to an unwonted height of faith. He recalled what the Sufferer was—a sinless man. So rebuking his comrade's madness, he said, "Dost not thou fear God, seeing thou art in the same condemnation? And we indeed justly; for we receive the due reward of our deeds: but this man hath done nothing amiss". Then filled with new-born conviction that the Sufferer beside him was indeed the Christ, was indeed capable of saving both himself and them, and would moreover in due time be willing to save them from death in a greater sense than ever occurred to his comrade, he turned to him and pleaded, "Lord, remember me when thou comest into thy kingdom".

What faith! What exquisite faith! To see a man in torment beside him, about to breathe his last, and still to acknowledge that man as his appointed Lord and King, perceiving at once the irony of his enemies' taunts and the truth of the inscription above his head! Small wonder that, sinner though he was, he made bold to plead, "Lord, remember me", and confessed his faith in the certainty of the ultimate coming of the long-awaited Kingdom by adding, "... when thou comest in thy kingdom".

His faith did not go unrewarded. There came the gracious answer—"Verily I say unto thee this day: With me shalt thou be in Paradise" (Luke 23:43) (Rotherham's version).* Always in Old Testament Scripture such a form of words as "I say unto thee this day" (cf. Deuteronomy 4:26,39; 8:19; etc.) was used to bring home with the utmost emphasis the solemnity of some great truth. This very Hebraism served the same purpose on this momentous occasion. What the penitent thief asked for, he received— an assurance that when the Son of man came in the glory of his Father with his angels, to reward every man according to his works, he himself would not be forgotten nor his faith despised. He, while the Saviour was yet suffering, had already accepted the salvation which his death was to bring to sinners; and in reward, to soothe his last hours of agony, he had the Saviour's own gracious reassurance—the King's own promise of free pardon—"Thou shalt be with me in Paradise". But the Saviour, too, in his own turn, had here in this man's penitence and unquenchable faith an earnest of that day when he would "see of the travail of his soul and would be satisfied". Thus were his own last hours soothed also, and though, as the darkness of death descended on him, he was constrained to cry, "My God, my God, why hast thou forsaken me?" yet it was with serene and kingly calm that he breathed his last, saying, "Father, into thy hands I commend my spirit" (Matthew 27:46; Luke 23:39-46).

---

* The grammar of the original Greek text gives full warrant for the English rendering of this verse. For detailed proof, see Bullinger's *Companion Bible* (p. 1505 of Commentary, and also Appendix 173).

12
EPILOGUE—THE LOVE OF CHRIST CONSTRAINETH US
Shining as lights in the world

HARD by the Cross stood a centurion whose grue-some duty it had been to supervise the execution of Jesus and the thieves who suffered beside him. By this stage in his military career he was doubtless inured to such spectacles of horror. Yet overcome by the unique pathos of this scene, and awed too by the earthquake which so terrifyingly rang down the curtain on it, this hard-bitten soldier was moved to cry, "Certainly this was a righteous man ... Truly this was the Son of God!" (Luke 23:47; Matthew 27:51-54).

Truth is in Jesus

Truer words were never spoken. This was a righteous man indeed, so righteous that even the grave, with its dread power, could not retain him. Jesus had breathed his last, comforted and sustained by the Psalmist's words, written long before concerning him, "My flesh also shall rest in hope. For thou wilt not leave my soul in hell; neither wilt thou suffer thine Holy One to see corruption" (Psalm 16:9,10). His confidence was not misplaced. Not many hours later, God raised him up, "having loosed the pains of death: because it was not possible that he should be holden of it" (Acts 2:24-27).

Had God not so acted, and Jesus not thus been proved to be indeed the Holy One, all his assurances to his disciples, so often and so confidently given, would have been no more than empty boasts and broken pledges. But on the other hand, the fact that his Resurrection so signally vindicated his repeated predictions of it, stamped all his deeds as having been wrought in God. It proved that he was all that he had claimed to be—the healer of sin and bringer of life, the ultimate arbiter, the very mouthpiece of God Himself. Not

263

in vain had he said, "He that receiveth me receiveth him that sent me", or claimed, "No man knoweth ... who the Father is, but the Son, and he to whom the Son will reveal him" (Matthew 10:40; Luke 10:22).

It is Jesus, then, and Jesus alone, whom men must accept as their Healer and Teacher. But he cannot be their Healer unless they first accept him unreservedly as their Teacher. "Unto him be hearkening", said the Divine Voice to the disciples on the Mount of Transfiguration (Luke 9:35, Rotherham), as already, centuries before, it had said to Moses, "I will raise them up a Prophet from among their brethren, like unto thee, and will put my words in his mouth; and he shall speak unto them all that I shall command him. And it shall come to pass, that whosoever will not hearken unto my words which he shall speak in my name, *I will require it of him*". (Deuteronomy 18:18,19).

Would that more saw things this way! but the majority, alas, show little or no inclination to heed what this Prophet had to say to them. Like "those by the way side", in the parable of the Sower, many no sooner hear the Word than "then cometh the devil, and taketh away the word out of their hearts, lest they should believe and be saved" (Luke 8:12). Tragic indeed is their indifference: they gain life now only to lose it for eternity.

Yet no less tragic is the folly of those who, claiming allegiance to Christ, and even professing him as their Healer, do not hesitate none the less to disregard his authority as Teacher. He, for example, honoured the Old Testament Scripture as the revelation of God's will, dependable in its smallest details, everywhere true and authoritative, a guide even to himself, the Spirit-endowed Messiah. Not so, many professed Christians: they despise the Old Testament as outmoded and unreliable, and make bold to flout its teaching and to accept only those parts of it which suit their own subjective fancy. Jesus also intimated uncompromisingly that men cease to exist at death, and perish utterly if they die in unbelief, but for all too long the bulk of Christendom has chosen instead to believe that man is born with an indestructible soul which goes on living after death. It was perfectly in keeping with his insistence on the mortality of sinful man that Jesus should also have believed and taught the doctrine of the Resurrection, but the majority of modern Christians either have too feeble a faith to believe it with him, or even have the presumption to deride the very notion. And, again, whereas Jesus foretold his ultimate coming in glory as undisputed King and final Judge of all the earth, few indeed of those who now claim him as their King believe that he will be their Judge, or accept robustly the doctrine of the Second Advent, far less make it the goal of their longings and a subject of their prayers. Some even cling still to the delusive hope (so subversive of his teaching) that the Kingdom of God will be set up on earth only as the outcome of a slow, progressive conversion of the world to Christianity. Most, too, this time in excess of zeal and reverence, claim for him a co-equality and co-eternity with the Father which are nowhere mentioned by Jesus himself, or by any of the sacred writers, for he ever acknowledged his dependence on, and subordination to, the Father, and it was not till well after the last New Testament Scripture was written that any one was either so rash, or so misinformed, as to designate him "God the Son".

The truth is, then, that from a relatively early date various false varieties of Christianity have come into existence, and by blinding men to the true facts have in time even come to rival the Christianity which was taught by Christ himself. Jesus, as the parable of the Tares is witness, foresaw from the outset that this would happen. As he said, it will not be until the divine "reapers" (the angels) are sent forth to gather up these "tares" (which in their first stages of growth were practically indistinguishable from the true seed) that the Christianity which is preserved for us in the gospels will receive world-wide recognition as the true faith, or that those who believe and obey it will shine forth as the sun in the Kingdom of their Father (Matthew 13:36-43). Meanwhile a host of counterfeit systems will continue to flourish and mislead those whose standard of judgement is not the Word of God but merely the testimony of men.

Faith that worketh

Let us be clear, however, as to what we mean when we speak of "the true faith". That term is more often than not used to distinguish a particular set of dogmas. This is indeed perfectly in order if those same dogmas faithfully set forth the doctrinal teaching of the Master. But since Jesus made that teaching the basis of his moral precepts also, so restricted a definition of "the true faith" is manifestly inadequate. That only can qualify to be described as "true Christianity" which is both a system of belief in harmony with the doctrinal assertions and presuppositions of Jesus, and also with them incorporates the moral teaching which Jesus everywhere predicated on them. Once more it must be stressed that, ultimately, the distinction commonly drawn between belief and conduct is artificial and misleading, for conduct is always some sort of belief in action. A few simple illustrations drawn from the gospels will help to make this clear, and enable us to rid our minds of the fallacy that "conduct" is of necessity an outward act. It may in fact take the form of an attitude of mind which vitally conditions outward acts.

It was this which Jesus sought to bring home to men in the Sermon on the Mount. Because, for example, the Law of Moses said, "Thou shalt not commit adultery", men all too readily concluded that they had observed this precept merely by abstaining from the actual physical act of adultery. But that, insisted Jesus, by no means followed. He declared, "I say unto you, That whosoever looketh on a woman to lust after her hath committed adultery with her already in his heart" (Matthew 5:27,28). That is, for Jesus, the wish was as bad as the deed, and as real a form of conduct as the very deed itself, and therefore subject to God's Judgement. In this, then, he did not modify the Law, but rather he enforced it with a terrible stringency. He in effect challenged men to act on their persuasion that all things are naked and open unto God—to be so convinced that He searches the heart and tries the reins that they shrink from displeasing Him as much by entertaining unlawful desires as by committing wrongful acts. In brief, Jesus called upon his disciples to be men and women of a

EPILOGUE: THE LOVE OF CHRIST CONSTRAINETH US

certain sort, performing what is right as the natural and spontaneous expression of their essential goodness, for, as he said, ultimately a man *does* what he *is*. Malice expressed, for example, is but the betrayal outwardly of malice cherished within, "for out of the abundance of the heart the mouth speaketh". It is this "abundance of the heart" which Jesus wants Christians to set aright, for it is the crucial criterion of their worth, and the actuating factor behind all they say and do, yes, even behind their hypocrisy on those occasions when the things they say and do are but an outward pose of goodness! "A good man out of the good treasure of the heart bringeth forth good things: and an evil man out of the evil treasure of the heart bringeth forth evil things" (Matthew 12:34,35). According to Jesus it is a law, not only of Nature in the wider sense, but also of a man's spiritual nature in particular, that "a good tree cannot bring forth evil fruit, neither can a corrupt tree bring forth good fruit". "Wherefore", said he of all pretenders and charlatans, "by their fruits ye shall know them" (Matthew 7:15-20). Then, as though that were not enough, he forthwith proceeded to show that it would be by these very same "fruits" that he himself would "know" them too in the Day of Judgement, for he added, "Not every one that saith unto me, Lord, Lord, shall enter into the kingdom of heaven; but he that doeth the will of my Father which is in heaven" (verse 21).

Jesus could not emphasize this profound moral truth too much, and it is significant that it is the theme of the last of all his parables, his final counsel in well-doing to those whom he was about to leave—to leave not only imminently through death, but also in a fuller sense when, a little later, he would go like a nobleman into a far country to receive for himself a Kingdom (Luke 19:12), or like a householder set off on a long journey after leaving his house, and giving authority to his servants, and *to every man his work*, and commanding the porter to watch (Mark 13:34). He told his disciples in this final parable that upon his return he would, as King of all the nations, set his sheep on his right hand and the goats on the left. "Then", said he, "shall the King say unto them on his right hand,

267

Come, ye blessed of my Father, inherit the Kingdom prepared for you from the foundation of the world". But strange to tell, these same would not have realized that they had done him service in the way that he declared they had! Nor, in contrast, would those on his left hand in turn be able to appreciate that they had failed to minister to him in his need when the opportunity had been theirs. "Then shall they also answer him, saying, Lord, when saw we thee an hungered, or athirst, or a stranger, or naked, or sick, or in prison, and did not minister unto thee? Then shall he answer them, saying, Verily I say unto you, Inasmuch as ye did it not to one of the least of these, ye did it not to me" (Matthew 25:31-45).

The essential stress of the parable is on the *unawareness* of both classes of disciple—unawareness of their wickedness in the one case and of their virtue in the other—and it is indeed ironical that so many should prosaically assume that the mere act of satisfying the physical needs of the hungry, the thirsty, the stranger, the naked, the sick and the imprisoned automatically ensures one a place among the sheep. To think thus is to miss the point of the parable. Its real lesson is that that virtue alone commends a man to God which is spontaneously performed, done out of the sheer joy of doing good. It is the lesson in another form of the parable of the Labourers in the Vineyard. The first-comers there worked to a contract. When the householder "had agreed" with these for "a penny a day" (generous payment this, let us note), they set to work in his vineyard. In due course they received what they alone had the right to expect—a penny. But others, engaged at the third, the sixth and the ninth hour respectively, consented to serve the householder not on contract, *but on trust*, relying on his assurance, "Whatsoever is right that shall ye receive". Lastly, at the very close of the day almost, yet others accepted his invitation to work, but they without even this assurance, so fully did they trust him! (See RV etc.). These last were paid first and received what had been promised to the contract-workers for a full day's work—a penny—for the householder as master of his own goods, accountable to no one, large-heartedly chose to requite their trust as well as their service. Against this the labourers engaged at the ninth, the sixth, and even the third hour, raised no complaint whatever. They were too content to accept the generosity of the householder toward themselves to protest against his munificence to others seemingly less deserving. But the commercially minded labourers, engaged at the beginning of the day, acting as self-appointed judges in their own interests, condemned the householder for not paying them an additional sum to which they by now considered his generosity to others to have entitled them. They received the curt answer which their self-interested spirit deserved, and their spokesman was promptly dismissed from the householder's employ. Thus did the last become first because their spirit of service was right; and the first became last because theirs was a spirit of hard-bargaining, self-righteousness and envy against others.

By this most effective illustration did Jesus soberly remind Peter—and so every other disciple too—to be on his guard against a sense of smugness at having made great sacrifice for the Gospel (Matthew 19:27—20:16). Less important than what disciples do, is the spirit in which they do it. God has assured them of a reward, and rightly so, but never must the reward be the dominant, let alone the sole motive of their service for their Master. It was such at this stage with Peter. And James and John were no better, for they clamoured shortly afterwards for the privilege of sitting the one on Jesus' right hand and the other on his left in his Kingdom. They were promptly reminded to leave their reward to God, as the uncomplaining labourers had been content to leave theirs to the householder, for Jesus said, "To sit on my right hand, and on my left, is not mine to give, but it shall be given to them for whom it is prepared of my Father". And to press home that the principle, "The last shall be first and the first last" is a fundamental law governing God's dealings with men, Jesus then expressed it afresh by saying, "Whosoever will be great among you, let him be your minister; and whosoever will be chief among you, let him be your servant" (Matthew 20:20-27).

Nor were these the only times when Jesus drew men's attention to this great spiritual truth. He did so again when remonstrating against some who considered their membership of the Chosen People to be sufficient to gain them salvation, warning them that in the final Day of reckoning much more would be required of them than the ability to say, "We have eaten and drunk in thy presence, and thou hast taught in our streets". He told them sternly that, to their grief and anguish, they would then find themselves "thrust out" from the Kingdom, and their place taken by Gentiles, their fate once more serving to prove the immutability of the law that, "Behold, there are last which shall be first, and there are first which shall be last" (Luke 13:23-30). Yet again while some time later he was present at a Sabbath feast in a Pharisee's house, he watched the conduct of the guests, and marked how they chose out the chief rooms. Once more he laid down this same law, this time saying, "For whosoever exalteth himself shall be abased; and he that humbleth himself shall be exalted". And when, a moment or two later, a smug guest said, "Blessed is he that shall eat bread in the kingdom of God", Jesus gave him as an extension of this principle a sober reminder in parable form that none of those who put their present comforts and pursuits first and the Millennial Supper last in their lives, will have the joy of tasting it (Luke 14:1-24).

Now it is self-evident that only in measure as men *believe* this great spiritual law will their *conduct* be brought into conformity with it, and they themselves come to qualify for membership of the Kingdom. It must be an integral part of any saving faith, for a faith which fails to actuate and inspire those who profess it is a barren intellectual creed, and "the true faith" never is nor can be this, even though it must command the intellectual assent of those who would be saved by it. The true faith is a faith that works, not in the bare sense that those who hold it also do their best to lead a life of righteousness conformable to it, but rather in the sense that it is the faith which actually imparts the *power* to lead such a life—in a word, *the faith itself transforms them*. Not until a man's faith has this effect upon him, even though he is able to demonstrate it in every detail to be according to the Word of God, can it begin to be for him, personally, the *true* faith. Its power over him is the criterion of its truth for him. He alone really believes that the Kingdom is of greater importance than everything else, who *gives* it a greater importance in his life than everything else; he alone is really persuaded that God is One who is led by his belief to serve Him with oneness, his very choice of loyalties being inspired by the precept, "Thou shalt worship the Lord thy God, and him only shalt thou serve" (Matthew 4:10); and he alone is convinced that he is saved by his faith whose faith succeeds in saving him from himself. The acid test of any creed which men profess as true is its influence upon them — and no creed which is top heavy with doctrine, because it is deficient in moral content, can exercise a truly saving influence. To adapt yet another axiom of the Master, we can here say once again, "A good tree cannot bring forth evil fruit, neither can a corrupt tree bring forth good fruit". What is wanted is sound conduct, springing from sound belief — "the tree good *and* his fruit good". A man's faith may be true as a matter of objective fact; but is it also true *for him?* That is the all important issue.

The lighted candle

Fearful indeed is the responsibility which the knowledge of the true faith, even in the purely doctrinal sense of the term, lays upon a man. This Jesus made abundantly plain when he had imparted to his disciples the meaning of the parable of the Sower. Knowledge, he said to them (*and so to us* also), brings light. But light is meant to dispel others' darkness beside one's own. "No man, when he hath lighted a candle, covereth it with a vessel, or putteth it under a bed; but setteth it on a candlestick, that they which enter in may see the light" (Luke 8:16). If man does not light a candle for nothing, neither does God. Those whom He graciously endows with the knowledge of His will and purpose are thereby placed under the inescapable obligation to impart that knowledge to those in ignorance. Indeed the more any one community insists that it alone possesses

the Truth the more proportionately do its members
condemn themselves if they withhold the knowledge of it
from others. To have jealously guarded the Truth and kept
it unsullied, and yet to have done no more than that, can
never suffice for God. Such an attitude has its rebuke and
condemnation in the parable of the Pounds. "Lord", said
the idle servant, sublimely unconscious of his guilt,
"behold, here is thy pound". He even went so far as to add,
"which I have kept laid up in a napkin". What irony was
this to have kept his talent in a towel normally wrapped
around the brow to keep the perspiration from the labour-
er's face as he toiled in the field! How cruelly did this man
condemn his own indolence by his own action. But, alas, it
had been with the worst, not the best, of motives that he
had done this, "For I feared thee", said he, "because thou
art an austere man: thou takest up that thou layedst not
down, and reapest that thou didst not sow". That is, he
knew that his Lord would tolerate neither loss nor waste,
and deemed it sufficient virtue to have conserved and kept
intact what had been entrusted to him. But he was quickly
and rudely disabused, and shown the implications of his
own conception of his Lord, by the Lord himself. "Out of
thine own mouth will I judge thee, thou wicked servant.
Thou knewest that I was an austere man, taking up that I
laid not down, and reaping that I did not sow: wherefore
then gavest not thou my money into the bank, that at my
coming I might have required mine own *with usury?*" So
the pound was taken from him. And what is more, it was
then handed to him who had used his pound to gain ten, in
special recognition of the latter's diligence. And when
objection was taken to this reward of diligence, Jesus
added solemnly, "I say unto you, That unto every one
which hath shall be given; and from him that hath not,
even that he hath shall be taken away from him" (Luke
19:12-26).

Now it is worthy of careful note that it was this same
divine law which Jesus went on to invoke when he had
interpreted the parable of the Sower. He did not stop short
at the similitude of the Candle, and its implicit lesson that
custodians of Truth have an obligation placed upon them

EPILOGUE: THE LOVE OF CHRIST CONSTRAINETH US

to bear witness to it. To show the disciples that that obligation was also a glorious privilege, he added, "For nothing is secret, that shall not be made manifest; neither anything hid, that shall not be known and come abroad". This, too, was for him a divine law, which not only explained his own advent and mission, but also guaranteed the eventual enlightenment of all the world. But were his disciples willing and bold enough to implement this divine intention? That was the operative question. Jesus would have them know, moreover, that their answer, either way, would be of eternal consequence. So he bade them ponder the matter earnestly. "Take heed therefore," said he, "how ye hear: for whosoever hath, to him shall be given; and whosoever hath not, from him shall be taken even that which he seemeth to have" (Luke 8:17,18). That is, as candles they had both to shine and to be pleased to shine, and if they were truly convinced that this was so they would neither fail to honour their duty nor have the inclination to forgo their privilege.

Here once again, then, to believe was to act. Not that to act would always be easy or pleasant! That it would frequently be the reverse had been made plain by Jesus to the Twelve when he sent them forth. There would be much to discourage them and to tempt them to withhold their witness—ostracism, persecution, even death, at the hands of ruthless adversaries. But "Fear them not", was Jesus' counsel. And why? Because God's purpose *will* be accomplished, come what may, as he next went on to remind them, by saying, "for there is nothing covered, that shall not be revealed; and hid, that shall not be known". If only, then, because their own enlightenment was but one outworking of this great truism it made their duty obvious. So Jesus then added plainly, "What I tell you in darkness, that speak ye in light: and what ye hear in the ear, that preach ye upon the housetops". But did their faith falter, and their resolution flag because there were many adversaries? Then let them bear in mind, as much to inspire as to warn them, that there were graver consequences to be envisaged than those which *man* might inflict upon them: "And fear not", said he, "them which kill the body, but are

not able to kill the soul: but rather fear him which is able
to destroy both soul and body in hell" (Matthew 10:26-28).
God is greater than man. In proportion as men believe this
truth so they will act upon it.

I in the midst of them

Have these things which were thus arrestingly revealed to
these first believers no meaning, then, for those who so
earnestly claim today that they are sole custodians of the
Truth, once for all delivered to the saints? "Ye are the light
of the world", said Jesus to them. If to them then surely
also to those who are their fellow-saints in these last days!
When these men first heard those simple words, little did
they dream what profundity of meaning lay in that one
word "world". They soon came to know however. "Go ye
therefore, and teach *all nations*, baptizing them in the
name of the Father, and of the Son, and of the Holy Spirit,"
was the commission laid upon them by the resurrected
Lord. At the time they received it the task seemed hope-
lessly beyond their powers but with it came the assurance,
"Lo, I am with you alway, even unto the end of the world"
(Matthew 28:19,20). At first, as "Acts" so convincingly
shows, the commission placed upon them was beyond even
their powers of comprehension: but the Lord was with
them and slowly but progressively the Infant Church came
to grasp that the Gospel was now, by virtue of the death of
Christ, the Gospel for all men, regardless of nationality.
Painful indeed was the process of learning that, "Then
hath God also to the Gentiles granted repentance unto life"
(Acts 11:18), and of realizing that, "There is neither Jew
nor Greek, there is neither bond nor free, there is neither
male nor female: for ye are all one in Christ Jesus"
(Galatians 3:28). But as that process proceeded, so also
grew the physical capacity of the Church to honour the
command, "Go ye therefore and teach *all* nations"—"all"
not merely in the sense that they no longer discriminate
between Jew and Gentile, but also in the strictly literal
sense that the uttermost parts of the earth were the only
boundaries set to their sphere of operations (Acts 1:8). We
distant Gentiles in this last epoch of human history, can

274

now in our day and generation rejoice in Christ only because these men and women of the early Church, who were at first so pathetically few in number, did their duty, spoke boldly "in light" and "upon the housetops", feared not what man could do to them, but waxed bold in the Lord whose hand, as promised, was with them in all they did (Acts 11:21). Believing that they were indeed the light of the *world*, they acted on that conviction and went *"everywhere* preaching the word" (Acts 8:4).

Jesus had said to them, "Go ye into all the world, and preach the gospel to every creature. He that believeth and is baptized shall be saved" (Mark 16:15,16). They did as bidden. They preached: so also do we. They taught that only those that believe can be saved: so again do we. They baptized: and so moreover do we. But they also preached in all the world, to every creature ... Do we do this too? Do we, to begin with, even *feel* that we, since we claim to be the light of the world of our day, have precisely the same commission to discharge as they? For as we really think about this matter, so we act, for here once again to *believe* is to do. To turn one's back upon the world as a wicked place whose contamination is to be avoided is far easier than to sally boldly forth to save others from its clutches, *everywhere*.

Not that our duty stops short at oral testimony. Conversion can be effected by more than word of mouth, for as the true Faith is a balanced blend of creed and ethic, so also can—and should—witness to it be given as much by a transformed life as by a cogent presentation of Scripture facts. Precept and practice should go hand in hand, and that not only in the case of the individual saint, but no less also of each assembly of saints and of the Household as a whole. To all who claim to be the light of the world today, the words of Jesus still have the same relevance as of old. "A city that is set on an hill cannot be hid. Neither do men light a candle, and put it under a bushel, but on a candlestick; and it giveth light unto all that are in the house. Let your light so shine before men, that they may see your good works, and glorify your Father which is in heaven" (Matthew 5:14-16). Any person, or community, that by fail-

ing to be true to the Faith in its totality brings shame upon
it, is guilty of treachery against the greatest cause of all,
and is accountable for that treachery to the Judge of all
the earth, for once again the law is absolute, "Unto whomsoever much is given, of him shall be much required"
(Luke 12:48).

The Infant Church acted on this law, and thereby found
Christ's promise to bless spiritual unity which springs
from faith in him, to be gloriously true. He had stated, "I
say unto you, That if two of you shall agree on earth as
touching any thing that they shall ask, it shall be done for
them of my Father which is in heaven, For where two or
three are gathered together (i.e. are *so* gathered, in unity
of mind and purpose), there am I in the midst of them"
(Matthew 18:19,20). This gracious promise fulfilled itself
in the experience of these earliest believers. "The multitude of them that believed were of one heart and of one
soul". So, as was meet, "great grace was upon them all"
(Acts 4:32,33). The same should therefore be true of us. We
share indeed their Faith—but do we also share their experience? Luke spoke in one breath of "the apostles' doctrine
... and fellowship", and nothing was more natural, for the
one was meaningless unless the other was its outcome
(Acts 2:42). And what was true then is still true today. May
we never forget that fact!

The mind of Christ

Of every generation of baptized believers it is true to say,
"Ye are all one in Christ Jesus" (Galatians 3:27,28). Yet in
no single generation has it been easy for believers to trans-
late their unity of faith into unity of fellowship. So to them
all in turn the words of Paul have come with unchanging
freshness, "I, therefore, the prisoner of the Lord, beseech
you that ye walk worthy of the vocation wherewith ye are
called, with all lowliness and meekness, with longsuffering, forbearing one another in love; endeavouring to keep
the unity of the Spirit in the bond of peace" (Ephesians
4:1-3). "Let your conversation", he said to the Philippians,
and so again to us, "be as it becometh the gospel of Christ:
that ... I may hear of your affairs, that ye stand fast in one

spirit, with one mind striving together for the faith of the gospel" (Philippians 1:27). "Fulfil ye my joy", he added, "that ye be likeminded, having the same love, being of one accord, of one mind. Let nothing be done through strife or vainglory; but in lowliness of mind let each esteem other better than themselves. Look not every man on his own things, but every man also on the things of others" (Philippians 2:2-4).

How sublime are these sentiments! Yet how difficult to put into practice! But Paul was perfectly aware of that; aware of the native frailty of the human will; aware that though the spirit is willing, the flesh, alas, is weak. Whence then were the Philippians, whence too are we, to acquire the strength to scale these heights? Paul went on to answer that inevitable question: "Let this mind be in you", said he, "which was also in Christ Jesus: who, being in the form of God, thought it not robbery to be equal with God: but made himself of no reputation, and took upon him the form of a servant, and was made in the likeness of men: and being found in fashion as a man, he humbled himself, and became obedient unto death, even the death of the cross" (verses 5-8).

This magnificent statement spans the whole of the Saviour's life, from birth to death, drawing out for us the fullness of meaning in his own gracious words. "Whosoever", said he, "will be great among you, let him be your minister; and whosoever will be chief among you, let him be your servant: even as the Son of man came not to be ministered unto, but to minister, and to give his life a ransom for many" (Matthew 20:26-28). Paul's appeal to the Saviour's humility, as evidenced in his sacrificial death, was thus but a reiteration of the Saviour's own appeal. Let us carefully trace the sequence of thought.

"God sent forth his Son, made of a woman", as Paul else-where expressed it (Galatians 4:4). That is, the babe born in Bethlehem was Emmanuel—God with us (Matthew 1:23): or, as Paul again has it, he was (subsisted) "in the form of God", for mystery though it is, "*God* was in Christ" (2 Corinthians 5:19). As that babe grew in years and understanding so he became increasingly aware of this tremendous truth, being already at the age of twelve so keenly conscious of who and what he was that he acknowledged no Father but God. Yet he was "God *with us*"; and so he laid no pretentious claim to equality with his Father, for he knew what else he was through having a daughter of Adam for his mother. What is more, he knew why he had "come" into the world with the mortal fleshly nature with which she had endowed him: it was for no other purpose than to minister and give his life a ransom. Of this he made confession when at Jordan in particular he "emptied himself" and "took upon him the form of a servant", thus associating himself, though sinless, with all other men even though they all were without exception sinners. Having thus resolutely declared himself to be one of them, he then went on to humble himself to the uttermost, and to empty himself absolutely, submitting himself, for their sakes, to a death which he alone among them did not deserve, but which could never have been of saving benefit to them had he in fact deserved it.

The marvel of it all is that, being "born of a woman", he had the will to disobey, and could at every stage—as a boy, on the banks of Jordan, in the ordeal of the wilderness, when provoked to show a sign, in Gethsemane—yes, and even on the Cross itself!—have chosen to disobey. Yet never once did he falter: though he was tempted in all points like as we are, it was always without sin (Hebrews 4:15). Thus was he able both to *suffer* for us and thereby to *save us*, and God could justly make him to be "*sin* for *us*, who knew no sin" (2 Corinthians 5:21). Thus, too, did he destroy death by death, and defeat sin in the very process of falling victim to it (Hebrews 2:14), for in the very act of being numbered with transgressors he succeeded also in bearing their iniquities and justifying many (Isaiah 53:11,12). This he did, as Peter so pithily puts the matter, when (though he "did no sin, neither was guile found in his mouth") he "his own self bare our sins *in his own body* on the tree" and so died as representative Man. He was one with sinners in nature, since "he also himself likewise took part of the same" flesh and blood as those whom he came to save (Hebrews 2:14). So when he died they as it were died also: and if they will but confess the fact in the symbolic death of baptism then their "old man is crucified with him, that the body of sin might be destroyed" (Romans 6:3-6). Or, to quote Peter once more, Jesus "his own self bare our sins in his own body on the tree, that we, being *dead to sins*, should live unto righteousness: by whose stripes ye were healed. For ye were as sheep going astray; but are now returned unto the Shepherd and Bishop of your souls" (1 Peter 2:24,25). Thus was he both "delivered for our offences", and then "raised again for our justification" (Romans 4:25).

The advantages are all ours. The humiliation, the shame, the stripes, the suffering, however, were all his. This the ambitious James and John duly learned—but not until they learned it did they appreciate why the Lord had appealed to his own imminent sacrifice in order to still their ambitious clamour and to teach them that lowliness alone is greatness (Matthew 20:20-28). The blunt fact which Paul wished the Philippians likewise to appreciate was that Jesus had died for them as well—yes, *died*—died even on a Cross, not shrinking from the utmost self-effacement for their good. If Jesus had done this for them had they the heart to do any less for Jesus? "Let this mind be in you, which was also in Christ Jesus", said he then, to reinforce his plea for unity based on humility and love.

All this is a pointer to us that if we in turn wish to do what is our reasonable service, we can acquire the resolve and strength to do so only by a contemplation of the Cross. The realization that Jesus died "for *me*", as *my* loving Saviour, is the one, the only, thing which can set God's power working mightily in any one of us. The strength to do as Christ did will originate not in our own unaided wills, but only in an appreciation of God's love in sending Jesus to live and die and live again for us. We can come to do service to Christ only to the extent that we appreciate how he came to do service to us.

Do we seek strength to endure unjust treatment and the grace to submit cheerfully to the loss of our lawful rights? Let the Cross, as Peter reminds us, be our inspiration. "For it is better", said he, "if the will of God be so, that ye suffer for well doing, than for evil doing. For Christ also hath once suffered for sins, the just for the unjust, that he might bring us to God, being put to death in the flesh, but quickened by the Spirit" (1 Peter 3:17,18). Let us ponder these words well, and not miss their essential point. We have it in that qualifying clause—"if the will of God be so". Not only, we note, did Jesus suffer wrongfully; he consented to do so (as Gethsemane is proof) *because it was God's will*. Can Christians, then, who benefit so richly from his suffering, complain when it is God's will that they should suffer like him or for him? That is the consideration which induces a victimised Christian to submit cheerfully to his irksome lot, and to endure each Gethsemane through which he may have to pass.

Do we seek vainly for the faith to believe that despite our sins and failures we are still dear to God? Then once again let the Cross be our inspiration, "For when we were yet without strength, in due time Christ died for the ungodly". That statement is simple, but its implications are staggering. For what are the facts? Men do not sign their lives away for others without good reason. None of us would readily consent to lose his life-blood and with it his life, so that another who was dying might live instead, unless he felt that that other *deserved* such a sacrifice. "For", as Paul says, "scarcely for a righteous man will one die: yet peradventure for a good man some would even dare to die". Considerations of *merit* are the mainspring of such self-denial as this. "But"—and here the contrast becomes so glorious—"But God commendeth his love toward us, in that, *while we were yet sinners*, Christ died for us". Christ died—gave all—for the utterly unworthy! For that is what we were. Now since God went to such lengths of mercy on Calvary is it conceivable that He will not still consent to succour us? Nay, "Much more then", says Paul to the fainthearted, "being now justified by his blood (i.e. being no longer entirely undeserving, thanks to God's grace already shown), we shall be saved from wrath through him". And as though that were not enough, Paul drives home the facts once more, "For if, when we were enemies, we were reconciled to God by the death of his

Son, much more, being reconciled, we shall be saved by his life" (Romans 5:6-10). Here is cheer for the downcast. Let us but appreciate how merciful God has been, and we shall never doubt how merciful He still is, and will continue to be. So "let us", as Paul bids us, put on "for an helmet, the hope (i.e. the robust conviction) of salvation. For God hath not appointed us to wrath, but to obtain salvation by our Lord Jesus Christ, who died for us, that, whether we wake or sleep, we should live together with him" (1 Thessalonians 5:8-10). Realizing this we can the better take to ourselves the reassurance of Jesus—"Fear not little flock, it is the Father's good pleasure to give you the kingdom". And doing so, we shall the less begrudge any sacrifice—be it of time, convenience, energy, money, pride, worldly happiness or worldly station—which the call of the Kingdom may cost us. If, for example, our meat makes our brother to offend, or our exercise of liberty puts a stumbling block in our brother's way, shall we not solemnly ask with Paul, "Through thy *knowledge* shall the weak brother perish, for whom Christ *died*?" and with him decide that "the kingdom of God is not meat and drink; but righteousness, and peace, and joy in the Holy Spirit" (1 Corinthians 8:11; Romans 14:13-17)?

And what if, far from being in the depths of despair, we are instead concerned with our spiritual superiority to others? Once more let the Cross be our guide. If we are contemptuous of another brother let us remember Jesus' telling parable to Simon the Pharisee, which began, "There was a certain creditor which had two debtors". There were *two* debtors. For Simon this was a revolutionary piece of news, when once he realized the creditor to be God! It meant that he, too, for all his complacency, was a sinner, no less than the woman whom he so despised. And what else did that imply? "The one", said Jesus, "owned five hundred pence, and the other fifty. And when they had nothing to pay, he frankly forgave them both". This was startling news indeed for the smug Simon, but how true!— "they had *nothing to pay*". That is, sinners can do nothing to save themselves, for even though their sin be slight, yet it is still sin, and makes them utterly dependent on God's

lovingkindness for the pardon of their debt. Only he loves
his Saviour much who appreciates how great a debt he has
been forgiven; and so only he is spontaneously indulgent
toward those sinners whom he adjudges worse than himself (Luke 7:41-47). And this holds good for the Christian's
attitude even to the unconverted. So easy is it for him to
despise those in the world simply because they are in the
world. But Paul's counsel to Timothy is, "I exhort therefore, that, first of all, supplications, prayers, intercessions,
and giving of thanks, be made for all men; for kings, and
for all that are in authority; that we may lead a quiet and
peaceable life in all godliness and honesty. For this is good
and acceptable in the sight of God our Saviour". Why does
Paul say it is "good and acceptable"? Because God our
Saviour "will have *all* men to be saved, and to come unto
the knowledge of the truth". And what evidence is there of
that? The simple fact that God is One! "For there is one
God, and one mediator between God and men, the man
Christ Jesus". And what of him? He is "Christ Jesus, who
gave himself a ransom *for all*" (1 Timothy 2:1-6). The
better we understand the Cross the more gentle and forbearing it makes us, and the more eager like God to seek
and to save that which is lost.

Yes, and the more willing it makes us to forgive those
that trespass against us, and the more anxious to further
that oneness which should unite all saints in holy and
affectionate fellowship. So Paul does not only exhort the
Ephesians to keep the unity of the Spirit in the bond of
peace. He also shows them how to do so: "Let all bitter-
ness, and wrath, and anger, and clamour, and evil speaking, be put away from you, with all malice: and be ye kind
one to another, tenderhearted, forgiving one another, even
as God for Christ's sake hath forgiven you. Be ye therefore
followers of God, as dear children; and walk in love, as
Christ also hath loved us, and hath given himself for us as
an offering and a sacrifice to God for a sweet smelling
savour" (Ephesians 4:31—5:2). What the Cross shows that
God has done, and that Christ has done, that also must
Christians do.

That spells death to the child of sin in every one of us. So there is no alternative but to join Jesus on the Cross, and put our sinful selves to death there with him, so that with him we might also rise, both now and also hereafter, to newness of life. That is precisely what he himself testified when he said, "If any man will come after me, let him deny himself, and take up his cross, and follow me. For whosoever will save his life shall lose it: and whosoever will lose his life for my sake shall find it" (Matthew 16:24,25).

Let us then face the challenge with which the personality of Jesus, his healing, his teaching and above all his suffering, present us, and say boldly with Paul, "I am crucified with Christ". For then we shall be able to add triumphantly, "Nevertheless I live; yet not I, but Christ liveth in me: and the life which I now live in the flesh I live by the faith of the Son of God, who loved me, and gave himself for me" (Galatians 2:20).

SCRIPTURE INDEX

285